Strategic New Product Development for the Global Economy

Also by Toyohiro Kono
STRATEGY AND STRUCTURE OF JAPANESE ENTERPRISES
LONG-RANGE PLANNING OF JAPANESE CORPORATIONS
STRATEGIC MANAGEMENT OF JAPANESE COMPANIES
TRANSFORMATION OF CORPORATE CULTURE *(with Stewart Clegg)*
TRENDS IN JAPANESE MANAGEMENT *(with Stewart Clegg)*

Also by Leonard Lynn
HOW JAPAN INNOVATES
ORGANIZING BUSINESS *(with Timothy McKeown)*

Strategic New Product Development for the Global Economy

Toyohiro Kono and Leonard Lynn

First published 2007 by
PALGRAVE MACMILLAN
Houndmills, Basingstoke, Hampshire RG21 6XS and
175 Fifth Avenue, New York, N. Y. 10010
Companies and representatives throughout the world

PALGRAVE MACMILLAN is the global academic imprint of the Palgrave
Macmillan division of St. Martin's Press, LLC and of Palgrave Macmillan Ltd.
Macmillan® is a registered trademark in the United States, United Kingdom
and other countries. Palgrave is a registered trademark in the European
Union and other countries.

ISBN-13: 978–0–230–00199–2   hardback
ISBN-10: 0–230–00199–8   hardback

This book is printed on paper suitable for recycling and made from fully
managed and sustained forest sources.

A catalogue record for this book is available from the British Library.

Library of Congress Cataloging-in-Publication Data
Kono, Toyohiro.
    Strategic new product development for the global economy / Toyohiro
Kono and Leonard Lynn.
       p. cm.
    Includes bibliographical references and index.
    ISBN-13: 978–0–230–00199–2 (cloth)
    ISBN-10: 0–230–00199–8 (cloth)
    1. New products–Management. 2. Product management. 3. Strategic
planning. 4. Business planning. 5. International business enterprises–
Management–Case studies. I. Lynn, Leonard H. II. Title.

    HF5415.153.K66 2007
    658.5′75–dc22

                                                      2006050835

10   9   8   7   6   5   4   3   2   1
16   15 14 13 12 11 10 09 08 07

Printed and bound in Great Britain by
Antony Rowe Ltd, Chippenham and Eastbourne

To our wives, Mizu Kono and Kuniko Yamada Lynn

Contents

List of Tables

List of Figures

Preface

There are a number of excellent books on new product development (NPD). We have learned from them, and we frequently mention them in this book. This book, however, is somewhat different from the others:

1. Our focus is on *NPD as a part of corporate strategy*. Many of the books on NPD give us excellent insights into how NPD teams might best be organized for creativity, or how to manage the various phases of the NPD process. This book is more explicitly concerned with how NPD fits the needs and strategies of the firm. To us the main criterion in judging the success of a new product process is *not* how "creative" the resulting product is, or how quickly it was developed. To be sure, these are important, but what matters most is how much the new product contributes to the strategic success of the firm. In this book we describe numerous instances where firms introduced brilliant new products, but did not profit at all from them. Sometimes other firms grabbed the market for the new product before the pioneering firm could even recover its cost of development. Sometimes management had no idea of what to do with a great new product, and failed to exploit it. In this book we pay a lot of attention to how NPD fits into the formulation and execution of company strategy. Indeed, we are concerned not only with the development of new products, but also with how a company can eliminate products that no longer fit corporate strategy, and that no longer support the future development of the company.

2. We present a *blend of cases, survey research, and theory*. The book presents more than 100 NPD cases. Cases provide a vivid way of making key points. We also put the cases into a broader context through the use of survey data and theory. One of our surveys was on NPD, the other on R&D. In constructing our theoretical frameworks we draw on both the English-language and the Japanese-language academic literatures. The surveys give a sense of how managers rate the relative importance of certain aspects of the NPD process and of R&D management. The cases help us to interpret what the responses to the survey mean, and the theory helps us to

understand how everything fits together. Together, the cases, surveys and theory help the reader see the main underlying principles of NPD.

3. While some books and articles give a detailed analytic model of a generalized NPD process, we describe *three distinctive models*. A feel for the nature of generic differences in NPD processes can be gained by thinking of the differences between developing a new medication, a new mayonnaise, and a new line of fashionable women's attire, for example. Each of these products requires a different approach to finding out what consumers need/want, what the technological possibilities are, and where crucial decisions are made about whether to go ahead with development or not.

The need for a medication that will treat a disease may be obvious, but the development of a safe and effective medication may not turn out to be possible. Here, most of the NPD process is concerned with finding a medication that works and is safe for as wide a range of people as possible. This typically involves reviews of huge numbers of molecules and extensive testing. The process is expensive, and most often does not actually result in a new product that can be marketed.

In the case of mayonnaise, the first step may be determining that eating habits or health habits have changed, and that this leads to a latent demand for mayonnaise with a different taste, or perhaps one that has a lower fat content. The technology may not be complex, but finding out exactly what consumers want can be extremely difficult. And, after the mayonnaise is developed there is a need to decide how to launch it (How much should be put on the market? What should the price be? How should the new mayonnaise be distributed? What kind of packaging should be used?).

Developing a new line of fashionable women's clothing poses problems of a somewhat different nature. New lines are needed each season and each year. The technology is pretty simple. The problem is that consumer needs are highly volatile. A firm in this industry has to be very quick to respond to changes in fashion, and to get its products into stores before the demand cools. Unfashionable products can only be sold at bargain basement prices, and products not in stock cannot be sold at all.

But while there are major differences in the development of such different products, there are also commonalities in such things as the need to link the NPD process to company strategy and in some of the sub processes used.

4. Much of the NPD literature centers on cases drawn from U.S. firms. We take a more *international approach*. The first author is Japanese, so many of the cases in the book are from Japan. We have tried to include some information from Europe and other parts of the world as well, but the emphasis of the book is on U.S. and Japanese companies. Over the past several decades U.S. and Japanese firms have produced many more successful new products than firms from other countries. Although there are some differences in management styles and personnel practices between U.S. and Japanese companies, we find that the same general principles of NPD apply equally well to both. Most of the Japanese companies mentioned in the book will be familiar to Western readers, but many of the Japanese cases have never appeared in print in English before.

5. As we near the end of the first decade of the 21st century, a number of developments have affected NPD processes. In this book we *highlight many of these current trends*. Creativity, for example, is perhaps more important than ever before. Accordingly, we devote considerable attention to the nature of creativity and to the organizational environments that are most conducive to creativity. The world has entered an era of globalization where markets and sources of technology are less defined by national boundaries than ever before. We discuss the impacts of this change on NPD. Another development is a rising demand for corporate social responsibility. It is not only desirable that new products be environmentally friendly, but it is increasingly a necessity – governments and society demand it. Finally, as was mentioned above, it is increasingly important that a company's product mix fits its strategies and aspirations. Not only do new products have to fit the strategy, but old products have to be evaluated as to how well they fit the company's strategy. Often old products, regardless of their links to company history and tradition, will have to be divested, or even discontinued altogether.

In writing this book we have been helped by a large number of people. We especially wish to thank members of the corporate strategy study group of the Japan Productivity Center. Thanks to this group we had the opportunity to hear the presentation of cases of NPD development at many companies, and to discuss them. We wish to thank the managers of the companies we visited, and those who responded to our surveys. The Japan Productivity Center helped us carry out the surveys. Professor Fumiko Kurokawa of Dokkyo University wrote the case on Corolla, Professor Inoue of Waseda University wrote the case on World fashionable apparel, and Professor Akihiro Takeda of Kansai Kokusai University wrote the pharmaceutical cases and did the statistical analysis of the results of the surveys. Much of Lynn's field work was supported by two grants from the National Science Foundation (SES-0080644 and SES-0242951) and one from the Kauffman Foundation. In all three of these projects his collaborator was Dr. Hal Salzman of the Urban Institute in Washington, D.C. Any opinions, findings, and conclusions or recommendations expressed in this book are those of the authors, and do not necessarily reflect the views of the National Science Foundation or the Kauffman Foundation.

Toyohiro Kono
Leonard Lynn

1
What is a New Product?

In this book we define a "new product" as a product that is new to the company. If the product is simply an improved version of a product the company already has on the market, it's not a new product for our purposes. On the other hand, if a product is new to the company, even though other companies already make it, we count it as a new product. Such products may not be new to the world, but they are crucial to the success of the company, and developing them is no simple matter.

Canon, for example, built a global reputation making film cameras, then copiers, PC printers, and digital cameras. Canon was not the first to make any of these products. But Canon improved them, and in the process enjoyed huge success. When another firm introduced auto-focus cameras, Canon developed a better auto-focus camera, one that could be used at night. Canon pioneered the inexpensive, low-maintenance personal copying machine. Canon also introduced the *bubble-jet printer* for PCs and digital cameras with an array of new features valued by customers. As a result Canon enjoyed rapid growth over a 20-year period – including Japan's depression decade of the 1990s. In 2003 it had sales of about $30 billion, and profits of over $4 billion.

While it was introducing successful new products, Canon was also dropping many products. Between 1995 and 1998 alone, it quit making personal computers, electronic typewriters, card readers, and LCDs (liquid crystal displays). Canon had spent large amounts of money developing these products. In the case of LCDs, Canon lost nearly $1 billion between the time it entered the market in 1984 and when it withdrew in 1998. But Canon disregarded its sunk costs once it saw that these products were not likely to generate much future growth.

New product development (NPD) separates the fate of the company from the life cycle of its products. By introducing products in the early stages of a product life cycle a company can achieve high sales growth and profits. By having a mix of products at different stages of the product life cycle, the company can have stable profits. So, strategic NPD is vital to the success of the firm.

Types of new products

There are a number of ways of classifying new products. These classification schemes can be useful in helping to identify new product opportunities and in planning new product development strategies for the firm.

Table 1.1 classifies new products based on two dimensions. The first is the technology used in the product. Is the technology the same as technology currently used by the firm? The second dimension is how the product is used and marketed. Does the product have essentially

Table 1.1 Types of new products

Use \\ Technology	Similar to existing products	Different	
		Related market	Unrelated market
Similar to currently used	(A) Existing product improvement, complementary product	(B) Marketing-and technology-related new product	(C) Technology related new product
Different from currently used	(D) Substitute, complementary product	(E) Marketing-related new product	(F) Unrelated New product

Examples from camera/photographic film company

Use \\ Technology	Similar to existing products	Different	
		Related market	Unrelated market
Similar to currently used	(A) ASA 400 color film	(B) Floppy disks	(C) Industrial chemicals
Different from currently used	(D) Video cameras, digital cameras	(E) Copying machines	(F) Housing construction

the same use as current products? Will it be used differently in related markets? Or will it have a different use in an un-related market.[1] The lower panel of the table gives examples from the camera/film industry of these different types of new products.

High speed color film (Cell A of the table) is an example of a new product that uses the same technology as an existing product, ordinary color film. Digital cameras and video cameras (Cell D of the table) are examples of new products that use a different technology to perform the same functions as existing products. Floppy disks (Cell B) are an example of a new product that uses a technology similar to that used in photographic film, but for an entirely different purpose. The market for floppy disks is somewhat related to the market for photographic film in that similar distribution channels can be used. Many of the people who buy cameras and photographic film also buy floppy disks. Film technology (Cell C) also has applications in industrial chemicals, an unrelated market for most firms in the camera/film industry. The new technologies used in the camera industry to produce digital and video cameras also found different uses in a related market, personal copying machines (Cell E), and in an unrelated market, housing construction (Cell F).

This classification system can be used in most firms with a relatively narrow range of products to analyze their mix of products and their new product needs, because the product life cycle changes either when a new technology is used for an existing purpose or when an existing technology is used for a new purpose.[2]

The system is less useful in analyzing product strategies for diversified companies. If a company is highly diversified, virtually any new product will improve or complement one of the company's current products (Cell A), or substitute for an existing product (Cell D).

New products in a company's traditional markets are in cells A and D in Table 1.1. New products for other markets tend to be highly disruptive to the company. They threaten power structures as they take resources away from those making and selling the traditional products. Similar problems can occur when new technologies are introduced because the new technologies may make the expertise of many managers obsolete. Thus, business history is filled with examples of leading firms that faltered when it came to handling disruptive technological transitions. Firms that led in the production of steam locomotives, piston engine passenger airplanes, vacuum tube radios and televisions, and typewriters, generally did poorly when customers turned to diesel locomotives, piston jet passenger aircraft, solid state electronics, and computerized word processors.[3] But when firms succeed in making these transitions, the payoffs can be huge. Because new market products are so disruptive, they need to have strong support from top management, and typically they have to be developed by special project teams or development departments rather than old-line units of the company. The different features of the two types of new products are shown in Table 1.2. The table also suggests how the organizational requirements for the two types of new products differ from each other.

Another classification system is shown in Figure 1.1 This system defines products as "new" based on the perspective of consumers. This diagram is a "market segment" or "product traits" map. A product filling any empty space in the market segment map can be considered to be a new product. The map shown in the figure represents popular brands of beer along two dimensions, light versus heavy, and less bitter versus highly hopped (or "full-bodied"). The size of the circles represents the number of consumers for each type of beer. A chart like this can be used to find opportunities for new products. In this case,

Table 1.2 New products for traditional and new markets

	Traditional market (A, D)	New market (B, C, E, F)
1 Organization	• Planning at division level • Less resistance in the organization	• Top down • Planning at head office • More resistance
2 Objectives and risks	• Increased market share • Similar life cycle position • Lower risk	• Increased sales and profits • Different life cycle • Higher risk
3 Information	• Improvement of existing technology and products	• Development of new • technology • Expansion of competencies
4 Ideas	• Improvement, incremental	• New business, not continuous
5 Time horizon	• Short or medium	• Long range
6 Evaluation and implementation	• Evaluation relatively easy • Internal development by product division • Overseas sales possible	• Evaluation difficult, tends to be risky • Alliances and acquisitions frequently used • Joint venture or subsidiary could be used • Domestic sales first

perhaps there would be a market for a new heavy and bitter beer, though it would not be a large market.

A limitation of the segment map is that it can incorporate only two, or perhaps three, product characteristics. A new product may have more dimensions than this. In such cases a "radar chart" can be used to define the product. Figure 1.2 gives an example of a radar chart that analyzes the key features of hotels. Through the use of conjoint analysis the features that are most important to consumers can be identified.[4] This information can be used to create an attractive new product. Marriot, for example, used this method to develop its Courtland-by-Marriot hotel chain.

Circles in the segment map in Figure 1.1 are based on the preferences of different types of beer drinkers. It is crucial that possible users be identified at an early stage of new product development. Canon decided to target private users who might need copying machines when it

Figure 1.1 Market segmentation and size of markets for different types of beer

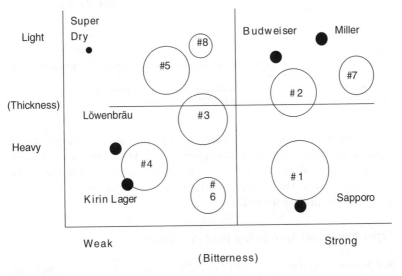

Notes:
(1) The circles indicate the number of consumers preferring different types of beer. Circle size indicates the relative number of consumers. The black dots show the location of various brands.
(2) Factors can be found by a factor analysis of survey results, or by using conjoint analysis (See appendix to Chapter 5).
(3) Locations can be determined by factor loading. The number of consumers in each group can be estimated by factor scores and by cluster analysis.

Figure 1.2 Radar chart – hotels

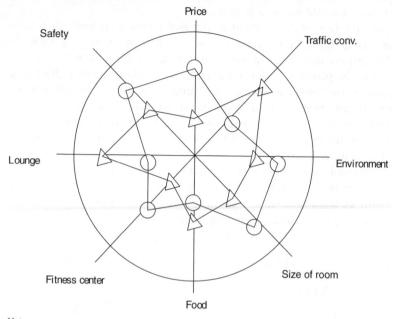

Notes:
1. Factor analysis, conjoint analysis, and multiple regression analysis of rankings can be used to identify key factors
2. Triangles represent the location on the chart of a typical city hotel
3. Circles represent the location on the chart of a Holiday Inn.

developed the PC10 and PC20 personal copiers. The Body Shop targeted environmentally conscious consumers in developing its cosmetics. Yamaha targeted people living in apartments when it developed the soundless piano. These were all adaptations of existing products that targeted new market segments.

Risks and rewards of being first in a market

Some new products really are new to the market, and some of these are spectacular successes. Examples include Sony's Walkman and Fuji Film's single-use camera. Both of these products were highly successful, and the companies that introduced them enjoyed huge success by being pioneers. Introducing products that are completely new to the market can be very risky, however, and there are numerous examples of failures. The English company, EMI, was first to introduce the CAT scanner. RC Cola was the first to sell cola in a can, and also was the first to introduce diet cola. Bowmar introduced the pocket calculator. De Havilland pioneered the commercial jet airliner. MITS introduced the first personal computer. Steve Jobs' Newton was one of the first PDAs. All of these products continue to be important parts of our lives, but none of the firms that pioneered the products profited greatly from them.[5]

Where did they go wrong? Sometimes the problem is that after paying the costs of developing a new product and taking the risk of failing with it, a company cannot keep other firms from copying the product once the market is proven. There was little to keep Coke and Pepsi from imitating RC's innovations. Indeed, larger rivals are often better poised to exploit the innovation than the innovator. GE had much better distribution and support systems than EMI in the U.S., by far the largest market and most profitable market for CAT scanners, and quickly took this market away from EMI. GE, and such firms as Philips and Siemens in Europe, were also better positioned to improve the technology (This case is discussed further in Chapter 2). Whether through patent rights or control over complementary assets such as distribution systems or manufacturing capability, the developer of a product that is new to the market has to be able to keep rivals from imitating the new product, at least until the developer has made a profit from it.

Sometimes the new product initially is not quite right for consumers. Rivals with a sharper sense of the market (or greater developmental capabilities) can gauge consumer response to the new product, then develop something that is a little better. Thus, Bowmar was soon over-shadowed by companies like Sharp that quickly entered the calculator market, and Newton was replaced in the PDA market by Palm. Companies that are followers in a market can be successful even when they do not supplant the pioneer. Sometimes they are successful because they add features that are valued by consumers. Sony's PlayStation followed Nintendo into the market, but it used CDs instead of tapes. This allowed the consumer a wider array of content. As we mentioned above, Canon successfully followed Konica into the market for automatic focus cameras by adding a device that made it possible for the auto focus to work at night.

But, of course, first movers are often highly successful. This requires that a profitable market for the product be maintained for the pioneer. This may be accomplished through strong patents or copyrights, trade secrets, distribution networks, or production capabilities that others cannot match. In the case of highly expensive new products, particularly for business use, it may be essential that the firm enjoy a high level of trust. If a company is introducing a new central air conditioning system for an office building or an automatic machine tool, the customers have to have confidence that the supplier of the equipment will make sure it works. When IBM dominated the market for business mainframes, it was commonly said that: "No one ever got fired for buying IBM." The idea was that other computers might be cheaper and more efficient, but, if they failed, the person choosing to buy them for a company would be in serious trouble.

Firms often can do well by pioneering "experience goods." These are products for which there is no apparent need before the product is introduced. But once people use these products they want them, and they may associate them with the company that first introduced them. An example is the Sony Walkman. Masaru Ibuka, then chairman of Sony, is said to have had the original insight into the potential for Walkman in 1978 when he visited two different Sony laboratories. One of the laboratories was developing small recorders, the other was developing more compact stereo headphones. As a music lover Ibuka could see a possible market for a combination headphone cassette recorder. The Sony Walkman also shows how a company was able to avoid losing a product to imitators. The Walkman was relatively easy to imitate, but Sony quickly developed a high number of variants of the Walkman for different customer niches. By the end of the 1980s Sony had introduced some 200 types of Walkman, all based on only half a dozen tape transport mechanisms. By constantly offering new versions of the Walkman, Sony was able to keep ahead of its competition.[6]

Recent trends

Four recent environmental changes are shifting the direction of new product development, and changing its impact on corporate performance. These are shown graphically in Figure 1.3.

Paradigmatic shifts in technology. Advances in such technologies as information technology (IT) and genetics are changing the rules of competition in many industries. In IT, for example, software has come to be more important than hardware in determining competitive strength. Pharmaceutical firms are using biotechnology in an effort to design new medications, rather than just using endless tests of natural substances to find those that may have medicinal value.

Figure 1.3 New demands facing developers of new products

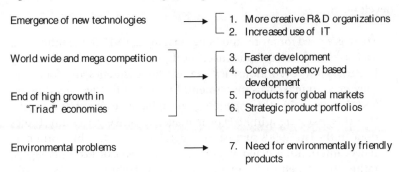

Global markets and mega competition. As the former socialist economies have joined the world market, and the World Trade Organization (WTO) continues to ratchet down trade barriers, firms are able to dream of selling to global markets, but they also must fear the rise of new competitors entering their home markets. A generation ago few would have imagined that powerful high tech/high fashion companies would be based in countries like Finland (Nokia) and South Korea (Samsung). Nor would many have expected that China would become the world's largest markets for such products as cellular telephones. The pressures to develop new products suitable for global markets are greater than ever before. This will be discussed in greater detail in Chapter 4.

End of rapid growth in the Triad economies. The rich economies of the Triad – Europe, the United States and Japan – have enjoyed slow growth, at best, over the past few decades. All the rich economies have aging populations. Since the 1990s, many Triad firms have followed strategies of concentrating on their competencies, making products where they have the strongest competitive advantage, and can add the most value. They have divested some products, and outsourced others. Chapter 10 gives more detail on how firms can withdraw from less promising activities.

The need to be "environmentally friendly." As populations and industrial output have grown, there have been stronger pressures on the environment. Citizens around the world are increasingly demanding that business firms be more environmentally responsible, both in the production processes they use and in the products they offer. This will be discussed further in Chapter 10.

These changes have had the following implications for new product development.

1. There is a need for more, and better managed, R&D. Some industries, such as electronics and pharmaceuticals, have always invested heavily in R&D. Now, even industries like textiles, cosmetics and food find they need to make this investment. In most industries spending on R&D is now higher than spending on capital investment. It is crucial that this investment in R&D be managed effectively. Certain studies done in the late 1990s suggest that high R&D spending by a firm may reflect internal inefficiency and excessive power of R&D managers, rather than an effective investment in new technology.[7] As we will see in Chapter 7, a firm's R&D and other creative activities must be carefully balanced between freedom and control.

2. IT (information technology) is finding broader applications. IT is having a pervasive impact on business. It is used to design and develop new products, to produce them, to give them new features, and to sell them. In developing new products, the internet and extranet are used to exchange design charts between component suppliers and car manufacturers. New ideas are solicited from consumers and retailers through the use of "electronic bulletin boards." The use of simulations has cut development times for drugs, cars and other products. CAD/CAM are widely used to make production more flexible and more efficient. IT has also dramatically increased the functions offered by many new products. We now expect our mobile telephones, for example, to serve not just as telephones, but also as cameras, television sets, games, personal data assistants and sources of music. Companies like Dell Computer and Amazon have pioneered new ways of using the internet for sales. Some firms like Dell are finding new ways to integrate sales and production.

3. The speed of development is increasing. To cope with today's mega competition, firms have to develop new products faster than ever before. Until recently it took more than 4 years to develop a new model car. Now this can be done in 1 year. Car makers achieve this by using common platforms across models, employing computer aided design, and using robots and other flexible manufacturing technologies. Because of all the safety testing and regulatory requirements imposed by governments, it takes about 10 years to develop a new drug, but it is still imperative that the pharmaceutical firms develop new products as fast as possible to secure patent rights and to be first to enter lucrative new markets. Firms use simulations, concurrent

engineering and alliances with other companies as important tools for shortening development time. The increased speed of development will be discussed in greater detail in Chapter 11.

4. Successful firms are identifying their core competencies more clearly, and concentrating on developing these areas. Firms are learning that in order to develop outstanding and successful new products, they must focus development on the creative activities of the company's R&D organization. These development efforts must be backed by an aggressive top management, and supported by a powerful strategic planning department and by strong production capabilities. Our research finds that successful companies have strong head offices, centralized control over research laboratories, and centralized marketing departments. Simple decentralization and product division systems do not work well. After the Japanese electronics giant Matsushita (Panasonic) recently centralized its research activities, centralized its marketing departments into the head office from the product divisions, increased its control over subsidiaries and consolidated many of its product divisions, its profitability increased dramatically.

5. Firms must develop new products for the world market. To be competitive anywhere, firms now have to be competitive in global markets. Both hardware and software have to be designed so they can be sold everywhere. Sony and Toyota have thrived by giving this policy high priority. Philips and Sony, for example, worked together to develop the standards for CD players. This allowed them both to sell CD players and disks to a world market. On the other hand Japanese cellular telephone producers have been handicapped on global markets, because telephones made to be compatible with Japanese national standards do not work in Europe and continental Asia. Firms from smaller economies like Nokia (of Finland) and Samsung (of South Korea) that had to focus on global markets were much more successful. Now the Japanese firms are trying to make their products compatible with the new global standards. The need to develop new products for the world market will be discussed in greater detail in Chapter 4.

6. Successful firms are increasing their strategic focus and product mix concentration. Given the slow down in economic growth in the Triad economies, firms are finding it makes sense to focus on products and activities where they have true competitive advantage. As Jack Welch, the legendary president of General Electric put it: "Don't own a cafeteria: Let a food company do it. Don't run a print

shop: Let a printing company do that. [Part of the CEO's job is] understanding where your real value added is and putting your best people and resources behind that."[8] Thus, Nippon Steel has withdrawn from the semi- conductor industry, Yamaha dropped the production of skis and tennis rackets, Canon discontinued production of LCDs. IBM has sold control of its PC unit to a Chinese company. Siemens has given up on the production of cellular telephones. And GE has stopped making home appliances, semiconductors and numerous other products.

7. Firms must provide more environmentally friendly products. There are increasing restraints on the use of products that are harmful to the environment. After it was discovered that Chloroflourocarbons (CFCs) are damaging the earth's ozone layer, the world's leading industrial nations agreed to restrict the use of CFCs. The refrigeration and air conditioning industries had to rush to find substitutes for Freon. Several European countries now require that recycling be considered in the design of automobiles. An automobile producer may be responsible for disposing of a car after it is worn out. After environmentalists in Japan opposed the introduction of Fuji Film Co.'s single use camera, Fuji redesigned the camera to make it easily recyclable, and organized a system so that the cameras are 100% recycled. Competition in the auto industry is beginning to focus on fuel economy and minimal emissions, thus leading automakers are racing to develop hybrid car and electric cars to gain a competitive edge. The need for new environmentally friendly products will be further discussed in Chapter 10.

New product development and corporate performance

Successful companies, such as 3M and Nitto Denko (which will be discussed in greater detail in Chapter 7) have been known for having policies requiring that 25% of their sales be accounted for by products developed in the past 5 years. Indeed, 3M now requires that 30% of sales be from products less than 4 years old. It is clear that in today's environment firms have to be flexible to survive. During the 1990s IBM changed its product mix from an emphasis on hardware to an emphasis on software. Its performance dramatically improved. As we shall see in Chapter 2, another American corporate giant, Westinghouse Electric, was slow to change and did not survive as an independent company. Two leading producers in the American color television industry in the 1960s were Motorola and Zenith. Motorola moved out of the television industry into cellular telephones and other products, and continues to be a business success. Zenith stuck to the television industry and no longer exists as an independent company.

Such Japanese firms as Aiwa and JVC were highly profitable a few years ago. They made, respectively, mini CD players and VHS video recorders. But they neglected the development of new products, and by 2001 they started to lose money. These companies may be recovering now, but often once a company's technology performance begins to decline its best engineers and researchers start to leave, and a fatal downward trend may begin.

To learn more about the effects of new product development on corporate performance we sent out a survey on new product development, Table 1.3 shows the results (Details about the survey are given in Table 1.4). Our survey encompassed 102 companies for which we had responses and could collect sufficient financial data to make an analysis. The table shows a clear relationship between new product development and financial performance. Companies that have a higher ratio of their sales accounted for by new products, also show better

Table 1.3 Corporate performance and ratio of sales accounted for by new products

Performance	No. of companies	New products as % of sales
High (P > 0.79)	23	33.09%
Medium (0.79 > P < 0.21)	30	27.37%
Low (0.21 < P)	49	18.94%
Average		24.70%

Notes:
1. Performance is measured by the following model.
   P = growth rate + ROS + EQ × 1/10
   Growth rate = growth of sales between 1990–2000 (if g < 0, g = 0)
   ROS = 10 year average of return on sales
   EQ = 10 year average of equity ratio
   1/10...utility value
2. The ratio of sales accounted for by new products is defined as sales of new products developed in the past 5 years divided by consolidated total sales in 2000.
3. For details about the sample, see Table 1.4.

Table 1.4   Survey on new product development: respondents

Distribution by industry

	Number of companies
Food	15
Textiles	10
Pulp and paper	5
Chemicals and drugs	26
Oil and rubber	8
Ceramics	7
Steel	1
Non-ferrous metals, metal products	8
Industrial machinery	18
Electrical machinery	28
Transportation equipment	19
Precision machinery	8
Other manufacturing	5
Service	2
Other	1
Total	161

Distribution by consolidated sales (2000)

Million USD	Number of Companies
More than 20,000	6
3,000–20,000	28
1,000–3,000	33
300–1,000	57
100–300	30
Less than 100	4
NA	3
Total	161

Notes:
1. Survey was carried out in November 2001.
2. Questionnaires were sent to 1,000 large manufacturing companies. One hundred and sixty-one usable responses were received for a usable response rate of 16%.

financial results. In our sample 33.09% of sales were accounted for by new products in higher performing companies, compared to only 18.94% in the lower performing companies.

Yet, we have to consider that new product development can also have negative effects on corporate performance. If a company has too many new products, it risks overflowing the shelves in retail stores and decreasing turnover. Shiseido, the cosmetics company, had this problem in the 1980s, and finally in about 1990 eliminated hundreds of its brands. Secondly, the cost of failure can be very high. Showa Denko, a chemical company, developed and sold a food additive made by a new technology drug. The side effects of the additive were serious, and Showa Denko had to pay nearly one and a half billion dollars in compensation to consumers. This case is discussed further in Chapter 10. Clearly, at a certain point a company may have more new products than it can adequately evaluate and launch.

Selected literature review

As should be clear from this chapter, there are many aspects of new product development. Each aspect is associated with its own literature. Some of the books and articles we have relied on for theory and cases are:

1. *Comprehensive studies of new product development emphasizing the development process.* Outstanding works include: Baker and Hart (1999), Cooper (2001), Crawford and Di Benedetto (2003), Kotler (2002), Kono (1987, 2003), Pessemier (1982), Schilling and Hill (1988), and Wheelwright and Clark (1992, 1995). For a provocative, critical review of the literature before 1995, see Brown and Eisenhardt (1995).[9]
2. *Quantitative analysis of new product development.* In addition to being taken up in many books on statistics, conjoint analysis is described by Asano and Yamanaka (2000), Okamoto (1998), and Crawford and Di Benedetto 2003).
3. *New product development cases.* Outstanding case books or papers include: Kurokawa (1997), Thomas (1995), Uchihashi (1978), Waseda University (2001), and Yamanouchi (1989).
4. *Research management.* Allen (1984), Burgelman et al. (2001), Narayanan (2001), Pelz and Andrews (1966), Tushman and Anderson (2004), Urakawa (1997), and Yamanouchi (1992).
5. *Creative organizations, personalities and processes.* Amabile (1998), Arieti (1976), Kawakita (1967), Levitt (1963, 2002), Leonard (1995), Senge (1990), Steiner (1965), Sternberg (1999).
6. *The diffusion of innovation.* The classic work in this area is by Rogers (5th edition, 1995). Also see Macadoc (1995).
7. *Corporate strategy and new product development.* Almost every book on corporate strategy touches on new product development. Some of these advocate ecological (Burgelman, 1991) or emergent models

(Mintzberg, 1987). In both cases much is made of the fact that new products may emerge outside the scope of current corporate strategies as middle-level managers find and promote new opportunities. As will be discussed at some length later, our research suggests the dangers of putting too much faith in these models. Firms need to systematically develop new products that are consistent with company strategies. Christensen (1997) and Christensen and Raynor (2003) suggest why it is difficult for established firms to deal with disruptive technologies. They offer some strategies managers of these firms can use to deal with this problem. Jonash and Sommerlatte (1999) show the need for integrating strategy and new product development.

Case: Shiseido Tactics hair dressing for men

This case illustrates the typical stages followed in new product development. It shows some of the difficulties of developing a new product. It also shows the process of segmentation by type of consumer. The product developed was not a "blockbuster" success, but a more typical new product success that continues to make acceptable revenues for the company.

Shiseido believes: "If you are just responding to consumer needs, you are already too late. Shiseido will offer products that awaken needs before the consumer is aware of them."

In the 1950s, pomade was a popular hair dressing for men. Pomade is an oily, some describe it as "greasy," mix that makes hair shiny and holds it tightly in place even on windy days. Early rock stars like Elvis Presley used pomade to give their hair a kind of sculpted look. Business men used it to make their hair look neat, with every hair in place. Long-extinct brands like "Vitalis" and "Wild Root Cream Oil" dominated the U.S. market for men's hair dressing throughout the 1950s. In the 1960s lighter hair liquids came into the market, and in the 1970s Shiseido's high-end brand "Bravas" became popular in Japan. In the 1980s, however, a new value system was emerging. It gave more importance to self fulfillment and self assertion. Internationalization was valued over tradition. To satisfy these new needs, Shiseido undertook the development of a new hair dressing for men. The company set the following criteria for the new product: 1. It should change the image of Shiseido to make it more fashionable with young men; 2. It should be high priced to signal high prestige and quality; 3. It should be international, appealing to markets outside Japan; and 4. It should re-invigorate the stagnant market for men's cosmetics.

A project team was formed at Shiseido. The team included a full-time leader and 15 part-time members sent from several departments. The project team proceeded through several steps:

Survey and identification of consumers. The team hired a market research company to do a survey of 1,000 men. Based on a cluster analysis of the responses to the survey and a large number of interviews, the team divided the respondents into four segments that accounted for about 80% of the market:

(a) Socially-active, open-minded, but not highly fashion conscious. About 24% of men were in this group.
(b) Fashion-conscious, very much concerned about their appeal to women. Most of these men are young, many are students. About 21% of men were in this group.
(c) Conservative, businesslike. Value a neat and clean appearance. Often middle aged. About 18% of men were in this group.
(d) Modern elite. Highly status and fashion conscious. Well-dressed. Concerned about the acceptability of their appearance to others. Often middle aged. About 17% of men were in this group.

Two of these groups, (b) and (d), were targeted for the new hair dressing. Men in category (b) are the most natural market for hair dressing, but as they grow older they tend to move to group (d), so it was important to make the new hair dressing appeal to group (b). Groups (b) and (d) are fashion leaders, influencing the choices of the other two groups as well. Naturally, there is a lot of competition to win over these groups.

Formation of a concept for the new product. The next step was to differentiate the new product from those already on the market. The team decided on the following characteristics.

• The fragrance should be subtle like that of other high-end cosmetics. It should be slightly sweet, and elegant. It should have the smell of fresh and natural green flowers.
• The product should be soft and easy to spread. It should have a nice feel and should promote healthy hair.
• The price should be at the high end, between $15 and $20 for a 300 cc (10 ounce) bottle.

Trial model products and testing. Once the new product concept was determined, many combinations of smell, touch, packaging and name were tested. Twenty-one different scents were tested in Japan, the United States and Italy. Out of the 21, five semi-finalists were selected, and finally one was chosen. When asked to associate words with the scent, respondents in the three countries said it was "young," "masculine" and "social." One hundred package designs were tested. These were narrowed down to six wooden mock ups. Several possible names for the new hair dressing were evaluated through tests in the U.S., U.K. and Japan. Some of these names were associated with music or sports, others with intellectual activities, strategy, games and love affairs. Finally, the name "Tactics" was chosen.

A new product evaluation committee, made up of top management, reviewed each stage of the development process. After Tactics had passed through these stages, it was launched nation-wide in Japan. There was no market testing, because each feature of the product had already been tested. There was some opposition at various stages to introducing the product. A marketing manager, for example, was convinced it would fail. In the end, however, all the testing that had been done helped to persuade people to go ahead with it. In all, the process of product development took about 2 years. When Tactics was introduced to the market, several sales promotion techniques were used. Large displays of the product were placed in front of retail outlets (Shiseido only sells cosmetics through selected retailers). There was an extensive advertising campaign. Some gifts were attached to the product, though it turned out this technique was not effective. Promotion by sales people turned out to be most effective.

Initial sales results for Tactics did not meet expectations. This was partly because the new product did not fit the traditional Shiseido image as a company making cosmetics for women. Of course, one of the goals for Tactics was to change the company's image. There was some criticism that the means used to promote sales were not appropriate. However, 20 some years after its introduction, this product is still sold in its original form. The Tactics case is typical. Like most new product, Tactics never became a hit product in Japan, or internationally. But, in terms of product longevity and overall sales it was a success.

2
Why New Products Fail

Often a new product development (NPD) process does not result in a new product. This may mean that the NPD process should be considered a failure. The company may desperately need the new product. But sometimes a NPD process can be considered successful because it prevents a money-losing product from being launched. Discontinuing development at an early stage may be the right decision. It may keep the company from spending a lot of money on a product that has poor prospects. In any case, no one should expect that every NPD process, or even most of them, will result in a product. To take an extreme example, the pharmaceutical industry screens an average of 10,000 molecules to find 250 suitable for preclinical testing. Of the 250 undergoing testing, only ten make it through to clinical trials, and only one is approved to go on the market. An effective NPD process is not one that makes a new product out of each new idea, but rather one that efficiently selects and develops the ideas that result in products that best fit the needs of the corporation and its customers.

So, an NPD process may be a failure because it fails to produce a new product, but it may also be a failure because it results in the launching of a new product that fails. A product is a failure if it is discontinued or divested without having made a profit for the firm. This doesn't mean that products have to be hugely successful. Indeed, some products may be taken off the market, but after they have made a profit. These would not be considered "failed products."

What causes new products to fail?

Even the casual observer can name examples of widely publicized new products by major firms that failed: "New Coke" was supposed to replace

"Classic Coke," Motorola's iridium project was supposed to result in a new global communications system. Oracle introduced a system to allow people to web-surf on their television screens. And, of course, there are thousands of failed new products that no one remembers.

Why do so many new products fail? And, what can be done to reduce the risk of a new product failure? To gain a better understanding of these issues we conducted an analysis of more than fifty cases of new product failure. We also carried out a survey of managers in Japan to get a better sense of what factors are the most common causes of failure. In our survey we asked managers to identify the causes of failure of new products that had been launched by their firms within the last 5 to 10 years. A "failed" product was one that was taken off the market because of a poor sales record, or one that had achieved a very low market share or rate of profit. Managers were asked to identify up to seven factors as contributing to the failure. Table 2.1 shows the results of our survey. Table 2.2 outlines the stages of the NPD process. The major stages include: 1. The formation of a development policy that fits the corporate strategy; 2. The collection of information and ideas to establish the new product concept; 3. The creation and testing of trial products; and, finally; 4. The launching the new product. By looking at the two tables together we can see how the specific causes of failures mentioned by managers occur at various stages in the process.

As can be seen from Table 2.1 a number of factors can contribute to failures in the NPD process. Sometimes the problem is at the very top. A strong company president may not support the development of new products that would refresh the company's product mix and allow it to do well in a changing environment. Or, conversely, perhaps a strong company president insists that the company continue to invest in new products that have poor chances for success. The president may be guided by emotion in such cases. There may be defects in the decision-making process, often because of insufficient market research or an inappropriate balancing of key decisions. This raises the question of why companies, including some with excellent reputations, make such poor decisions. The problem might be systemic at the senior management level, including the CEO and his or her top management team. Perhaps the management team is not properly structured to work towards the overall good of the company, or it may fall victim to decision-making pathologies. The company may have internal management problems that lead to a failure in the NPD process, such as poor coordination between product departments or insufficient cooperation between the groups developing, manufacturing and selling the new product. It may be that the new product does not fit company strategy

Table 2.1   Factors leading to new product failures

		% of respondents mentioning
Top management problems	• Top management unsupportive or arbitrary in support of new products	7.50
	• No product champion at top	20.00
Inability to muster critical core competencies	• R&D capability	26.88
	• Production technology	9.38
	• Marketing capability	46.88
	• Sales channels, cooperation	30.00
Poor decision-making	• Insufficient market research	55.00
	• Market too small	43.13
	• Poor fit with consumer needs	40.63
	• Too technology oriented	36.25
	• No series of product groups	14.38
	• Did not persist in development	15.63
	• Defective development process	3.13
Poor cooperation internally	• Not enough cooperation between R&D, production and marketing departments	23.75
	• Insufficient investment in R&D and advertising	5.63
Insufficient follow-up and product differentiation	• Product not unique	43.13
	• Poor quality (insufficient R&D, unsatisfactory evaluation)	18.13
	• Price too high	52.50
	• Emergence of competing products, too severe competition	28.75
	• No clear segment	8.75
	• Bad timing of release (Last stage of life cycle, imitation product, too slow development)	18.13

Note: Based on survey of 1,000 large manufacturing firms in all industrial categories carried out in November 2001. One hundred and sixty-one usable responses were received (a response rate of 16%). See Table 1.4 for details about the sample.

well, or that the company fails to incorporate it into its mainstream activities. Related to this, the firm may lack the core competencies needed to succeed with the new product, and it may be unable to build these competencies. Sometimes firms fail with new products because they do not take advantage of possible alliances with other firms that

Table 2.2   Stages of new product development

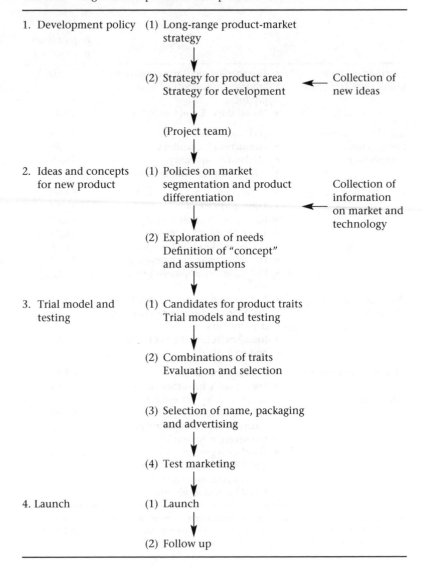

1. Development policy   (1) Long-range product-market strategy

(2) Strategy for product area   ← Collection of new ideas
    Strategy for development

(Project team)

2. Ideas and concepts for new product   (1) Policies on market segmentation and product differentiation   ← Collection of information on market and technology

(2) Exploration of needs Definition of "concept" and assumptions

3. Trial model and testing   (1) Candidates for product traits Trial models and testing

(2) Combinations of traits Evaluation and selection

(3) Selection of name, packaging and advertising

(4) Test marketing

4. Launch   (1) Launch

(2) Follow up

could help make the product a success. Finally, there may be problems with the follow up of the product launch, or with pricing, or because of the rapid emergence of strong competing products.

Passive or arbitrary top management

Crucial new products may not be developed at all because of a lack of support from top management. On the other hand, unsuccessful products may be launched because top management arbitrarily insists that the company stick with a new product, long after others are skeptical. In our survey numerous respondents mentioned top management problems as a cause of new product failures. Twenty per cent complained about a lack of product champions at the top, and 7.5% said products had failed because top management was either unsupportive or arbitrary.

Although other factors were mentioned more often, failures of top management in new product development can have enormous consequences for the company. New product development can be expensive, and cannot be undertaken without strong support at the top. On the other hand, when the wrong products are emphasized the company can lose opportunities and find itself in serious trouble.

Passive top management. Consider the case of Westinghouse Electric. This company was established in the late 19th century and, until the 1980s, was the most important American competitor to General Electric (GE). Westinghouse enjoyed extraordinary success in developing new products over much of its history. Its founder, George Westinghouse, was a great rival of Thomas Edison – and many considered Westinghouse to be the greatest engineer of his generation. During the 20th century Westinghouse Electric was granted more U.S. patents than all but two other companies. Westinghouse built the world's first AC (alternating current) power generation station, made the world's first commercial radio broadcast, pioneered the first diesel-electric railway car, built the first industrial atom-smasher, developed the electronic amplifier to improve x-ray images, built the first commercial PWR nuclear plant, and provided the cameras that made it possible for the world to watch man's first walk on the moon in 1969. In the mid-20th century Westinghouse, like GE, was a household name in much of the world – making everything from washing machines and light bulbs, to nuclear power plants and railroad equipment. But, while GE aggressively reshuffled its product mix in the 1980s, Westinghouse was slow to do so. Today, Westinghouse is no longer an independent multinational active in a wide range of industries. It is a subsidiary of an English company and specializes in nuclear power plant products. The Westinghouse brand name survives in a few products made by other companies. Westinghouse's former rival, GE, remains one of the most admired companies in the world.

Unfortunately, for their employees, suppliers and other stakeholders, there have been a number of companies like Westinghouse. Another example is provided by Nippon Columbia. This company was a highly successful manufacturer of electronic audio equipment and a producer of musical records, tapes and CDs in Japan. Unfortunately for the company, its top management focused on which new singers it should promote for its CDs, and did not pay enough attention as Sony and other manufacturers moved into its markets for audio players and musical recordings. Nor, despite the attention it gave to new singers, did the top management team do a very good job of introducing new trends in music.

Arbitrary top management. While passive CEOs can be disastrous for companies, especially during times of rapid change, a CEO who is too autocratic and aggressive can lead a company to develop products that fail catastrophically. To be sure, nearly 16% of our respondents attributed new product failures to insufficient tenacity. So a company can give up too quickly on a new product. But a company under an arbitrary leader can meet disaster by persisting too long in trying to make a product succeed. The president of Mazda automobiles (who was also a grandson of the founder of the company), Kohei Masuda, pressured his company to persist in basing the production of most of the company's cars on rotary engines long after it became doubtful that technical problems could be solved to make these cars economically viable within a reasonable time. When the oil crisis of the early 1970s made rotary engine cars, which had low fuel efficiency, even less popular with the public, Mazda was close to bankruptcy and Mr Matsuda resigned. Later, management control of Mazda was taken over by the Ford Motor Company.

One of the most innovative new products of recent years was Iridium. This was a concept developed by engineers at Motorola. Primarily funded by Motorola, Iridium launched 66 satellites in low-earth orbits to provide voice, messaging and paging services that could be routed almost anywhere on Earth. It was said that eventually a person in a rowboat in the middle of the Pacific Ocean, or on a camel in the middle of the Sahara Desert, could use an Iridium telephone to call anywhere in the world. The project was launched in 1987 under Robert Galvin, son of the founder of Motorola and the company's long-time CEO. In 1993 Chris Galvin, Robert Galvin's son, became president and CEO of the company. Under Chris Galvin, Motorola kept investing heavily in Iridium even after it was becoming apparent that the project was unlikely to make money within a reasonable amount of time. There were also growing concerns about what would happen when the orbits of Iridium's satellites began to deteriorate, making it necessary to replace them. How much money would it take to replace the satellites, and how much would Iridium have to charge its customers to pay for the replacements? Finally, in 2000, Iridium was declared bankrupt. Investors lost some $5 billion, and Motorola was sued by various creditors.

To avoid a situation where a company leader stays on too long, the founders of Honda Motors, Soichio Honda and Takeo Fujisawa, decided to retire on the 25th anniversary of the establishment of the company. Honda was 66 at the time and Fujisawa was only 62. Both men withdrew from active management of the company, and also barred their children from working there.

Poor decision-making by top management team

Several of the factors most often mentioned by our respondents as accounting for the failure of new products relate to poor decision-making by senior managers. The top management team may have failed to collect adequate information, ignored important information, or given too much weight to some factors over others. Often, for example, it turns out that the firm developed and launched a new product without first finding out if there is an adequate market for the new product.

In 1985, Coca Cola launched New Coke, and announced it would no longer sell Coke based on the company's traditional formula. New Coke was developed because Coca Cola managers had been concerned that they were losing market share to Pepsi Cola. They spent millions of dollars on research to develop a beverage that might compete better with Pepsi. New Coke, however, was a spectacular failure. The company received thousands of telephone calls from people who did not like the change, and sales of New Coke were much lower than expected. The company had to revive "Old Coke," calling it "Classic Coke." While Coca Cola had done extensive taste testing in developing the New Coke (and many people did prefer it to the traditional Coca Cola), Coke did not do market testing to see how people would react to the elimination of the traditional Coke. They failed to consider the psychological meaning of Coke.[10]

Coke, of course, survived this debacle. Schlitz Beer, once the largest producer of beer in the U.S. and second in sales only to Budweiser as late as 1976, did not survive its inadvertent introduction of a new product. Schlitz' chemists developed a new rapid brewing process that sharply cut the cost of producing beer. The new process also changed the taste of the beer. Schlitz, however, did not bother to find out how well its customers liked the new taste of the beer. Over the first several months after the fast-brewed beer was introduced the reduced production costs allowed company profits to double. Unfortunately, Schlitz's customers did not like the new beer. Rumors spread that the company was selling "green beer," and Schlitz customers switched to other brands. Schlitz never recovered.

In 1994 a Japanese city built the "Seagire" project. Seagire included a 43 story hotel, the world's largest indoor swimming pool, and a 98 hole golf course. It cost nearly $2 billion. Unfortunately, Seagire could not attract many guests. It went bankrupt in 2001, and was sold to an investment firm for one-fourteenth of what it had cost to build. The city had not carried out adequate research to make sure there was a market for this type of resort.

Canon introduced an interesting new product called "Synchro-reader" in 1984. This was a special kind of paper. A letter could be written on one side of a piece of the paper, while the other side could be used for audio recordings. Canon recruited many electrical engineers to help develop this product. It built a large production facility. The stock market was impressed, and Canon's stock price jumped about 60%. The problem was that special machines were needed both to "write" and to "read" these letters. The machines cost over $1,000. The company had not undertaken market research to test the willingness of consumers to spend so much on this technology, and in fact there were few buyers. The product failed. Interestingly, Canon was able to make the most of this failure. The company learned the need for careful market research before investing heavily in the later stages of the NPD process. The company president made a point of taking responsibility for the failure of the product launch, so that those who had been successful in developing the technology would not be blamed for the failure to carry out adequate market research. This helped foster a creative culture in the company for the future. While Canon had invested heavily in the development of competencies for this new product, these competencies proved to be useful for other products as well. The company was able to use its new electrical engineers in applying electronics to cameras and office equipment, and the new production facility was used to manufacture other new products.

In the late 1970s GE spent some $50 million to develop Halarc, a revolutionary new light bulb that lasted ten times longer than the traditional light bulb, and used far less energy. To no one's surprise, except GE's, consumers were unwilling to pay $10.95 for a light bulb, no matter how revolutionary. GE's management, like Canon's, was smart enough not to blame the researchers for this misstep, indeed many were given bonuses and promoted as rewards for their technological success.

While it might seem to violate common sense for a company to invest in a new product without making sure there will be a market for the product, it is not unusual for firms, even well-managed firms like Canon and GE, to fail to do adequate market research before investing heavily in the development of a new product. Some 55% of the managers responding to our survey said that within the last 5 to 10 years new products at their firm had failed in part because there had not been adequate market research. Perhaps not surprisingly then, more than 40% of the failed products turned out to have a poor fit with customer needs, or else they did not have a large enough market to succeed. How is it that a management committee can decide to proceed with the development of a new product without first making sure the product is likely to meet customer needs? Or that it will have a large enough market to make development worthwhile?

Composition of top management teams

Many new product failures are the result of decisions made by top management teams where important information is left out of the decision-making process, or if this information is collected, it is not given adequate attention. There are a number of reasons this happens. Some relate to a structure of management committees that is commonly used, others to processes that occur within the committees.

Management committees comprised of the heads of product divisions. Although a company's board of directors holds the legal right to make certain decisions affecting the rights of shareholders and involving some other areas, the management committee is the actual decision-making body for most operational decisions in U.S. firms, as well as for most firms in Japan, Europe and the rest of the world. At many companies the management committee is made up of product division managers. The problem with this is that the heads of product divisions generally have a vested interest in putting their division's products on the market, even if this may not be in the overall best interest of the firm. Indeed, they will most likely see greater potential for products they are familiar with than those offered by other divisions. As a result, decisions to initiate or continue a NPD process may depend more on the power of the division head, or on various bargaining processes, than on what is best for the firm. We find that successful companies avoid these problems by having small management committees with members who represent general management rather than product divisions. Such firms as Emerson Electric, Alcan, Nitto Denko and Sanyo Electric all have small management committees of this sort.

Management committee members are too specialized, and lack conceptual skills. A problem at many companies is that members of the top management committees are too narrowly specialized. Often the blinders of their specializations keep these managers from seeing possibilities outside their specialties. Some insight into the skills needed by top managers is given by a survey of 116 company presidents. The results are shown in Table 2.3. We believe that the attributes of successful

Table 2.3 What makes a good company president?

A. Conceptual skills	% mentioning
1. Broad vision, international vision	20
2. Long-range vision and flexibility	37
3. Aggressive initiative and decision-making, appropriate decisions under risk	32
4. Work and study hard	8
B. Human skills	
1. Clear statement of goal and guidelines	27
2. Willingness to listen to other's opinion	24
3a. Impartiality, unselfishness and faithfulness	37
3b. Ability to use employees' capacity fully	24
4a. Likeable personality	15
4b. Abillity to build up a team and create harmony	18
C. Good Health	32

Notes:
(1) Respondents were presidents of 116 large manufacturing companies
(2) Percentages total more than 100 because respondents could mention more than one item.
Source: "Top Management," a series of articles published in *Nihon Keizai Shinbun*, between 1980 and 1989.

company presidents are also needed for management teams to succeed. Top management needs to have both conceptual and interpersonal skills. The most important conceptual skills include having a broad and long-term vision, and flexibility. Important interpersonal skills include the ability to give a statement of goals, a willingness to listen to the opinions of others and impartiality. A successful management team member does not necessarily have to understand every technical detail about a product, but he or she does need to have the imagination and breadth of vision to see possibilities. The successful team member must be open-minded and more concerned about the overall good of the company than the interests of divisions or specialties of the company.

"Group think" in top management committees. Top management committees can also make bad decisions about new products because they become victims of "group think." The notion of "group think" was developed by the psychologist Irving Janis based on his study of several disastrous U.S. foreign policy decisions including the failure to anticipate the attack on Pearl Harbor, the chain of decisions that led to growing U.S. involvement in the Viet Nam War, and the decision of the Kennedy Administration to support the Bay of Pigs Invasion in Cuba. Janis concluded that the bad decisions involved in these disasters were not caused by the stupidity or bad motives of individuals. Indeed, the decision-makers were generally dedicated and highly-intelligent. Rather, the problem was group think, a pathology of group decision-making processes. Later scholars have concluded that group think has also been a factor in bad business decisions, such as those that led to the bankruptcy of Enron.

What is "group think"? Janis defined it as "a mode of thinking that people engage in when they are deeply involved in a cohesive in-group, when the members' efforts to achieve unanimity override their motivation to realistically appraise alternative courses of action."

Decisions affected by group think are faulty because they are made based on an incomplete survey of alternatives and objectives. The decision-makers don't carefully examine the risks associated with the choice they prefer. They don't carefully consider initially rejected alternatives. They are biased in how they process information. They don't develop contingency plans. In the case of NPD it is easy to see manifestations of these problems, for example when the NPD team doesn't do enough marketing research, when it does not identify realistic markets, or when it fails to consider possible alternative products. What causes a group of smart people to make mistakes that look foolish to outsiders? And, what are the situations in which group think is most likely to occur. Typically group think takes place when the group is somewhat insulated, so there are not many external sources of information and opinions. The group is likely to be highly cohesive – the members have high regard for one another. The group is led by a directive leader. This leader is highly respected by the other members, who want to follow his or her lead. Groups can become victims of group think because they do not have norms requiring methodical decision-making procedures. There is typically an environment of high threat. The group feels it has to act.

The conditions conducive to group think are present in many top management groups. The company president may have had many successes in the past, and thus be directive. Other members of the team will often have been appointed by the president. We have seen how firms like Motorola and Madza came to grief because they persisted too long in following the policies of strong CEOs. Team members do not want to risk becoming outsiders by disagreeing with what they see as the prevalent way of thinking in the group. These pressures for members not to express disagreement may lead to an illusion of unanimity. If the company is large and has a long history, the group may have a collective sense of invulnerability (despite the obvious threats their decision is supposed to address), with the result that individual group members do not understand how much is at stake in the decision.

How can we escape from group think? Janis states nine remedies, but we can consolidate them into two groups.

(1) Provide opportunities for criticism and objections. Create the role of critical evaluator, someone who is given the responsibility of reexamining the proposal. Perhaps an outside expert can be invited to do this. After a conclusion is tentatively reached, ask everybody to critique it. If it is too difficult to get members to do this in front of the entire group, ask them informally to give their opinions before the presentation. Informality gives people the opportunity to give their true views without being seen as disloyal to the group.

(2) Increase the number of decision alternatives. This can be done, for example, by assigning two teams to the same project. Then give each team the opportunity to criticize the other team's plan. Honda sometimes uses two teams to develop versions of the same car. If one team runs into a dead-end, the other may still be successful.

Advantages of group decision-making. It needs to be stressed that while group think can be a problem, this does not mean that group decision-making should be avoided. Janis points out, as do other researchers, that group decision-making offers a number of advantages over individual decision-making. In groups a wider variety of information and ideas are brought out. As a result, the planning concept will generally be much better than if it were developed by a single person. Group discussions can lead to very productive brain storming. Members can stimulate each other to generate more ideas, especially if there are processes so that premature criticism is not allowed to kill the creative atmosphere.

Coordination of product divisions

Product failures often result when a firm's product divisions are too independent. The delegation of authority to product divisions works well for operational decisions, but authority should be centralized for strategic decisions. We have found in various studies that a strong head office is needed to create a strong company.[11] This is because there are important differences between strategic decisions, such as introducing new products, and the operational decisions involved in running the business day-to-day. The basic differences are outlined in Table 2.4.

Past experience is generally the best guide in making good operational decisions. This is not true when something completely different, like the development of a new product, is being done. Generally the product divisions are the repositories of past experience – which may make them poorly suited to making good decisions on strategic directions such as the introduction of major new products. There may also be a wasteful duplication of efforts between the product divisions. The performance of Matsushita Electric Co. (producer of Panasonic, National, and other globally well-known brands) declined during the 1990s because the company's product division structure gave too much independence to the divisions. Similar products were developed in different divisions, and they competed with each other. For example, car navigation systems were independently developed and sold by three different Matsushita divisions. In 2000, a new company president, Kunio Nakamura, saw this as a problem and reorganized the company. He merged subsidiary companies into the various divisions and consolidated the divisions under three groups at the head office. He centralized marketing functions under the head office's marketing department

Table 2.4 Differences between strategic decisions and operational decisions

	Strategic	Operational
Subject of decision	Corporate goals, domain, organizational structure	Production planning, marketing planning
General features	Ill structured Issues are not self-evident	Well structured Problems arise cyclically
Goals	Future results Discontinuous	Current results Incremental
Information	Outside, future	Mainly from inside, past record
Idea generation	No precedent New combination	Repetitive Selection of best practices
Time horizon	Long term	Annual
Evaluation	Complex, risk and conflict Involved	Easier, can be repeated
Where decisions are made	Head office	Divisions

and consolidated many of the company's laboratories. By 2003 Matsushita's financial performance had improved sharply.

An example of strategically centralized leadership is provided by Emerson Electric. Emerson is a large multinational enterprise with some 120,000 employees around the world. The company has six business groups and 30 product divisions. It makes such products as household waste-disposal units, compressors for air conditioning systems, and electrical motors. Despite the size and complexity of the company, the head office, which is located in St. Louis, is not very large. Emerson's small top management team maintains strategic control by spending a whole day each year with the head of each division, discussing the company's long-range strategy. Given the number of divisions, it takes more than 5 weeks in all just for these first round day-long meetings. The long-range plan is followed up every month. Top management spends about 60% of its time on planning. This is one form of centralized management.

To be successful at the centralized formulation and orchestration of corporate strategy, however, top management must have the staff support needed to collect information about opportunities and threats in the changing environment. Top management cannot be expected to collect and evaluate all the information it needs to develop informed strategies by itself. Nor can it rely on its product divisions to do this. As we have seen the product divisions have their own concerns. Successful companies such as Canon, Sony and Matsushita tend to have strong strategic planning departments, while less successful companies often do not.

Cooperation between R&D, production and marketing, and with other firms

Nearly a fourth of the respondents in our survey of managers said their firm had experienced new product failures because of a lack of cooperation between R&D, production, and marketing. Some others mentioned a lack of adequate support for the new product in R&D and advertising. Many other scholars have also pointed to the poor interface between R&D, production and marketing department as a serious problem.[12]

Firms sometimes launch unsuccessful products because management of the firm's R&D is not strategically oriented. Successful products seldom come from environments that give too much freedom to researchers. Nor do they come from overly controlled environments. The balance between freedom and control is key. A famous example of too much freedom that resulted in a high level of creativity, but did not benefit the company, is provided by Xerox Corporation's Palo Alto Research Center (PARC). In 1973 scientists at PARC developed the first personal computer – years before IBM or Apple. In 1976 PARC developed a system of hardware and software that some say was not matched until Apple introduced the Macintosh 5 years later. And yet, Xerox was unable to make good use of these new products. Ironically, a company that had built its success by pioneering new technology was unable to exploit two key new technologies. Thus, from the standpoint of Xerox these technically successful products, for which there eventually proved to be huge markets, were "failed products." Much has been written about why Xerox failed to make a success of the first personal computer (e.g. Smith and Alexander, 1988). The research center was too isolated from the rest of the company, both geographically and managerially. PARC was in California, Xerox's top management was in Connecticut. Top management was not entirely aware of what PARC was doing, and did not fit the center into the mainstream planning of the company. Nor did the researchers develop products that fit what the leaders of the company expected.

The poor interface between R&D and other parts of a company can also occur because members of the R&D department have more education, and thus higher status, than members of the production and marketing departments. Because they look down on their colleagues in these departments, the R&D people may act without adequately considering their information and opinions. One company where this happened was Asahi Breweries, one of Japan's major producers of beer. Until about 1960 Asahi had about one third of the Japanese beer market. Over the following years the tastes of Japanese beer drinkers changed, and Asahi's market share dropped to below 10% in the mid-1980s. The recipe for beer was the sole responsibility of Asahi's R&D department – which had no interest in taking advice from the marketing department. The R&D department developed new beers, but these did not sell well. Things were made worse by a kind of vicious cycle. Asahi beer did not sell well, so the stock of beer got older. By the time the beer reached consumers it was often stale. This further hurt the brand image.

A new president came to Asahi from the company's major bank in 1982. The new president established a project team to study the problems of the company. The team carried out extensive market research. A study of 5,000 consumers was made to find out which aspects of beer taste were most important to the market. The team found that "richness" and "smoothness" had become the most important taste characteristics of beer. Consumers no longer preferred beer that was bitter and heavy. As a result of the marketing research, the company introduced the new Asahi Draft Beer in 1986, and then Asahi Super Dry in 1987. Before launching the new beers, the president ordered a complete recall of the old draft beer from 130,000 stores. The old beer was thrown out at a cost of $10 million.

Thousands of Asahi employees from all departments were sent out into the streets. They gave samples of Asahi Super Dry beer to about one million people. The new beer was a huge success. Asahi's market share jumped from 9% to 40% in 1990. In 2000 it was still the leading brand in the Japanese market. This case shows the importance of a market orientation, of cooperation between R&D and other departments and of how a change in corporate culture can be made.[13]

One approach to enhancing cooperation between departments is to transfer employees from one department to another. Some companies send new R&D employees to work in production or marketing. Other companies set up cross functional product development teams with members from the various departments.

Increasingly firms also need to cooperate with other firms to successfully launch a new product. This is often the case when it comes to getting a new industry standard established. A famous case of failure is that of the old Sony Betamax video recorder. Until about 1980, the Betamax dominated the market. Many still believe the Betamax was technically superior to the rival VHS system that ended up controlling the market. Sony's mistake was that it did not offer patent rights for the Betamax to other manufacturers. In response, Matsushita and Japan Victor developed the VHS video recorder, and shared patents rights to this technology with other firms around the world. As more and more firms produced VHS recorders, the firms marketing pre-recorded video tapes increasingly used the VHS standard. Once VHS was dominant in the selection of video tapes available, the fate of the Betamax was sealed. Other companies making hardware requiring support from software, such as DVD and CD players, and PCs have found it necessary to build coalitions of firms by sharing their technology.

In some industries companies are finding they need to cooperate with other firms in R&D because of the costs. In the pharmaceutical industry, for example, it typically costs $800 million or more to develop a new product – yet, as we have seen, only about one of 10,000 possibilities for a new drug typically is successful. Firms can work together to share the risk, and to speed the development process. Clearly there are potential problems when working with other companies. One is finding a fair way to allocate the rewards of a collaborative effort. Hitachi Ltd., for example, invented a computer system to map DNA. It sold its patent rights to this technology to Genetics, a venture business in the United States. Genetics succeeded in producing a DNA map of mankind and made a large profit, but Hitachi did not get much from this collaborative effort.

There are also risks of alliances between companies being too rigid. The loyalty of Swiss watchmakers to the producers of their mechanical components caused the Swiss to be slow to move to electronic watches. In Japan several electronics firms had a special arrangement with NTT, which had long had a monopoly on telephone service in Japan. These firms made the traditional black rotary dial telephones, and they did very well for many years. When the telephone industry was deregulated other firms, such as Sony and Matsushita, were much quicker to market colorful touch-tone telephones. The NTT "family" companies had been sheltered from competition because of their special relationship with NTT, and had not needed to be innovative for decades. Now it was difficult for them to develop new products.

Developing or acquiring core competencies

Sometimes a company's technological competencies and marketing capabilities are not appropriate for the new product. More than a quarter of our respondents mentioned problems in R&D capabilities, for example, as contributing to the failure of new products, and nearly half mentioned a lack of marketing competencies. These problems occur when a firm does not have the core competencies needed to succeed with the new product, and fails to develop or acquire these competencies.

Just what are core competencies? They include three components: 1. corporate culture, including values and norms; 2. management systems; and 3. technical systems. These three elements correspond to conceptual skills, human skills, and technical skills.[14] Core competencies are the bases of competitive power and provide a foundation for the creation of new corporate strategies. Core competencies are hard to imitate, are commonly used by a company in several key products, and allow a company to offer products and services which are demanded by consumers. But when there are changes in technology or in consumer demands, core competencies have to change so that these changes are transformed from threats to opportunities.

A few years ago Sears tried to enter into the insurance, investment banking and real estate businesses, but failed. These were not areas of competency for Sears, and they were not areas where Sears could easily acquire competencies. Sometimes an existing brand image can be a handicap that must be overcome with strong marketing. A few years ago a leading producer of shochu, a traditional Japanese liquor made from potatoes and various grains, imported beer-making technology from a German firm, and tried to enter the beer business. The beer the company produced may have been of high quality, but consumers could not get beyond their association of this company with its traditional product. They said the beer smelled like shochu. The company should have anticipated this problem, possibly through market research, and decided whether it had or could develop the marketing competencies to handle it.

Seiko, the highly successful Japanese watchmaker, entered into the production of eyeglasses and machines tool. Seiko failed in these industries because it lacked the core competencies to succeed in them, and it did not develop these competencies. Seiko was highly successful, however, when it entered into the PC printer business. The difference was that this time Seiko invested adequate resources into research and marketing. Furthermore, Seiko had been producing quartz watches, so it had basic electronics capabilities to build on. This case shows that core competencies can be reinforced, depending on the amount of resources spent and on synergies with existing competencies.

Developing core competencies. Many companies fail to rejuvenate their core competencies through inertia, an inability to act because of a lack of strong central leadership, or incrementalism, making only small changes that are inadequate responses to changes in the environment. Figure 2.1 diagrams some of these failures and their root causes.

Figure 2.1 Dynamic changes in core competencies

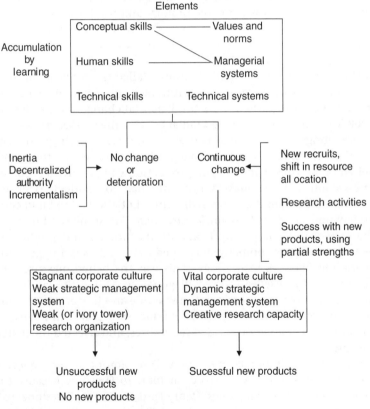

(1) Inertia
     Example: Swiss watchmakers' failure to change technology in 1970s.
(2) Inefficient deployment of core competencies.
     Example: Three competing car navigation systems developed at Matsushita in 2000s.
(3) Incrementalism
     Example: Firestone tires in 1980s

Swiss watchmakers, for example, had dominated world markets for high quality watches for generations. They stumbled when the industry shifted to electronics technology, such as the use of crystal quartz technology. One problem for the Swiss watchmakers was that they depended on components supplied by small manufacturers who could not change their traditional mechanical technology. Like the Swiss watchmakers, Seiko in Japan produced mechanical watches, and initially had no competencies in electronics. Seiko, however, was guided by a strong strategy that involved the selection and development of key competencies. The company worked with a university, and recruited electronics researchers. After intensive research, it produced a large crystal quartz clock. Eventually, it was able to scale down this technology and produce a small, electronic wrist watch. The scaled down quartz technology worked far better than the electric motors and tuning forks used by many other electronic watchmakers.[15]

The American tire company Firestone failed to survive as an independent company because it sought to make incremental changes in its key technology when more fundamental change was needed. In 1968 Michelin put steel belted radial tires on the market. These tires offered longer life and made cars easier to drive at high speeds. The problem for traditional tire makers like Firestone was that steel-belted radial tires made old tire production competencies obsolete. The established tire makers not only had to conduct extensive research to develop their own radial tires, but also had to build completely new facilities to manufacture them. Firestone tried to avoid the expense of completely changing its product and production technologies. The company developed a tire that was an extension of the old bias tire technology. This was the belted bias tire. The belted bias tire used a crossed diagonal cord (like the cloth in a necktie) to provide a more comfortable ride and longer life. It could be produced in the company's old factories. Unfortunately for Firestone, the market demanded radial tires, and rejected the belted bias tire.

Even Firestone's long-term customer Ford Motor Company rejected the new tires – this was a particular blow to Firestone because the founders of the two companies, Henry Ford and Harvey Firestone, had been close friends, and the Ford and Firestone families had intermarried. These ties notwithstanding, Ford needed to put radial tires on its cars to remain competitive. Firestone soon had to give up on belted bias tires, and rushed to develop radial tires and to build new facilities to make them. The company invested nearly $150 million in new plants in the early 1970s. However, perhaps because development had been rushed, Firestone's radial tire technology proved to be defective. In 1978 the company had to recall a record-breaking 8.7 million tires at a cost of another $150 million. The company was fatally weakened, and in 1988 it was acquired by Bridgestone.

Before 1970 Firestone was a widely admired company. Its production facilities were excellent. It was noted for its employee benefits and its bottom up decision-making style. Its close ties with Ford were also an important strength. Despite all these strengths the company failed. A major reason for the failure was that the company was too slow to re-orient its competencies to a new technology vital to its business.[16]

A company's core values can greatly influence its ability and willingness to change its core competencies. GE and ICI changed their product mixes and competencies dramatically, while such companies as Westinghouse (as we have seen), Hitachi and Toshiba did not. Hitachi and Toshiba continue to produce home appliances and semiconductors, even though these product lines are losing money. The most important value to Hitachi and Toshiba is not profits, but contributing to society by providing high technology products and protecting the welfare of employees. These policies can result in unprofitable products. If a firm's guiding value is protecting the jobs of its employees, it may be slow to close product lines and plants. Indeed, concern about its employees may have been a factor in Firestone's slowness to change to the new radial technology. The change was hard on workers skilled in the old bias ply tire technology. Whether this policy is wrong or right depends on your assumptions about to whom the company belongs and what the role of the company in society should be. As we saw with Firestone, however, if a firm risks its survival it may not be able to implement its other values.

NPD core competencies also reside in marketing, and firms often fail when they try to enter new markets because they do not adequately develop their marketing capabilities in the new area. This can be particularly difficult when firms have been in a high growth industry or a high growth economy where marketing capabilities were less necessary for success. Management may not fully appreciate the importance of marketing capabilities. Many Japanese companies found themselves in this situation as Japan entered an era of slow (and sometimes negative) growth after about 1990. Most Japanese companies at the time had previously enjoyed success because of their strengths in engineering and production, rather than in marketing. The central management problem had been rapidly increasing production of high quality products, not selling them. When markets stopped growing, the central problem changed. Now firms had to find ways to sell their products in the face of heavy competition. Some sought to enter new markets. In the food industry, for example, some firms tried to move into the growing Japanese market for mayonnaise. This market had been dominated by Kewpie, noted for making a Japanese-style mayonnaise, and by various American brands, selling American-style mayonnaise. Most of the firms trying to enter this market failed because they were unable to differentiate their products. As we will see later, another Japanese firm, Ajinomoto, was able to successfully enter the mayonnaise market by using marketing know-how it acquired from an American partner. After the Cold War ended, some U.S. firms failed when they tried to market their products to civilian rather than government markets. These firms had developed strong competencies in dealing with government bureaucrats and in meeting extraordinary technical requirements (such as designing integrated circuits that would survive nuclear explosions). They were not very good at cost control and marketing.

Acquiring core competencies.   As we have seen, some firms successfully add necessary new core competencies, but many do not. We have already seen some of the ways firms change or reinforce their core competencies. They may recruit new employees who have key knowledge (Canon and Seiko, for example, recruited large numbers of new electrical and electronics engineers to help in the development, respectively, of auto focus cameras and crystal quartz watches). They may change their allocation of resources by making new capital investments, or by reinforcing research activities. The old-line Japanese tire maker Bridgestone, unlike Firestone, quickly did this and was able to develop a radial tire. A success in new product development can reinforce some competencies, and indeed can change whole areas of core competencies. This happened, for example, when Asahi Breweries developed its Super Dry beer. Asahi had been noted for brewing traditional German style beers. Super Dry beer took a different approach that was an immediate hit with younger beer drinkers.

Other companies have been very successful in adapting to a changing environment by aggressively changing their core competencies, and their product mixes. England's ICI provides a good example. As Table 2.5 shows, this company has drastically changed its product mix over the last 24 years. Products accounting for more than 90% of

Table 2.5 Change in product mix at ICI: 1978–2002

Year	1978	1982	2002
Sales (million pounds)	4,533	12,100	5,645
Profits (million pounds)	504	565	564
Products	%	%	%
Agricultural	17	11	–
Fiber	8	–	–
Chemical materials	18	3	–
Explosive	3	5	–
Organic chemicals	10	15	–
Paint	9	13	35
Petrochemicals	16	23	–
Pharmaceuticals	6	14	(to AstraZenca)
Plastics	13	10	–
Others	2	6	–
Industrial products	–	–	14
Home care	–	–	9
Starch	–	–	31
Flavor	–	–	11

Source: ICI annual reports

its sales in 1978 were no longer made by the company in 2002. Although ICI's sales did not increase over this period, the company maintained profitability in the face of a harsh business environment. ICI changed its product mix by divesting some product divisions and acquiring others. It gave up on the concept that ICI should be the UK's heavy chemicals champion. Over this period the number of its employees decreased from 151,000 to 35,000. At first glance this may make it seem that the company served shareholders at the expense of employees, but the majority of the ICI employees kept their jobs. It was just that their divisions were now part of other companies. Some 60,000, for example, went with the pharmaceutical division to AstraZeneca, the highly successful pharmaceutical company. If ICI had not changed its product mix many more employees might have lost their jobs.

Launching problems

Sometimes a new product is successful in the market, but must still be considered a failure because the firm developing it does not make much profit from it. More than a quarter of the managers responding to our survey mentioned problems such as the emergence of strong competitors shortly after the launch of a new product as leading to the failure of the product. This can occur because of insufficient product differentiation or because there are few barriers to the entry of competitors once they see that there is a market for the product.

Product differentiation. An emerging challenge in some industries is the increased modularization of component parts. Assemblers of automobiles, computers, and electrical machinery are finding that their components require increasingly high levels of technology. Rather than undertake the (perhaps impossible) task of building competencies in all the new areas critical to their product, they turn to component suppliers to provide these competencies. This contributes to the strength of the assembler. Toyota, for example, benefits greatly from its close relationship with Nippon Denso. GE, Dell, Siemens, Ford, and most other multinationals are increasingly outsourcing component parts, and even engineering and design work, to companies that can provide these goods and services at lower cost.

The risk in some industries is that as more and more components are standardized, there will be a loss of product differentiation. The final product may become a commodity. This has happened, for example, with personal computers. In 2004 personal commuters had become commoditized to the point that IBM sold off its PC division to a Chinese company. The PC came to be an assembled package of standard computer chips (usually from Intel), software (usually from Microsoft), and a few other readily available components. There was little difference between the PCs offered by different companies, and brand names came to have little importance. The producers had to depend on price competition rather than product innovation and differentiation to keep their market share. Not all industries, however, face the same risk of a loss of product differentiation. A critical difference is whether the interface of components is standardized or not. In the case of automobiles, while some of the components may not be distinctive, the overall product is. The interface of modular components is not standardized. Automobiles are a product characterized by "integral architecture." Corporate decision-makers have to consider carefully what category a proposed new product might fit into, and evaluate the risks accordingly.

No barriers to entry for competitors. As was mentioned in Chapter 1, the English company EMI pioneered production of the CT scanner (also called CAT scanner), yet lost control of this market before it could fully profit from it. EMI introduced the CT scanner in 1972. The company received a flood of orders. Margins on sales were around 30%, and everything looked very promising for EMI. But competitors saw the success of the CT scanner and quickly entered this market, EMI's market share (and profits) plummeted almost immediately, and the company had to sell its CT scanner business to another company. In Chapter 1 we described how EMI was weaker than GE in the U.S. market, and how this contributed to its failure to capitalize on its new product. There were other problems as well. EMI was not able to stay ahead of its competitors technologically. Three giants in the electronics industry, GE in the U.S., and Siemens and Philips in Europe, aggressively worked to further develop the CT scanner, cutting the time required for a CAT scan and sharply reducing the cost of a scanner. EMI was not able to maintain a technological lead that would have served as a barrier to the entry of these other firms into this market.

Other firms have also lost the advantage of being first to market with important new products because competitors quickly offered equal or better versions of the same product. Konica, for example, was the first to develop an auto-focus camera, but soon lost much of this market to Canon because Canon developed a camera that could measure distances and focus even when it was dark.

Maintenance of a technological lead can help protect the market for a new product. As was mentioned in Chapter 1, Sony developed 150 different versions of the Walkman within 5 years of launching the product. And, Walkman so far has succeeded in keeping ahead of its competitors.

Types of entry barriers. Several types of barriers can keep competitors from moving into the market for a new product. A firm might build a large-scale production facility, so that little room is left for the products of competitors. The Korean company Samsung followed this strategy by investing in a large LSI production facility. A firm might have an advantage over potential rivals in production, sales or distribution costs due to access to raw materials, superior market channels, better production technology or other factors. As we have seen, product differentiation is an effective way to keep control over a market. This might be attained through a strong brand. A firm may be able to control the technology that supports the new product, possibly by holding patents or proprietary knowledge. High exit barriers can also be barriers to entry. Other firms will be cautious about investing heavily to enter a new market if

Figure 2.2   Causes of new product failure

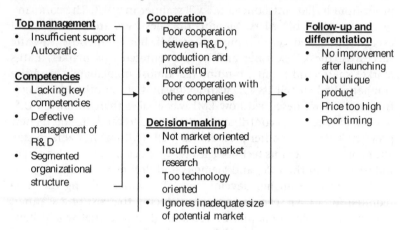

Top management
- Insufficient support
- Autocratic

Competencies
- Lacking key competencies
- Defective management of R&D
- Segmented organizational structure

Cooperation
- Poor cooperation between R&D, production and marketing
- Poor cooperation with other companies

Decision-making
- Not market oriented
- Insufficient market research
- Too technology oriented
- Ignores inadequate size of potential market

Follow-up and differentiation
- No improvement after launching
- Not unique product
- Price too high
- Poor timing

the cost of failure could be very high. Finally, as we have seen in the case of Sony and the Walkman, a firm can continue improving a product to the point that other firms can't keep up. Failure to do this resulted in the failure of what should have a major new product success for EMI.

We have discussed a large number of factors that can lead to the failure of a new product. These factors are shown schematically in Figure 2.2. We will discuss them in greater detail in the following chapters.

Selected literature review[17]

In this chapter we have drawn on a number of scholars, and on a number of published cases of new product failure. Levitt (1963, 2002) examines why new idea creators are often poor at implementing their ideas or at operating businesses. Amabile (1998) shows how reliance on control and order can undermine the employees' ability to generate and implement powerful ideas. Nutt (1999) says that half the decisions made in organizations fail. He analyzes why operational decisions are not implemented. The two major reasons are insufficient information and defective motivation. Janis (1972) explains the problem of "group think" in group decision-making process. Amabile et al. (2002) analyze success and failure when time pressures are strong. Rumelt (1982) analyzes the role of synergy in the success and failure of diversification. A number of books give case studies of new product development failure. Smith and Alexander (1988) describe PARC and Xerox. Nikkei (2004) describes how Canon found it needed to re-organize its product development processes. On modular architecture and integral architecture, see Baldwin and Clark, 1997; Christensen (1997) and Christensen and Raynor, 2003) describe numerous cases where firms concentrated their R&D on making incremental improvements that would satisfy their traditional customers, and missed opportunities for develop new markets. Much of the literature on core competencies was originated by Prahalad and Hamel (1990). Also see Leonard-Barton (1992). We drew on Kawade (1989) for information on Bridgestone and Firestone.

3
New Product Development Processes

The successful development of different types of products requires that different NPD processes be used. Some products, for example, are technology intensive, such as copiers and pharmaceuticals. Some are market intensive, but in markets where consumer preferences are relatively stable, such as cosmetics and mayonnaise. And for some products, consumer preferences are crucial, but are highly dynamic. An example is fashionable women's clothing. The successful development of new technology intensive products requires considerable technological testing. With market intensive products extensive market testing is needed. And, when the product involves a high level of demand uncertainty, it is necessary to use a trial and error experimental approach involving several cycles of short production runs and dynamic market feedback.

In this chapter we discuss the NPD for each of these three types of product and give case examples for each type. We also describe various NPD sub-processes, and present cases that illustrate several of the processes and sub-processes.

Developing technology intensive products

With technology intensive products the emphasis of NPD is, of course, the development of the technology that delivers the characteristics desired in the new product. Here we offer two very different cases of how successful technology products were developed.

Case: The Canon personal copier

One of the best documented cases of the successful development of a technology intensive product is Canon's small "personal copiers," the

PC10 and PC20. These were the best selling copiers in the world until 1987.[18]

Decision to develop the new product and organization of the project team. In the 1960s Canon was a highly successful producer of high quality cameras, but the market for cameras was mature, and top management worried that the company was overly dependent on a single product. In 1965, as part of its long-range plan, the company made the strategic decision to enter the copier business. Top management reasoned that a copier could be thought of as a large-scale camera – so Canon's technological competencies were well-suited to this new product. Copiers were also a growth product. Canon's entry into the business was successful, and by 1979 copiers accounted for 35% of the company's sales. In 1980 Canon saw huge market potential for smaller copiers. A project team was organized at a plant next to the company's head office. This team, called "Task Force X," included 200 members appointed by Canon's CEO. This was the largest NPD task force organized at Canon since the company had developed its highly successful AE-1 camera some years earlier. The earlier success was posed as a model for the new project, and Task Force X took as its slogan: "Let's create the AE-1 of copiers."

Task Force X was made up of three groups. Group A was responsible for design and technical development. Group B was responsible for the development of production technology. Group C provided staff support, with a coordinating committee, a steering committee and other groups responsible for cost, quality, patents, etc. The steering committee coordinated the team's activities, schedules and budget. Most of the Task Force team was brought in from the development department, but the team was cross functional. Most team members worked full-time on the project. The overall development process is shown in Figure 3.1.

Information collection and product concept formation. After the development policy was decided, the team began to collect information. To evaluate the potential demand for small copiers, the team estimated the number of offices with fewer than five people working in them, the likely demand for desktop copiers from large corporations, and the expected demand for small copiers in households. The team decided that a small copier that would meet the demands of these market segments should:

1. Weigh less than 20 kilograms (44 pounds)
2. Cost less than 1,000 U.S. dollars.

Figure 3.1   Canon copier development process

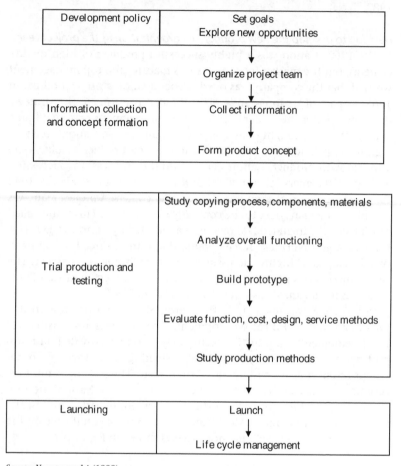

Source: Yamanouchi (1989).
Notes:
(1) Many ideas were presented during trial production and testing.
(2) Many feedback and spiral processes took place during development.

3. Be "maintenance free," i.e. be designed so that maintenance could be done by simply replacing components.
4. Be sold, not leased like other copiers.

The creation of the product concept was done only after there had been an extensive collection of information. This was a critical starting point. It is where the goals for the project were set.

Trial production and testing. Several activities took place during trial production and testing.

1. Studies of which copying process to use, what components would be needed and what materials would be used.
2. Analysis of the overall copying function of the machine.
3. Building of prototypes to evaluate the copier's functioning, its cost, and its design and service requirements.
4. Studies of production system for the copiers.
5. Design of a mass production system for the copier.

During the first two of these phases the components of the project were closely examined. Many ideas were presented and many experiments were carried out. During the third and fourth phases, the various components were integrated. The entire process can be thought of as having consisted of three sets of activities: goal-setting; analysis of the components needed to reach the goals; and integration of the components into a total system.

Product Launch. In accord with the product concept, the copiers were to be sold, not leased. A service support system designed to accommodate small business and household owners of copiers was established. Sales began.

Success factors. The new copier was a huge success because: 1. The developers effectively used market research to identify a market niche (i.e., a maintenance-free copier for less than $1,000); 2. The Task Force achieved good cooperation between the development and production departments; 3. The Task Force was staffed by young engineers who came up with many new ideas (indeed they produced nearly 600 patents); 4. The manager of the development department was an effective product champion, working hard to improve communications between top management and the young engineers.

Case: Development of an antibacterial agent

Tarivid is a broad spectrum oral antibacterial drug. It is used in the treatment of nearly 50 different diseases, and is effective against urinary tract infections, infectious diseases of the intestine, as well as pulmonary infections and intractable infections. It was launched by Daiichi Pharmaceutical Company in 1985, and quickly took the lead in the market for antibacterial agents. By 1991 it had sales of about $400 million. It was sold in 119 countries.

The development of a new medicine is distinctive in at least three important respects: 1. Generally, the need for the new medicine is known before product development begins; 2. Development times are very long – usually 10 to 15 years and; 3. Partly because of the long development times, but also because of the special needs to ensure the safety of the medicine and to gain regulatory approval for it, development costs are extraordinarily high – a widely reported estimate for 2005 was that it cost over $800 million to develop a new medicine, and sometimes much more. The overall process of development of a successful new medicine typically involves screening about ten thousand molecules to find one that results in an approved drug.[19]

New Medicine Development. The development of a new medicine can be thought of as comprising three sub-processes (see Table 3.1). (1) Drug discovery, (2) Pre-clinical testing, and (3) Clinical trials.

During drug discovery a number of promising new compounds are either discovered in nature or created in the laboratory. The compounds are screened in test tubes and by testing on animals. These

Table 3.1   Development of a new medicine

Phase 1 Drug discovery (2–3 years)
Target identification (gene and compounds)
Study of physical and chemical traits
Screening

$\downarrow$

Phase 2 Preclinical development (3–5 years)
Pharmaceutical studies (absorption, distribution, metabolism, excretion)
Animal tests

$\downarrow$

Phase 3 Clinical trials (3–7 years)
Phase 3.1 (safety tests)
Phase 3.2 (effectiveness tests, small scale)
Phase 3.3 (effectiveness tests, large scale)

$\downarrow$

Process chemistry and production
Registration
Sales and marketing

---

tests are used to determine the compound's effectiveness, toxicity, absorption distribution, and its effects on metabolism and excretion. During clinical trials the compound is administered to humans to further evaluate its effectiveness, and to determine appropriate dosages and methods of application. In Phase I the test subjects are healthy volunteers (usually men with an average age of about 30). In Phase II a broader, but still limited number of test subjects is used. These are people who have the condition the drug is intended to treat. One group of these subjects receives the drug, the other is given a placebo. In Phase III the drug is tested in several hundred to several thousand patients who have the disease or the condition the drug is supposed to treat. Phase III typically lasts several years. Some 70% to 90% of the drugs that enter Phase III testing are approved.

During the development of a new medicine, the compound being studied can't be changed. This is a special feature of drug development. When a new car is being developed the design and the modules can be changed. But when a new drug is being developed, the compound is either used or it is not. It can not be modified. Thus a large number of compounds must be tested to find an effective and safe new drug.

Exploratory process. The exploratory process includes three stages: finding a compound with the specified characteristics (the lead compound), constructing a system to test the compound, and synthesizing the compound. In research on antibacterial agents, the system of testing is well established. Bacteria on a plate is tested using different compounds. Research concentrates on producing the compounds to be tested.

There are two design processes. The first selects the compound platform ("the parent compound") necessary to activate the desired compound structure. The other finds ways to increase activity. Finding a parent compound with antibacterial activity is extremely difficult. The company constructs the compound from the natural library or from something found in its accumulated research. Or the company may select it from a known parent compound. Once the parent compound has been selected, the next stage is to find ways to increase activity. After the design has been determined, the compound is actually produced. Antibacterial activity is measured and assessed, and in a process of trial and error a promising compound is finally identified.

Development of Tarivid. Daiichi Pharmaceutical Company started to develop antibacterial drugs in 1964 by experimenting with Wintomylon (nalidixic acid), a first generation quinolone, from Winthrop Laboratories. Over the next 20 years, Daiichi experienced a series of failures and accumulated a large amount of experience. Early on the company composed "DJ-1611," a synthesized antibacterial, but this compound was not easily absorbed through the bowel, and did not attain an effective blood concentration. Through a structural conversion "DB-2563" was composed, but it failed clinical trials. Next "DJ-6783" was tried. This compound did far better in animal tests of absorption than the earlier compounds, but researchers could not show that it was effective in human clinical trials. Development was discontinued during Phase II.

New goals were established. The researchers now sought: (a) A compound with high antibacterial activity that also (b) allowed high blood concentrations, and (c) was less subject to metabolic action.

The New Approach. Daiichi began exploring a new generation of quinolons. A new-quinolon antibacterial agent had first been introduced by Kyorin Pharmaceutical Co. in 1978. Daiichi started developing its own new-quinolon antibacterial agent. The new-quinolon had the same antibacterial activity, but at a lower blood concentration.

Designing a chemical compound. In the exploratory research phase of new medicine development, the first step is to design and create the compound. Most of the candidate compounds are eliminated during the development process. To minimize the uncertainty involved in this process a large amount of information must be collected and reviewed. Researchers need to examine both explicit information and tacit knowledge that has been accumulated in the company, patent information, and information in the published literature. By combining a variety of information and knowledge, Daiichi identified promising new chemical compounds. One piece of useful information, for example, came from studying a compound patented by another company, Otsuka Pharmaceutical. This compound was not suitable for use as a medicine, because the central action was too high. But Daiichi's researchers were able to modify the compound to overcome this problem.

Creating a chemical compound. After a chemical compound is designed it must be composed. In the 1980s, this typically took a week to 10 days. This particular compound, however, presented special difficulties, so the design process took 4 months. The researchers found they could obtain Cl with an intermediary, but it was difficult to replace the intermediary with Cl. Finally, a member of the research team happened to read a paper on the halogen reactions of a material with a benzene ring. This helped the researcher find a new way to compose the compound.

After Tarivid. Many rival companies entered this market because Tarivid was so successful, but Daiichi continued development work. The researchers knew that Tarivid was composed of two optical compounds (S&R). After considerable difficulty they managed to separate these compounds. They found that S was the effective component. Indeed the separated S portion had twice the effectiveness of the old Tarivid, with fewer side effects. It was also more water-soluble. The company applied for a patent on the S component.

During preclinical and clinical tests, and the rest of the development process, the S component was found to be an ideal oral antibacterial agent. It had high antibacterial effects and few side effects. This new compound was named Cravid, and in 1992 it was launched to replace Tarivid.

Success factors. This case shows some of the uncertainty involved in developing a new medicine. The key to reducing this uncertainty is effectively finding and using as much relevant information as possible. Antibacterial research had gone on for decades, so Daiichi had accumulated substantial knowledge about synthesized antibacterials. The company also had rich experience in creating compounds which are not affected by bodily metabolism. Daiichi also carefully monitored outside sources of information. It monitored patents held by other companies such as Otsuka and Kyorin, and new scientific developments published in academic journals. It used this knowledge to create a new compound.

Coping with technological uncertainty. As it continued to do research, Daiichi accumulated more knowledge. It also increased its ability to collect useful information from outside the company. These capabilities allowed Daiichi to effectively test the level of concentration of the antibacterial agent and the antibacterial activity during the early stages of development. They did not, however, help Daiichi evaluate tissue penetration. The greater the amount of knowledge that has been accumulated, the harder it is to cope with major technological changes. There are several ways of dealing with this problem.
(1) Bootleg research. A common mantra of successful researchers is: "challenge common sense." And yet researchers find it difficult to do research that has not been formally assigned to them. To overcome this limitation, many organizations allow researchers to spend a certain percentage of their time doing research in other

areas – bootleg or under-the-table research. The development of Tarivid was initiated in this manner by a small research group.
(2) Strong top management support. At Daiichi, the laboratories were directly under the president. He had the flexibility to allocate resources to bootleg projects like this one.
(3) Overcome formal project limitations. Daiichi gave high priority to developing a new synthesized antibacterial agent. It mobilized a large number of researchers, but the formal project teams were not able to produce an agent that was more effective than Tarivid. Under conditions of high technological uncertainty, formal project organizations may not be effective in developing a successful product.[20]

Developing marketing intensive products

With certain products, such as food, automobiles, cosmetics and clothing, technical features don't matter as much as emotional satisfaction, social meaning, taste, color, smell and design. Packaging and the brand name are also important. These are "marketing intensive products." Sometimes technology intensive products become marketing intensive over time. Many home appliances, for example, have reached the point where the competing products all have similar technical features. A generation ago a new refrigerator or range may have succeeded because it had unique technical features, but now success more often depends on styling and other intangibles that the market likes. Viking, SubZero, Fisher Pakel, Wolf and some other appliance brands are regarded as prestigious, despite ratings for performance and reliability that are average at best. Because of their style and prestige they can command huge price premiums.

In developing marketing intensive products two important concepts should be kept in mind: product differentiation and market segmentation. Needs (wants) differ depending on the customer's age (Generation X'ers don't like the same kinds of cars that Baby Boomers like), or the situation (stylish clothing for the office is different from stylish clothing for going out). In developing marketing intensive products the team has to come up with product premises, test their validity, and find the product most suitable for the targeted use. This is a continuous testing process.

Case: Ajinomoto mayonnaise

A successful market intensive NPD product is illustrated by the experience of a leading food product company, Ajinomoto. Ajinomoto intro-

Figure 3.2 Development process for marketing intensive product (Ajinomoto Mayonnaise)

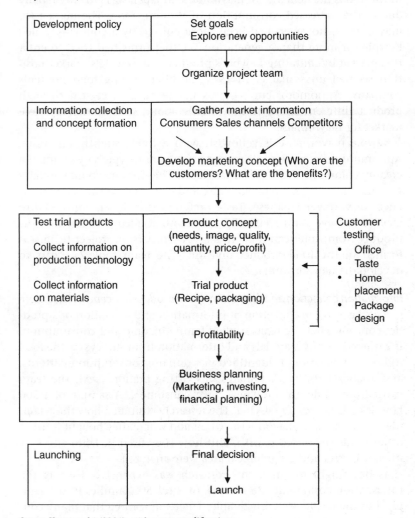

Source: Yamaguchi (2001), with some modifications.

duced a new style of mayonnaise in Japan in the 1960s, and then successfully introduced two other new mayonnaise products in the 1990s. The overall process by which Ajinomoto developed the new mayonnaise is shown in Figure 3.2.

Decision to develop the new product and organization of the project team.
In the 1960s the demand for mayonnaise in Japan was growing rapidly
due to the increased consumption of Western food. The market for
mayonnaise, however, had been monopolized by a company called
Kewpie for more than a generation.[21] Other firms had tried to enter
this market by imitating Kewpie's product, but Kewpie's market position seemed unassailable. In 1967, another leading food products
company, Ajinomoto, entered this market and succeeded through
product differentiation. It now holds about 30% of the Japanese
market for mayonnaise.

Kewpie mayonnaise is yellowish with a thick, slightly tart taste.
Ajinomoto differentiated its mayonnaise from Kewpie's by giving it a
creamy color and a softer, less tart taste. The Ajinomoto mayonnaise
was more like American mayonnaise and better suited the taste preferences of younger Japanese. Taste preferences in Japan continued to
change, however, and eventually Ajinomoto decided to differentiate its
product from American mayonnaise. A ten person project team was
formed in the food product division. The team took $2\frac{1}{2}$ years to
develop the new mayonnaise.

Information collection and formation of the product concept. There were
three stages in the collection of information and formation of a product concept. First the team studied family income and consumption.
It gathered census materials and information from surveys by the food
industry association. It identified mayonnaise consumption patterns,
and analyzed the market shares of existing brands. Next, the team
carried out in-depth interviews with consumers. A sample of 1,500
families was randomly selected. The researchers studied how these families thought about mayonnaise, when and where they bought it, what
other foods they used it with, and how they used it. Differences by
income cluster and geographical area were analyzed.

As one might imagine, this research was expensive. Getting the
information cost about $35 for *each* of the 1,500 families in the sam-
ple, but the results were invaluable. The team learned that many consumers were dissatisfied with the mayonnaise that was then on the
market. These consumers wanted a soft, tart taste. This formed the
basis for the new product concept.

Development and testing of a trial product. Ajinomoto used its food and
production technology expertise to test possible features of the new mayonnaise. It produced samples of mayonnaise with tastes falling into

twenty "groups" of tartness, each with several variants. Many other combinations of taste characteristics were also tested. The product premises were used to decide which combinations to try. Laboratory staff members were the first to test the new product. Next, it was given to a panel of housewives. The opinion of each housewife was collected in interviews. Finally, the new product was placed in homes, and opinions were solicited from each member of each of these households.

A survey company collected a variety of other information. This company studied the functioning, shape and design of packaging. Pictures of possible packages were tested, than wooden and plastic models were made and tested. The survey company studied potential prices. A price point was selected based on the production cost and the prices of rival products. It was decided to set the price 10% higher than the main rival product to see whether consumers would accept this price. Then sales channels were examined to determine what sorts of refrigeration were available, and what margins were required.

Product Launch. The product was launched on a trial basis in the Tokyo area. A panel survey of the distribution channels was used to determine the inventory and turn-over ratios. A survey was done to evaluate POP (point of purchase) advertising, showcase design, and the impact of special service by sales people. This information helped the company improve its advertising and sales promotion methods.

The product was finally launched $2\frac{1}{2}$ years after the formation of the product concept. Sales were started in the Tokyo area. After a year, success of the new mayonnaise had been confirmed, and it was marketed all over Japan. Sales in the second year reached about $100 million.

Ajinomoto's new mayonnaise succeeded for several reasons. The company followed its creed of "better and different" to develop a differentiated product concept. It collected a large amount of relevant information to provide a good basis to form ideas. The ideas were tested, and then fleshed out. At first the product was distributed directly from the manufacturing plants to retail stores. This ensured that the mayonnaise in stores would be fresh. After a year, the mayonnaise was also distributed through wholesalers. Over a million dollars was invested in advertising during the first month of sales. Through the multiple effects of advertising, other sales promotion activities, and publicity (such as sending press releases to newspapers and other periodicals), diffusion of the brand name reached 86%. Finally, it should be noted, mayonnaise is a product that fits Ajinomoto's brand image in Japan. It had synergy effects with the company's other products.

Two new Ajinomoto products. In 1995 and 1996, Ajinomoto launched two new products in an effort to further expand its market share. One of the new mayonnaises has less fat and is oriented to dieters. The other, "Ajinomoto Pure Select Mayonnaise," has an improved taste. Here is how "Pure Select" was developed.

Information collection and formation of product concept (The new product concept is discussed in more detail in Chapter 5). Ajinomoto carries out large scale marketing research every 3 years. In the mid-1990s the company found that in Japan some 25% of mayonnaise is used in salads, 41% to garnish vegetables, and 34% in other ways. Consumers most wanted mayonnaise to be tasty (30%) and smooth (9%). Twenty-eight per cent wanted it to be low in fat. In developing a new product to meet these preferences, Ajinomoto decided to target the tastes of younger consumers.

Production and testing of trial product. To achieve the product concept, the soy bean oil traditionally used in mayonnaise was replaced by rape seed oil. Three-year-old malted vinegar was used so the product could be kept fresh for up to a week. Thirty kinds of samples were produced and tested over a year before the final product was chosen. The plastic bottle containing the mayonnaise was made a little harder to make it distinctive, and "Pure Select" was chosen as the new brand name. Testing was carried out with customers. The new mayonnaise cost more to produce, but managers decided to keep the price the same.

Case: Development of the Toyota Corolla

The Toyota Corolla was introduced in 1966. By 1999 some 28 million Corollas had been produced, dwarfing the production runs of such cars as the Model T Ford and Volkswagen. In this case we will see how the ninth generation Corolla was developed. Cars are complex products, made up of many systems and components. Consequently, many departments are involved in designing and developing a new car. This case shows how Toyota departments and suppliers worked together to develop the new Corolla.

The product development department of Toyota is composed of five development centers (see Figure 3.3). Three of the centers (FR, FF and RV) specialize in the development of different types of cars. The fourth develops engines and the fifth develops electrical systems. Members of the FF center worked with the fourth and fifth development centers in the development of the Corolla. The project team was cross functional,

Figure 3.3   Toyota organization chart (as of 2003)

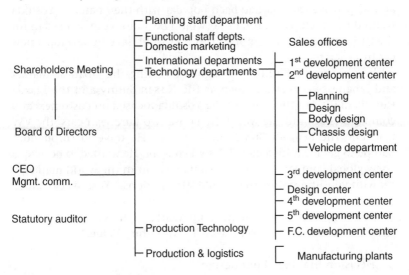

Source: Organization chart published by Toyota.

with about 20 full-time members from the design and experimental departments, assembly plants, and suppliers. These were key members from each department. Others from the design, chassis design, experiment and power-train departments also worked with the project team as part-time members. The project leader was the chief engineer, Mr Takeshi Yoshida.

Many departments participated in the early stage of development. This made concurrent engineering possible. This process may be called "design-in" or "concept-in."

1   Marketing research and concept creation

The project was started in 1997, and the new Corolla was launched about $3\frac{1}{2}$ years later. The first step was to get a good sense of Corolla's current brand image. Customers and dealers were asked what they thought of the Corolla. The results showed that people thought of Corolla as a safe and dependable car, but one that was "commonplace, inexpensive, mediocre, and lacking in charm." Yoshida wanted to create a new image. He did not refer to the history of the car in creating the concept of the new Corolla – the old concept for the old Corolla had been created from the producer's viewpoint, not the consumer's. To younger consumers, Corolla was an inexpensive car that had been popular with their parents. Yoshida wanted to develop a Corolla that would be a new compact sedan for the 21st century. To accomplish this he would have to develop a new car from scratch.

The old Corolla had been designed targeting the Japanese market and Japanese competitors such as the Nissan Sunny and the Mazda Familia (326). For the new Corolla Yoshida focused on customers and competitors around the world. He chose two European cars, the VW Golf and the Peugeot 306 as benchmarks. He traveled throughout Europe to get ideas for a global design concept. He wanted to develop a "new global compact car which would be a hit in the world market, a car with youthful styling that would stir emotions." Yoshida explained this concept not only to top management, but also to members of the project team, each department, component suppliers and dealers. The tentative name for the new car was "New Century Value."

2   Decision-making about design

When Mr Yoshida was appointed chief engineer (CE) of the project team, a full size mock-up of the 9th generation Corolla had already been made. This design by the 2nd development center had been selected from among three alternatives. But Yoshida did not accept this design. For one thing, customers could tell at once that it was only a little different from the 8th generation Corolla. Even worse, it had been designed for the Japanese domestic market, and it did not fit the new globally-oriented image he wanted the new Corolla to have.

From the beginning Toyota's top management supported Yoshida's proposal to start over and redesign the car. There was a competition among five designs, two from the 2nd Development Center, and one each from the American, European, and Tokyo design centers. The one from the European Design Center was selected. This model had a short nose and high roof. It fit the image of a car for young drivers, and was expected to be well received in the world market. An interior design was selected from at least six alternatives. The interior of the Corolla wagon was given special attention. There was a careful analysis of the "benchmark cars," the VW Golf and the Peugeot 306. Ideas were solicited not only from members of the design staff, but also from other employees. One result was that the gaps where parts fit together were cut in half to give the dashboard, hood, doors and other parts the look of a high quality car. A special challenge was that this new standard of quality had to be achievable not only in Japan, but at all 15 Corolla production centers around the world. The goal was not merely to improve fuel economy, brake performance, and crash resistance standards over those achieved in older models, but to move towards absolute "ought-to-be" values. High standards were set for basic performance. Eighty "very important controlled components" were newly designed.

3   Trial production and use of IT

Toyota had worked with component suppliers since 1997 to develop a computerized car design system. This system, "Visual and Virtual Communication," allows a product developer to use a computer to check the fit between components, operating feasibility, and body appearance. In addition, it can create three dimensional displays showing the product, equipment and workers in production simulations. This makes it possible to identify problems with the product or production system before prototypes are made.

Use of IT enabled Toyota to shorten the development period. Changes in design charts are never completely accurate, so in the past physical models had to be used so that final adjustments could be made in the design. This added time and expense to the development process. Now the design can be finalized through the use of IT.

4   Cost reduction

A cost reduction committee was organized in 1998. The committee was led by an executive director, and included ten directors responsible for various technologies. This cross functional team also included members from component suppliers, production plants and procurement departments. They met once a month and, because of the make up of the team, were often able to make key decisions on the spot.

Cost reduction was also carried out at the grass roots level. An accurate measurement was made of the cost of each car produced. To reduce the cost of components, a team made up of people from procurement, technology and production was sent to suppliers. The teams did a cost analysis at the suppliers, and suggested cost reductions. Through these activities they were able to reduce costs by 30%. Toyota maximized the use of standard components across different cars, which gave the suppliers economies of scale. These cost reduction activities were applied not only at the production plant, but also in sales channels; and not only in Japan, but also in the U.S. and in Europe.

Success factors. The success of the Corolla project can be evaluated in terms of four areas of competency: technical, market, human resource, and organizational.

The project was highly successful from the standpoint of three main aspects of technological competency, the speed and efficiency of product development, the level of quality control and the effectiveness of cost control. As we have seen, the support of top management, Toyota's large technology data base, and the project's effective use of IT, led to a fast and efficient NPD process. A high level of quality control and effective cost control was also achieved. In its 2001 survey JD Power Co. ranked the 9th generation Corolla as having the highest quality of any compact car. Finally, value engineering and value added activities allowed a strong control over component costs.

The project was also highly successful from the standpoint of marketing. Several factors contributed to this success. Toyota had accumulated a large amount of market information, and used it effectively in this project. Since the introduction of the 3rd generation Corolla, Toyota had conducted extensive surveys, and used this information in the development of new cars. The company has a special survey department to analyze user needs. This department is continuously collecting information on sales, and on the quality record of cars. The 9th generation Corolla project also effectively responded to customer needs. The project manager himself visited dealers to listen to their opinions and talked to customers to get their views.

Toyota also demonstrated a high level of human resource competency in several aspects of the project. Top management made speedy decisions, had a clear vision, and strongly supported the product concept. The recruitment of project managers was also handled well. Young engineers were recruited from engineering departments and trained as assistant project managers. Some were promoted to project manager after training, the others returned to their former departments.

The project also showed Toyota's high level of organizational competency. Cross functional teams were used to integrate the development activities of several departments. Rapid development was attained by carrying out product and process engineering, production and marketing in parallel. This also contributed to further cost reductions and improved quality. Toyota was able to transfer successful systems from one project to others. By transferring cost reduction activities to other design and development projects, Toyota reduced the ratio of the cost of components and materials to sales from 65.8% to 63.2%.

Major processes of car development and feedback system. New car development includes four major processes: (1) concept creation, (2) product planning, (3) product engineering and (4) process engineering. In the first and second of these processes a rich imagination is needed. The project team is given more freedom and decision-making authority, and is allowed the time needed to arrive at a good design. In the last two processes, speed and accuracy are most important.

These four processes generally flow in sequence, but there are also feedback loops. If it appears problems are coming from the previous stage, it is necessary to go back and fix them. In a concurrent engineering process, there is not as much feedback as with a relay system, but some kind of feedback is still needed.

To speed up development and enhance the efficiency of car development, Toyota has set standard times for development. When the car uses a new platform, for example, the time to mass production should be 18 months. When the platform is similar to that used for an existing car, the time to mass production should be 15 months. When the platform is the same as that of an existing car, the time should be 12 months. Automakers have found that product differentiation can often be achieved, even when the same platform is used.[22]

Developing dynamic market products

Fashionable apparel and some other products have rather different characteristics from technology and market intensive products. The technology for these products does not take long to develop, and, while market acceptance is crucial, the product features desired by the market are highly unstable. The cost of development is not very high, but potential losses due to unsold inventory are very high. A trial and error, or spiral, model is most suitable for the development of products of this type. Figure 3.4 illustrates this model of NPD.

Companies selling fashionable apparel traditionally started to prepare for the design and production of a new line of women's apparel about 10 months before the beginning of a new season. Unfortunately, by the time the season actually started they often found that much of their clothing was no longer fashionable, and could only

Figure 3.4 Spiral model of new product development

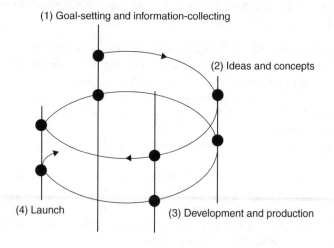

(1) Goal-setting and information-collecting

(2) Ideas and concepts

(4) Launch

(3) Development and production

be sold at bargain sale prices. Five Fox Company, a Japanese apparel company, succeeded in this market by taking a different approach to this form of NPD. Five Fox starts to design and produce small lots of apparel just 1 or 2 months before the season begins. If the initial response to a line of apparel is good, Fire Fox increases production. If not, it collects new information on what consumers want, and redesigns the clothing. Five Fox's suppliers work round the clock, if necessary, and can manufacture articles of newly designed clothing within 10 days. Since Five Fox relies heavily on direct sales channels and on its sales corners in department stores, its sales channels are short. This gives it a sales and production system that resembles a production-to-order system. As a result of these practices, 75% of Fox Fire's apparel can be sold at list price. Since its sales per unit of floor space is large and the turn-over ratio is high, department stores welcome the company's products.

Of course this kind of fast NPD cycle time could not be applied overall to the development of new technology intensive products, since the development of new technology requires a long lead time. However, in the early stages of development similar processes can be used. Small changes in design can be made in response to consumer demands, and adjustments can be made in the production system. Even after a product is launched, improvements may be needed. Thus, some sort of feedback system or spiral system is needed for every new product.

Case: World Company – The development of fashionable women's apparel

The demand for fashionable women's apparel depends both on fashion trends and the season. It's difficult to come up with a hit product every time, but if a company makes a mistake in forecasting demand and manufactures too much of an item, it will have a lot of dead stock. On the other hand, if the company is too conservative in its forecasts, it will lose potential sales. Before 1990 many apparel manufacturers produced goods one quarter at a time, and tried to sell them out during that quarter. Planning started about 1 year before the season. Samples were shown at exhibitions for retailers. Orders were taken, and stock was produced before the season started. This system had the advantage that production could be planned, and there were economies of scale in production. But companies often produced too much, or not enough of particular lines of apparel.

In Japan many companies had especially serious overstocking problems during the recession of the 1990s. In response the World Company adopted a quick response system. World shortened the lead time between planning and production to make it easier to forecast fashion trends. For example, in the case of a line targeted towards career women, a planning concept is presented only 6 months before the release. Because the lead time is so short, the designer can integrate the latest fashion trends into the product concept. Four months before the beginning of the season, inside monitors evaluate the plans, give them evaluation points and rankings, and project a tentative volume of production for each item. Three months before the season there are market tests. In the case of the spring outfits to be displayed in February, for example, test sales are carried out in December to forecast demand.

During the season, sales at the retailers are tracked by a Point of Sales (POS) system. Features such as the color, materials, and designs of good selling outfits are analyzed every week. Decisions are made about which should be discontinued and which should have increased production. During this analysis, the elements of success are analyzed, and outfits with new designs are produced every week. Because of the short production cycle, it is possible to change more than 40% of the products within 2 weeks. The cycle is 1 week for simple repeat production, and 2 weeks for outfits where the design has changed.

World uses a scheduling method called "cassette merchandizing." A "cassette" is a group of similar types of outfits. The contents of a

Table 3.2 Old and new schedules for development of fashionable apparel

Old system	Month	New system (Quick response)
	February	
Information collection	March	
Master plan	April	
Materials and design	May	
	June	
	July	
Samples	August	Information collection
	September	Master plan
Exhibition	October	Materials and design
Ordering materials and	November	Exhibition
Production		Accurate response
	December	Test sales
	January	Correction of plan
Store sales	February	Store sales

Figure 3.5 Development process using experimental design

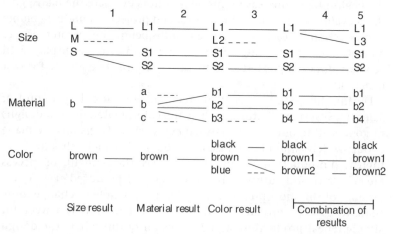

Notes: (1) Dotted lines indicate unsuccessful elements, to be discontinued.
(2) L1, S1, S2 indicate go on to next stage without testing, to reduce number of tests.

cassette are planned before the season begins by considering past data and projecting future trends. Planning includes the mix of colors, types of cloth, designs, sizes and other specification, overall product mix, and combinations of outfits to be placed in the shops. Examples of planning items include: "during nth week, examine competing products at the stores", "during n+1st week, study the color balances of outfits of competing companies at the stores." These action items are noted on the cassette boxes.

NPD principles. A season's performance largely depends on the sales of hit products. World calls these "ace products." The "Mrs." line includes fewer than 20 ace items, but these account for 70% of the sales for that line.

It is not necessary to identify Ace products in the first week of the season, but it is important that elements of ace products be quickly identified. Before the season, a number of combinations of elements are tested by using the experimental design method, and before the season, the combination of elements making ace products is found. Table 3.2 shows the time schedule for identifying ace products. Figure 3.5 illustrate the overall process that is followed.

Three elements define women's skirts: the type of cloth, the color, and the length. The most variable element is length. At the beginning lengths are tested to find consumer preferences. Lengths are tested in S, M and L sizes. During the first week, sales are relatively slow, so small lots of different combinations of each of the three lengths are tested with a particular color and type of cloth. It may turn out, for example, that short skirts are the most popular, medium the least, with long in the middle. In the second week, sales increase, so the number of combinations is increased. Two lengths, three types of cloth and one color are combined for a total of six combinations to be tested. This time the most popular cloths are identified. In the third week, sales increase again, so combinations of two lengths, three types of cloth and three colors can be used to make 18 combinations. This time the most popular colors are identified.

By this method, the best mix of design elements for the peak period is found. On the cassette box, the tasks for each week are indicated. Fashions do not completely change with the season. Some Ace products are sold over two seasons. A cotton version of a "Mrs." beige knitwear coat, for example, sold well in August and a wool version of the same coat sold well during the Fall.

A member of World's planning department says that what matters is overall performance during the year, not performance in a single season. It is not necessarily best for the company to sell out its merchandise during one season. The plan of one season should be carried over to the next season. It is important to have plans which can be phased into the next season.

Implications of this case. World's ability to achieve a short feedback cycle was not the only success factor in this case. Weekly planning helps discover Ace products for the peak season. The planning should not be too short-range oriented, however. Short cycle planning such as weekly planning is most effective in combination with quarterly planning and the use of the continuous experiment method.[23]

Commodity goods and differentiated goods

We have distinguished amongst technology intensive, market intensive and dynamic market products, it is also useful to categorize products as to whether they are "commodity goods" or "differentiated goods." Commodity goods lack hard to imitate distinctive traits. Examples include most raw materials, standard components, standard semiconductors, personal computers, and medicines for which patents have expired. Lots of firms can make commodity goods, and competition tends to be based on price. Firms succeed with these products by lowering their costs. In recent years many companies have done this by building production facilities in China, India or other countries with low labor costs. Sometimes they have outsourced production to other companies. Differentiated goods include automobiles, robots, fashionable women's apparel, and patented drugs. These goods have distinctive styles, images, or technical features that are difficult to imitate. With these goods a firm can command a price premium. The challenge for a firm specializing in differentiated goods is to keep its products from becoming commodity goods for as long as possible, and/or to keep developing a stream of new differentiated goods.

Manufactured commodity goods often have a modular architecture, while differentiated goods often have an integral architecture. A product with a modular architecture is made up of components with standard interfaces. Production or assembly is easy. Examples include personal computers and most home appliances near the end of their product life cycle. There tends to be severe price competition for these products, and their manufacture has often moved to countries with low labor costs. On the other hand, products with an integral architecture have components whose interfaces are not standardized. Examples include automobiles and robots.

Most raw materials, like cement or nylon, are commodity goods. However, raw materials that are highly specialized, are patented or are made by a process that uses an integral architecture, can be differentiated products. Examples include the very fine nylon fiber used to produce silky cloth, and carbon fiber produced from burned acrylic fiber. Patented medicines are also differentiated products, but when their patents expire they become commodity goods. Generally, if a raw material is made by a production process that is modular, standardized, and easy to copy, the raw material is a commodity good. Nylon and polyester fiber were once differentiated goods because they were made by proprietary production processes. Now that the processes for making these products are no longer proprietary, these products are commodity goods. And, indeed, most of the production of these products has been transferred to China.

Commodity goods tend to have a U-shaped profit curve, or "smile curve." This means that most of the profits from these products come either from the beginning or the end of the value chain, but not from the middle. In the PC industry, for example, Intel (at the beginning of the value chain when it designs a new chip) and Microsoft (at the end of the value chain when it develops a new generation operating system) have made large profits, but the PC manufacturers have not. In the case of copiers, profits are made from designing new copiers, and later from servicing them and from the sales of toner and color cartridges. Apparel companies such as the Gap and Benetton make profits, not from the efficient production of their clothing, but by having exclusive sales channels all over the world. One might think that a company producing commodity goods in the middle of the smile curve should integrate forward to a more profitable place on the curve. Most find they are unable to do this. A synthetic fiber company, for example, may be able to produce cloth, but that doesn't mean it can easily move into the production of women's apparel or men's suits. It does not have the related competencies.

Basic NPD processes

Despite their differences, the three NPD processes we have described have much in common. All of them start with the collection of information on technology "seeds" or market "needs." In seeds oriented development the job of the NPD team is to find a use for a new technology. There was initially no application, for example, for a new carbon fiber developed by Toray. Later, NPD teams were able to develop uses for the carbon fiber, first in golf club shafts, then in airplane wings, and then in an expanding number of other applications. Completely new products, such as "post-it" note and cornflakes were invented by producers finding new uses for existing technologies. CAD/CAM was suggested by producers. Even women's apparel and home appliances can be marketed as "proposals for a new life style," and thus can serve as the seeds for new fashions. In all these cases, innovation is driven by companies finding new applications for technologies they have on hand or have learned about.

With needs oriented development the potential demand for a new product is forecast, a product concept is created, and the NPD is begun. This is the general model for success. Even in the case of seeds oriented development, it is necessary to study consumer needs. Generally speaking, when the producer knows more about the product than consumers, a seeds type of development can succeed. When the consumers know more, as in the case of fashionable women's apparel and home appliances, needs oriented development is more likely to succeed. Yet even in this case, research suggests, it is necessary to give special attention to "expert consumers" – those who have visions of future trends.

After information is collected about the seeds or needs, a "product concept" is constructed. The goal of development is to satisfy the primary function of the product concept. Next, the architecture of the total structure is designed, showing the relationships between the parts. The architecture is divided into parts. In the case of a copier, for example, the architecture would be broken down into components and materials. In the case of an automobile, the process goes from design to components. In the case of cosmetics, it may go from design to the development of creams and perfumes. Finally, the parts are integrated into a whole, and the new product is tested. If this process is not followed, the new product is likely to fail, as we saw in Chapter 2 happened in the case of the $2 billion Seagire resort project.

IT plays an increasingly important role in each type of NPD process. The use of computers and the internet, have greatly improved the speed and quality of development. We look at this more closely in Chapter 11, but a few examples can be given here. POS needs can be explored through the internet. New ideas can be solicited through the intranet. Design charts can be exchanged with component suppliers through the extranet. Computer simulations are used to develop drugs and chemical products, allowing researchers to predict the effects and traits of new products. The use of CAD and CAM are also becoming increasingly important.

Some NPD sub-processes

Despite important differences in how different types of products are developed, some sub-processes are commonly used for all types of products.

Sources of new product ideas. Not all ideas for new products come from product development teams. In the movie business, for example, most scripts come from outside the studio. Even when these new product ideas (the scripts) come from outside, however, the scripts are carefully evaluated with respect to market needs. Technical development is carried out, and there is a final market testing process. After the movie is completed, it is shown at "sneak previews," and, depending on the opinions of the audience, small modifications might be made. The title may be changed, for example, and certain scenes may be re-edited.[24]

As we will see in Chapter 4, many companies now outsource the development of some aspects of NPD to other companies. They may even get new product ideas from companies in foreign countries. These ideas from outside traditional sources within a company can be assessed and used effectively as long as they are in accord with the company's long-range plan or strategy. Comprehensive planning and serendipity can co-exist – but they must complement each other.

Another source of new product concepts is "bootleg development," where someone in a development department works on a project that is not officially authorized. There have been many well-publicized successful cases of bootleg development. Nissan's management did not officially authorize development of the Z sports car, for example. The development team produced the car by modifying an existing chassis and combining components from other cars. Nissan sold more than 1.4 million Z's in 10 years, and the car is now considered a classic. According to one member of the team that developed the car, the Z succeeded because top management *did not interfere* with its development. Similarly, Casio did not officially support development of a digital camera. But when Casio "bootleggers" developed a digital camera, the company began manufacturing it. The new camera immediately sold out in the US.

As we have seen, Asahi's best selling "Super Dry" beer was developed after intensive marketing research, under a top down process. However, another Asahi success, "Honnama," was developed through a bootleg process. Honnama is a brew with a malt content of less than 25% malt. This allows it to be taxed at a lower rate than conventional beer in Japan. But, because Honnama has a low malt content, Asahi's top management did not consider it to be a "real" beer, and so did not encourage its development. An Asahi researcher managed to improve the taste of the low malt beer by mixing in an extract of barley and other ingredients. The top management team was surprised by the good taste of Honnama. The new product was officially launched and immediately became the second biggest seller in the Japanese market.

Because of the prominent success of bootleg projects like these, it might be thought that those laboratories which host the most bootleg projects will be the most creative. Indeed, under *certain conditions*, allowing plenty of freedom to bootleg researchers will enhance creativity. The caveat, however, is in the "certain conditions" that must be met. It is essential that the freedom bootleg researchers enjoy is consistent with the corporate strategy. The Nissan Z, Casio digital camera, and Asahi Honnama were all new products that fit easily into company strategies. On the other hand, in Chapter 2 we saw how Xerox was unable to profit from extensive (and expensive) projects that were too far removed from corporate planning. Xerox learned from this failure, and research at Xerox's PARC facility is now more closely controlled by corporate strategy.

Missile and spiral types of NPD. One can think of NPD processes as falling into two categories, "missile type projects" and "spiral types projects." Once a missile is launched there is no calling it back. Similarly, once a company commits to a missile type NPD project, it is essentially committed to carrying the project through to completion. In the case of projects to develop new commercial aircraft, new car platforms, or new large scale computers, for example, huge investment is required during the early stages of development. These investments cannot be recovered until the project is launched. Once the early stage investments are made, the future of the company may depend on the success of the project. In these projects it is essential that careful market research and technical testing be carried out early on for the investment to succeed. As we saw in Chapter 2, the developers of the Seagire amusement center did not do adequate market research and testing, and consequently were faced with a disastrous failure.

Spiral type NPD is suited to products where details about market demand are not clear, and the required initial investment in development is relatively small. This was the case, as we have seen, with fashionable women's apparel. Plans can be changed even at the last stage of development.

Protecting new products. In Chapters 1 and 2 we described cases where firms had developed new products that were very successful, but quickly lost market share (and the lion's share of profits) to other firms that moved in. Certain strategies can reduce the chances of this happening. Some products can be given an image that other companies cannot easily imitate. This might be a feeling that a certain mayonnaise is healthy, or that a certain lipstick has a special aura. It could be an image the consumer has of a company. Because of The Body Shop's reputation for environmental responsibility, for example, some consumers feel that a person who uses The Body Shop products is a good citizen. "Invisible traits" like these are mostly planned for the product during the development stage.

Of course, firms sometimes use patents to protect a new product. All too often, however, the disclosures required in patenting can allow competitors to "invent around" the patent and come up with a similar product. It is easier to protect a proprietary production processes. Anyone can buy a new product and try to reverse engineer it, but a firm can keep others from observing its production processes. When the production process becomes widely known, as happened with the processes used to make nylon, polyester and acrylic fiber, the products become commodity goods. The processes used to make highly fine fibers are still more tightly controlled, and the production of these fibers remains profitable.

Another strategy to help a firm profit from its new products is horizontal specialization. A company might, for example, outsource production while keeping tight control over design and sales. Dell does this, outsourcing production of most of its PCs to companies in Taiwan. As we have seen, "Five Fox" also does this in the ladies fashion industry.

Finally, a firm must be careful that it is not blindsided by others taking different technological approaches to its markets. When a new and very different technology is used, well-established firms may find it difficult to respond. Sony was not a significant producer of portable radios in the early 1950s. This market was dominated in the U.S. by such companies as Sylvania and RCA, and in Japan by Toshiba and Hitachi. By moving into this market with the new transistor radio, Sony quickly grabbed market share away from the market leaders. New firms have also grown quickly at the expense of established market leaders with the introduction of new products as disparate as nylon stockings (replacing silk), vinyl pipe (replacing lead), PCs (replacing mainframes), digital cameras, small disk drives, and artificial leather.[25]

The Stage-Gate System. Some firms use the "Stage-Gate system" in the NPD process to systematize some of the NPD steps we have discussed.[26] The Stage-Gate system divides the NPD process into five stages (plus a "pre-stage") and five gates. Each gate has systematic and explicit criteria for the decision about what to do next with the project. The alternatives are "go," "no-go," "hold," "recycle" and "rework." "Hold" means to stop the process for now, but to consider it again later. Recycle or rework means to send the product back to the previous stage to be redone.

As Figure 3.6 shows, during the pre-stage ("discovery") preparatory work is done to discover opportunities and generate ideas for new products. This is accomplished by carrying out research and collecting ideas from customers and others. At Gate 1 the ideas are evaluated based on such criteria as strategic fit and market attractiveness. During Stage 1 (Scoping), a quick and inexpensive review is made of the idea being considered. A rough concept of the new product is developed based on preliminary market, technical, business and financial assessments. At Gate 2 the strategic fit and feasibility of the new product are evaluated. During Stage 2 a business case for the project is built. Surveys of user needs, competitive analyses, and detailed technical assessments are all used to more clearly define the new product. The project plan is created. At Gate 3 it is decided whether or not to commit substantial resources to the project. The potential costs and benefits of the project are evaluated by financial or economic models such as NPV (net present value) or IRR (internal rate of return).

Stage 3 is development. The physical development of the product is carried out in parallel with marketing activities. In-house tests are made. Market analyses are conducted, and customer feedback is sought. The results of these studies are fed back to technical development. Gate 4 reviews the progress and attractiveness of the product. A more detailed financial evaluation is made. Stage 4 tests and validates the entire plan. In this stage, prototype or sample products are made.

Figure 3.6 The stage-gate model flow chart

Pre-stage		Stage 1		Stage 2		Stage 3		Stage 4		Stage 5	
Discovery, idea generation	Gate 1	Scoping	Gate 2	Build business case	Gate 3	Develop-ment	Gate 4	Testing & valida-tion	Gate 5	Launch	Post Launch Review

Source: Cooper, 2001. Also, other writings by this author.

Field trials are conducted. There may be pilot production. Evaluations are made of customer acceptance of the product, and of how it will be produced and marketed. At Gate 5 the decision is made whether or not to launch, mass produce and mass market the new product. Stage 5, the final stage, consists of the product launch and the post-launch review.

The Stage-gate system provides a useful checklist of many of the things that need to be done for successful NPD. The system, however, does have its limitations. It puts most of its emphasis on the evaluation process, and pays less attention to the creative and technological development processes. The model assumes that there is a standard development process, regardless of the type of product. It ignores differences, for example, between technology intensive, marketing intensive, and dynamic market products. The system says little about the organizational aspects of development.

Speed of development

A firm must both quickly come up with the new product concept, and then develop the product more quickly than its rivals. This is true whether the firm is in an industry where new product development takes a long time, or a short time. It takes about 12 years to develop a new medical product, but if a firm is just 1 day behind a rival in developing a patentable product, it will not get the patent. In most industries the time required to develop new products is constantly being reduced. The time it takes to develop a new car, for example, has dropped from more than 5 years to only 1 or 2 years. This is even true with the development of a car based on a substantially different technology, as when Toyota developed its hybrid car in only about 3 years.

In our cases we have seen some specific examples of how NPD teams were able to accelerate the development process. Here we will make a few more general comments.

Table 3.3 Factors accelerating NPD process

	%
1. Support of top management/product champion	51.55
2. Clear goals, development themes and schedule	83.23
3. Use of IT (CAD/CAM, information exchange through internet)	17.39
4. Based on core competencies	44.10
5. Alliances and cooperation with outside organizations	45.96
6. Acquisition	1.66
7. Concurrent engineering	48.45
8. Full-time project team	52.80
9. Sufficient budget, staff, and capital investment	41.61
10. Common use of components	9.94
11. Control of progress and use of simulation	22.98
12. Other	1.86

Source: See Table 1.7. Respondents selected five items in response to question: "What factors were most important in accelerating the speed of new product development?"

It is widely believed that cooperation between departments, such as through the use of concurrent engineering, and the enthusiasm of the project team are the most important factors in speeding the development of a new product. These factors are clearly important, but our survey shows that other factors are even more important. As Table 3.3 shows, we found the most important factors were having clear goals, having the support of top management and a product champion, and using a full-time project team.

The support of top management and a powerful product champion are critical in NPD because short-term and sub-unit goals may conflict with investment in NPD. Most new products do not produce an immediate profit, and the development of new products can be disruptive for day-to-day production and other operations of a company. NPD must be promoted by someone who has an overview of the broader, longer-term strategy of the firm, and the power to promote these longer-term interests. It is important that the project have clear goals and a targeted completion date, but some flexibility of goals and schedules is also important.

Cooperation between related departments. Cooperation between R&D, production and marketing is critical to the success of NPD. This may seem obvious, but in some firms the NPD process follows a one way stream. The new product goes from development to production, to marketing. The prestige of the R&D department may be so high that the production department is pressured to make whatever R&D has developed. Marketing then has to sell whatever is produced. As one observer puts it, the design is simply thrown over the wall to the next stage.[27]

There are several barriers to close cooperation between departments in the development of new products:

1. Since the line departments have their own profit responsibilities, they are reluctant to cooperate in the development of a new product that will not make a profit for a long time, if ever.
2. It is easier to perform routine daily tasks than to risk the uncertainty of doing something new.
3. Department managers may be afraid that the new product will cannibalize current products.
4. New products may make the skills and knowledge base of current employees obsolete (Recall the Firestone case in Chapter 2).
5. The department may fear that so many company resources will be poured into the new product, there will be little left for current products.

It often takes very strong support from top management and powerful product champions to overcome these barriers.

Two means of achieving cooperation are widely used. Some firms use cross-functional project teams composed of members from the R&D, production and marketing departments. In our cases, for example, cross-functional teams were used by Toyota and Canon. Another technique is the use of a concurrent engineering system, where various departments and key suppliers simultaneously work on different aspects of a new product. As we saw, Toyota efficiently used concurrent engineering in the development of the 9th generation Corolla.

Cross-functional teams. Cross-functional teams have been effectively used by a number of companies for a wide range of products in different industries. Honda and Ford use cross-functional NPD. When Fuji enjoyed quick success with its new single-use camera, Kodak used a cross-functional team to quickly develop a comparable product. Its camera was on the market within a year. The use of a cross-functional team also helped Kodak to respond to environmentalist complaints about the environmental impact of disposable cameras. Kodak was quickly able to modify the camera so it could be recycled (they also quit calling it a "disposable camera").[28] Some times problems arise with cross-functional NPD teams because the members who were dispatched to the project team are unsure about what will happen to them after the project is completed. This should be addressed.

Concurrent engineering. With concurrent engineering, people in the R&D, production, and sales departments work in parallel to develop a new product. This accelerates the development process. It also cuts costs by eliminating the need for work to be sent back to an upstream department to meet the requirements of a downstream department. In the case of improvement products, if the manufacturing plant includes a development department and produces the products by a cell manufacturing system, a production to order system can be established.

Concurrent engineering often involves suppliers or customers. We saw this in our Toyota Corolla case. Sometimes confidential design charts are shared with them. Other forms of cooperation can also speed development. When Toray developed a new soft contact lens, for example, its marketing department was able to gain the cooperation of a hospital. For concurrent engineering to involve suppliers or customers, the partners obviously have to have a close relationship – something that may not be possible if components are acquired through arms length competitive biding by various vendors.

Enthusiasm of the project team. The speed of development greatly depends on the enthusiasm of project team members. The team may need to be motivated to work very long hours in order to meet project schedules. There must be encouragement from top management and the rest of the company. We will further explore this point in Chapter 5.

4
The Globalization of New Product Development

One of the most dramatic developments in NPD over the past 10 to 15 years has been the globalization of new product development. Today some of the largest and fastest growing markets for new products are in countries that were not truly part of the global economy a generation ago. China, for example, is now the largest market for cellular telephones. China and India are the world's fastest growing markets for automobiles and many consumer appliances. China, India and other emerging economies are also, increasingly, centers of excellence for the technologies key to certain products. Major new challenges for managers of NPD include both finding ways to develop products for a wider range of global markets than ever before, and drawing on the capabilities of human and technological resources that were largely ignored in the past. This chapter deals with these challenges.

The new globalization of NPD and how it is different

In deciding how best to make use of the new opportunities in globalized NPD, it is useful to understand what is different about this new form of globalization, and where current trends seem to be leading.

Older forms of global NPD. A generation ago NPD was almost exclusively carried out in the home countries of the multinationals. And almost all of the multinationals were headquartered in the "Triad" nations of the U.S., Japan and Western Europe. To the extent NPD took place in other countries, it seldom amounted to much more than adapting Triad products to the more primitive conditions in other countries. A German automaker in Mexico, for example, redesigned its cars for service on rougher roads. A U.S. appliance maker in India redesigned its washing machines to cope with the more extreme electrical power surges common in that country. Sometimes products were re-designed for production by less advanced machine tools and less-educated workers. Some countries had less stringent safety standards than those in the Triad, and some multinationals redesigned products to the laxer standards in order to cut costs. Underlying this form of product development was the notion of the product life cycle. Firms could eke out further profits from products that were becoming commodity items in their home markets, by adapting them for use in poorer countries.

In the 1980s and 1990s the Triad firms found that it was necessary and desirable to begin globalizing NPD. It was necessary because the Triad firms were increasingly serving global markets, and the firms that were closest to their customers were best at developing products for them. It was desirable because it made it possible to draw on the human resources and technologies available in other countries. The mix of new demands and new technological inputs was extremely fruitful. In the 1980s, for example, Procter and Gamble introduced Liquid Tide, a new detergent that allowed clothes to be washed clean at lower temperatures. Since energy costs were low in the U.S., technology to allow the washing of clothes in cold water had not been given high priority for development there. The situation was different in Japan, and Procter and Gamble's R&D facilities in Japan were able to draw on Japanese technology to develop a cold water washing ingredient. The water in much of the United States, however, is higher in mineral content than that in Japan, and requires softening before it can be used to wash clothes. Europe also has water with a high average mineral content, and the best water softening technology was being developed in Belgium, where Procter and Gamble also had an R&D center. Procter and Gamble combined the technologies from its R&D centers in the U.S., Japan and Europe to develop a new detergent that could wash clothes at low temperatures using water high in mineral content.

P&G benefited from globalizing its NPD by taking advantage of globally distributed centers of technological excellence. Other multinationals found other reasons for locating aspects of NPD in different advanced economies. In the 1990s Ford decided to develop a "global" car. By putting together a trans-Atlantic NPD team Ford was able to develop a sense of which consumer needs were global and could be incorporated into the basic platform for the new car. The car developed by the trans-Atlantic team was the Ford Mondeo (Contour/Mystique in the United States). More than a million of these cars were eventually sold in nearly seventy different countries. Kodak used a consortium of people from companies in Germany, Japan and the U.S. to develop a simple to use "drop and close" 35-mm film and camera system. Kodak wanted a multinational team working on this project because they hoped to establish a new global standard for the system. When Corning decided to develop and commercialize products based on its ability to immobilize enzymes on glass beads, it used a team including members from the U.S., U.K. and France. One reason for this was that it wanted people with experience dealing with the different feed-stocks being used in different countries. Even more important, the company found it did not have all the necessary talent for the team at any one site.

But, while there are many examples like this of the globalization of new product development, before the mid-1990s most of them were restricted to globalization within the Triad economies. Multinationals from the U.S., Japan and Europe rapidly set up research and engineering development centers near each others' universities, markets and manufacturing centers. Most "global" NPD teams, however, even when they were composed of people from different countries, worked at the same site. Or, if they were at different locations, they worked independently on discrete components of the project. A new, qualitatively different, globalization of technology development began to gain momentum in the 1990s. The new globalization extends to many of the emerging economies, and often it involves people simultaneously working on the same NPD project while separated from each other by thousands of miles.

The new globalization of NPD.[29] Several factors are contributing to the new globalization of NPD. Some of the most important of these are listed in Table 4.1. A trend underlying these factors is the dramatic liberalization of the world trade environment that began in the 1990s. During the 1990s more than 1,000 changes were made in laws worldwide to facilitate foreign direct investment (FDI). In 2002 alone, more

Table 4.1 Factors encouraging the globalization of new product development

> Needed to access fast growing emerging-economy markets
> Allows access to newly developing centers of technological excellence
> Enables multinationals to overcome shortages of well-trained science and technology human resources at home
> Enriches technology by exposure to different engineering paradigms
> Allows expansions of technological capability at relatively low cost

than 200 regulatory changes were made in seventy different countries to facilitate FDI.[30] Countries like India and China, that had been reluctant to host foreign firms, suddenly began eagerly seeking foreign investment. By the beginning of the 21st century, FDI was increasing at a rate of about 20% a year, reaching more than $7 trillion. FDI brought large amounts of foreign capital, new technologies and new management methods to the emerging economies. To attract FDI, the emerging economies increasingly opened their markets. Multinationals in virtually every industry raced to establish production facilities in at least some of the emerging economies.

As the emerging economies strove for modernization and economic development, they worked to improve the quality of their science and technology human resources. In India, for example, the government created the Indian Institutes of Information Technology Colleges. An engineering manager at a U.S. multinational told one of the authors that there is not much difference between hiring a graduate of a leading U.S. engineering program and a graduate of one of the Indian Institutes. Indeed, he said in some areas the Indian graduate might be better trained than the American. In an interview in Fortune magazine in January 2004, the leading business thinker Peter Drucker commented that the medical school in New Delhi is perhaps the finest in the world. China has also invested heavily in the education of scientists, engineers and managers who can assume leading roles in foreign enterprises in China, and also in China's new multinationals. In 2005 as many as 325,000 Chinese reportedly earned engineering degrees, compared to around 70,000 in the U.S.[31] As opportunities have increased in the emerging economies, more and more young people who might earlier have gone overseas for their education have instead gone to institutions in their home countries. Moveover, many who had been successful technologists, entrepreneurs, or managers in the Triad economies have returned home.

Some of the emerging economies have also drastically increased their spending on the development of technology. While U.S. spending on R&D rose by 50% between 1995 and 2001, R&D spending tripled in China over the same period. In 2003 Chinese were awarded 5,300 patents in the United States, far more than the combined number for the older East Asian tigers of Taiwan, South Korea, Hong Kong and Singapore.[32]

Triad multinationals have moved quickly to capitalize on the availability of world-class technology and science and technology human resources in some of the emerging economies. The attractiveness of setting up product development centers is further enhanced by the fact that salaries for engineers and scientists can be 70 or 80% lower than in the Triad. At many multinationals hiring freezes were imposed at Triad facilities, but managers were allowed to hire new engineers and scientists in countries like China and India. Figure 4.1 suggests the extent to which this offshoring of technology activities has occurred.

Meanwhile the advance of information technology made it increasingly possible for engineers and scientists scattered around the world to collaborate on the development of new products. As a consequence, multinationals began opening R&D and product development centers in the emerging economies. Motorola has 19 R&D centers just in China, with others in India and other countries. Other multinationals with R&D centers in China include Cisco Systems, IBM, Intel, Texas Instruments, GE, Alcatel, Hewlett Packard, Astra-Zeneca, Siemens, Procter and Gamble. Most of these companies have centers in India as well.[33] Figure 4.1 shows the flows of R&D spending by U.S. firms and their foreign affiliates to countries around the world.

While the corporate offshoring of activities is often attributed to firms seeking lower cost workforces, it has to be emphasized that the globalization of NPD has often been driven even more powerfully by Triad

Figure 4.1   Industrial R&D spending flows of U.S. and foreign affiliates, by world region: 1998

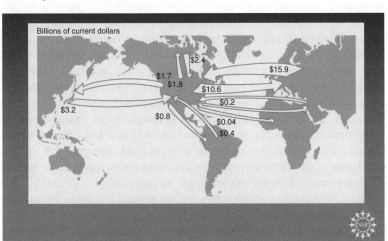

Source: National Science Board, *Science and Engineering Indicators – 2002*

firms seeking centers of excellence for certain technologies in a world where cutting-edge technology is no longer monopolized by the Triad. GM located some of its development activities in South Korea to take advantage of South Korea's strengths in new materials technology. India is now a global center of software development and, increasingly, of pharmaceutical research. China is becoming a center for the development of cellular telephones and other telecommunications technologies. Nokia recently transferred a major part of its third generation software development from Finland to China. According to a recent report, China now has some 700 foreign R&D centers. For some time Southeast Asia has been a center for the development of hard drive production technology – working in coordination with product development centers in the United States.[34] Advanced aerospace work is now being done in Brazil. The British pharmaceutical giant GlaxoSmithKline is partnering with the Indian company Ranbaxy to conduct clinical trials in India.

While sometimes the new product development activities are carried out at different sites in a relatively autonomous manner, often they are highly integrated. GE, for example, has a project team to develop micro-turbines that includes eight core-members – four in the U.S., three in China and one in India. Hewlett-Packard's development in 2003 of the ProLiant ML150, a new computer server for small businesses, suggests how new product teams can take on a broad geographical spread. Initial design for the server was done in Singapore. The product concept was approved at the company's offices in Houston. The concept design was done in Singapore, but engineering design was done in Taiwan. The product is now made in Singapore, Australia, China and India, and is sold all over the world. Factors that made this global development team approach viable and attractive included government incentives from Taiwan and Singapore, and relaxed visa requirements in several countries. An NPD manager of a U.S. multinational in Beijing told us that frequently governments in China, at both the national and local levels, subsidize research being done by Chinese companies working with foreign multinationals. He said these subsidies have encouraged his company to locate more of their NPD activities in China.

The globalization of NPD offers the advantages of proximity to markets, access to a variety of national innovation systems, and low-cost high quality science and technology human resources. Many managers are finding it also offers an additional advantage. Because of differences in cultural backgrounds, educational systems, and motivations, engineers in different countries sometimes bring different approaches to

NPD. A blending of these approaches can greatly enrich the NPD process. Some engineering traditions emphasize technical performance more highly. Others emphasize customer satisfaction. Engineers in some countries are trained to minimize capital costs, while others are trained to minimize the use of human resources.

Finally, there is another reason we might expect dramatic increases in the expansion of NPD activities in emerging economies. In a recent best seller, C.C. Prahalad calls the attention of multinationals to "the fortune at the bottom of the pyramid."[35] Prahalad argues that multinationals are overlooking the opportunity to make substantial profits while improving the lives of hundreds of millions of people. He points out that while people in the emerging economies have low per capita incomes, they have huge aggregate purchasing power. He says innovative approaches to product development can tap into these markets, while providing tremendous benefits to the people in them. Prahalad presents numerous cases to show how this can happen. A bank, for example, found a way to profitably extend its services to low income groups in India. An entrepreneur in Nicaragua developed low cost renewable energy systems that could be sold to peasant farmers. Cemex, the world's third largest producer of cement found a way to add special services that made it possible to profitably sell cement in Mexico to the poor for housing construction.

Special problems in global NPD

While the opening of new markets and the increased access to new human and technological resources for NPD provide wonderful new opportunities, there are special challenges in making the fullest use of these opportunities. Since this is a new area, other challenges will doubtless arise. Table 4.2 lists some of the risks that have been mentioned most often so far. Here we suggest how important it is that these be taken into consideration, and discuss how some firms have dealt with the challenges posed.

Table 4.2 Special difficulties/risks in globalizing new product development process

---

➢ Uncontrolled incrementalism
➢ Loss of control over NPD capabilities
➢ Weakening of NPD capabilities
➢ Loss of intellectual property

Coordinating global product development. Earlier we discussed the need to closely coordinate NPD with corporate strategies. Recall how Xerox received little benefit from the development of important new technologies at its PARC facility because these new technologies were not incorporated into Xerox's broader strategies. The challenge of coordination becomes even larger when activities are scattered not just across a country, but around the world. It is essential that there be frequent face to face meetings by those responsible for various technology development activities. Matsushita Panasonic (like most multinationals) has major overseas R&D laboratories in the U.S., U.K., Germany and a number of other countries. Just in the last few years the company has built or invested in five high-technology product development centers in China. To help coordinate these activities the company has global R&D meetings in Japan and overseas each year. The presidents and vice presidents or directors from all the overseas laboratories participate. They not only exchange technical and market information, but also establish personal relationships with each other. Strong personal relationships are particularly important when managers are coming from highly diverse backgrounds and are working in very different environments. Technical exhibits have been set up at Matsushita Panasonic to help managers at the head office maintain a high level awareness of what all of Matsushita Panasonic's laboratories are doing.

Coordinating global NPD "virtual teams". At one time multinationals almost always divided global projects into discrete units. The firm might be operating in many countries, but specific NPD projects were handled by a team at one site. This still is the most common practice. Now, however, as we have seen, there are increasing efforts to have "virtual teams" whose members may be scattered around the world. A wide range of new communications and data sharing technologies have made this possible, but the limitations of these technologies must be clearly recognized.[36] Coordinating the activities of any virtual team can be difficult, but it can become even more difficult when members of the team are from different cultures.

One study found, for example, that cultural differences complicated the functioning of cross-national virtual teams in several ways that managers had not anticipated. The managers of one global team found, for example, that American and French members differed in their approach to problem solving. The French preferred to make a thorough analysis of an entire problem before acting. The Americans preferred a trial and error approach. They would take a promising approach and see if it worked. The managers of another global team found that the American members were comfortable questioning project leaders, and generally preferred informal discussions to formal presentations. On the other hand, the Japanese members of the team seldom questioned managers, and preferred formal information exchanges.[37] Of course there are the additional complications caused by language differences. In one case familiar to us, a Japanese participant in a U.S.-managed project felt insecure about the quality of his English. He did not want to admit this to the Americans or to his Japanese co-workers. As a result he routinely delayed communicating until he could have his English checked, and sometimes completely missed requests for information. Language problems may be compounded because many electronic media do not offer rich feedback (such as the chance to observe puzzled expressions or pauses). It is essential that cultural differences be understood as much as possible and taken into account.

Given the relative recentness of the development of electronically mediated global NPD teams, and the dynamism of the relevant technologies, it may not be useful to go into extensive detail on this topic, but early research on virtual teams suggests a few points.

Several studies suggest that it is critical that the members of the team get to know each face to face before they form a virtual team. They need to develop a common set of work standards and interfaces, they need to set project goals, develop project plans and define roles and responsibilities for each team member, and they need get to know each other as people. It is also useful for team members to have experience seeing and working in each other's environments. Even when firms recognize this, however, they often seem to forget. Once a virtual NPD team is up and running, managers may find it difficult to persuade those in charge of budgets to continue to fund international travel. If team members are replaced, little thought may be given to having the replacements travel.

Generally, it seems the efficiency gained by having face to face meetings begins to wear off after several months, and the performance of virtual teams begins to decline. Early research also suggests that management practices effective in managing face to face teams, may be less effective in the case of virtual teams. It seems more important, for example, for leaders of virtual project teams to concentrate on project facilitation, rather than close surveillance. While "heavy weight" project managers may be highly effective in some NPD settings, they do not seem to be effective in the case of virtual teams.

Other issues in managing cross-national virtual NPD teams. Discussions with global NPD managers suggest that certain problems are beginning to emerge as firms come to rely on virtual NPD teams. One is a possible deterioration of the work environment, especially for those working in the Triad economies. Two prominent examples of a deteriorated work environment might be mentioned. First is the issue of working hours. One of the widely touted advantages of globally distributed projects is that globally-distributed team members can hand off a project from members in one time zone to those in another, and thus shorten the time to development. The converse, however, is that team members may find themselves coming into the office early, leaving very late, or working from home, in order to have telephone or video conferences with their colleagues in different time zones. Members of global NPD teams tell us they typically have routine meetings by telephone or video conference with team members in other countries at least once a week, plus additional trouble shooting and other meetings. Traditional working hours for a team member in the Eastern Time Zone of the United States might be 9:00 AM to 5:00 PM. In China this would translate to from 10:00 PM to 6:00 AM. Different companies deal with this differently. Some rotate teleconference meeting times so team members in different countries are equally inconvenienced. One firm gives global cell phones to globally distributed virtual team members so they can call each other from their homes (which, of course, still intrudes on their 'off-duty" time). In the excitement of participating in a global project team members may not object strongly to these inconveniences at first, but several we talked to questioned how sustainable these projects can be.

Issues of equity also arise – particularly when product developers in emerging economies may have salaries that are 70 or 80% lower than equally qualified fellow team members in Triad economies. While salaries have been rising in the emerging economies, a significant gap seems like to remain for decades. A long-term consequence of this may be downward pressures on Triad salaries. There may be growing resentment on the part of those in emerging economies receiving lower salaries, and those in the richer economies as their salary increases diminish.

Finally, managers tell us it is increasingly difficult to find qualified product development managers in emerging economies. A manager in charge of product development at a multinational's site in China told us, for example, that he has to have the requisite technical skills, the ability to read legal documents and negotiate in Chinese, and the ability to work in a multinational. The first two of these qualifications might seem obvious, but the third was also a challenge because ways of doing things varied so much between domestic companies and multinationals. He said, for example, that commitment to deadlines and quality standards were far higher in the multinationals.

The risks of global NPD

Aside from the difficulties in effectively establishing, coordinating and maintaining global product development teams, there are also some risks that must be kept in mind. It should also be kept in mind, however, that possible risks should not deter careful consideration of global NPD possibilities. After all, there may be even greater risks in not pursuing this approach.

Intellectual property rights. A number of Western and Japanese firms have suffered from the lack of strong intellectual property rights protection in China, India and other emerging economies. Honda had to stop a Chinese scooter manufacturer from selling a lower-price (and presumably lower quality) copy of a Honda scooter under the brand name "Hongda." This not only took sales from Honda, but also may have damaged Honda's brand equity. Honda also found a Chinese manufacturer producing an SUV that looked almost identical to a Honda SUV, but sold at only half the price. A manager from a European automobile company told one of the authors that recently in planning a joint venture in China, managers at his firm believed they needed to recoup their investment within 5 years. They are convinced that all of their technology will have "leaked out" within that period.

China, Brazil, India and other countries are coming to understand that a weak intellectual property rights regime hurts their own efforts to build strong technology creation systems. For one thing it discourages foreign firms from placing high technology activities in their countries. For another, many of these countries are accumulating their own intellectual property that they want to protect. In 2004 Indian companies applied for nearly twice as many patents at the World Intellectual Property Organization as they had in 2001. China, as we have seen, has also sharply increased its investment in the creation of new intellectual property. China, India and other emerging economies have, in fact, moved to enhance the protection of intellectual property rights. Nonetheless, there are continuing complaints that these countries have not gone nearly far enough. Regardless of their intentions to comply with WTO standards, administrative issues still stand in the way. Local officials may not understand or share the view of national leaders that they have to protect foreign owned intellectual property. There may be conflicts of interest that prevent enforcement of laws. It seems highly unlikely that the intellectual property rights problem will be solved any time in the near future.

And, if it is difficult to protect intellectual property in general, it might seem completely impossible in the NPD process. Here the problem may be further aggravated by employee turnover. A manager complained to one of the authors of losing technology in India to competing multinationals as employees left to take higher paid offers at other firms. In this case the company had an NPD facility in an industrial park, which was also home to many other multinationals. It is easy for employees to change firms. A dilemma often faces companies. If the firm tries to protect its technology by not having local employees in other countries work on it, the work being given the local employees is likely to be less challenging – increasing the chance that valued local employees will leave. This seems to have been a particularly difficult problem for Japanese firms. Matshushita Panasonic and other Japanese companies have reportedly found it difficult to hire good engineers because there is an image in countries like China that employees of Japanese companies have to work long-hours and that local employees are unlikely to be promoted.

Despite these issues some firms have been successful in organizing multinational NPD projects without the loss of intellectual property rights. Some offer special training and incentives to employees to protect intellectual property. Motorola ties promotions to the ability to generate ideas that result in patents. The Japanese electronics giant Matsushita uses what they call a "black box" technology approach. Matsushita protects its products with patents and designs them so they can't be taken apart and analyzed. It also makes sure each of its employees in China is only familiar with one part of a multi-step production process. A manager at a U.S. firm in the auto parts industry told us that her firm makes sure there are plenty of "missing pieces of the puzzle" in decided what product development activities to locate offshore. Sometimes firms can maintain high product introduction rates to keep ahead of local competitors. Sometimes brand names or reputation can maintain a firm's market share. Much of this will sound familiar – the techniques are often the same as those used against any set of competitors.

Outsourcing parts of development and losing core competencies.[38] Many firms are now outsourcing some of their NPD. One study found that between 1995 and 2001, major U.S., Japanese and European firms had doubled their dependency on external sources of technology. The author of that particular study characterized this increasing dependence on external technology as the most important change by multinational companies around the world.[39]

In some industries the outsourcing of NPD is motivated by costs. As we have seen the cost needed to develop a new drug is extremely high, and there is no guarantee the firm will profit from the new drug. As a result, firms in the pharmaceutical industry often want to share the cost, and thus the risk, of developing a new drug with other companies. In a number of industries economic pressures have been forcing cuts in R&D budgets. This has also added an incentive to outsource key elements of NPD. Many firms are trying to be more strategic in just what parts of NPD they do in-house. The chief engineer at one large company is quoted as saying: "We want to be the technology leaders, but not the technology driver."[40] This company wanted to decide what technology to develop and how to use it, but not do the actual development work itself. Some companies choose to focus on highly strategic NPD, while outsourcing more routine projects, such as product development intended simply to extend the life cycle of a product. The company Solectron, for example, specializes in this type of NPD for the electronics industry. Some firms outsource the design of low-end products to fill out a product line. They may, for example, need to add a low-end digital camera to the line of higher priced cameras they really want to sell. Otherwise, they can't get shelf space at large retailers like Best Buy and Circuit City.

Many of the firms doing outsourced NPD work started out as contract manufacturers, evolving from OEMs (original equipment manufacturers) to ODMs (original design manufacturers). A Taiwanese owned company we visited in Southern China, for example, began as an OEM making a product to the specifications of a U.S. firm. As more and more manufacturing technology was transferred to the plant in China, the U.S. product designers had to work with those in China to design their products for increased manufacturability. In time detailed design functions were increasingly transferred to China. Not all OEM and ODMs are in emerging economies. Some are in Triad economies. Flextronics, for example, began in the 1990s manufacturing for other companies, and then moved into product development work. Although Flextronics, like many of the ODMs is not well-known to most people, it is a huge company with some 90,000 employees around the world. Flextronic designs and makes products for such firms as Casio, Hewlett-Packard, Motorola, Xerox, Microsoft, and Nortel. In 2002 Flextronic started aggressively building up its NPD capabilities – putting together a 7,000-engineer product design staff in India, China, Southeast Asia, Ukraine, Europe and Latin America. The CEO of Flextronics says that design itself is now a commodity. He claims that his company can develop a new cellular telephone for about a third what it would cost an integrated cell phone producer.[41]

A number of companies have developed specialties in certain types of NPD for other companies. Many of these companies are based in Taiwan. Quanta Corporation, for example, is now the world's leading designer and producer of notebook PCs. Recently Indian companies, including HCL and Wipro, have become major factors ODMs. Indeed it is expected that India's total revenues from contract R&D may reach some $8 billion by 2008.

Even large companies with strong NPD capabilities are outsourcing some of their NPD work. Honeywell has outsourced some of its core processor design work to IBM. Such companies as Boeing, General Motors, Procter and Gamble, Eli Lilly, GlaxoSmithKline, Hewlett-Packard and Motorola have also outsourced some of their design work. Most notebook PCs, MP3 players and PDAs (personal data assistants), are now designed and manufactured by ODMs.

While many firms have realized substantial savings from outsourcing some of their NPD work, there are risks. As the supplier of NPD for a firm builds up its own capabilities, it may become a competitor. Motorola, for example, contracted design and manufacturing work for its cell phones to BenQ, a company in Taiwan. A few years later BenQ started selling cell phones in the fast-growing Chinese market under its own brand name. Motorola had to cut off its relationship with BenQ to protect its position in China. There may be disputes about who actually owns the intellectual property developed in outsourced NPD projects. There may be a hollowing out of a firm's own NPD capabilities. Indeed, the head of product development at one company told one of the authors that there was so much outsourcing at his company, that he is no longer sure what competencies he can draw on within the firm. Firms that outsource NPD also risk losing the incentive to maintain their competencies in the outsourced area. Finally, when competitors outsource some of their NPD to the same design firm, they may end up with products that are not well differentiated. At one OEM plant we visited in China, there were separate show rooms for the competing products the OEM made for four different multinationals. Clearly, decisions to outsource NPD should be carefully considered in the context of company strategy.

Conclusion

In a growing number of industries NPD is globalizing. Firms have to serve global markets that are more diverse than ever before. They have to place some of their NPD activities near these new markets. There are also new opportunities to draw on new technological and human resources and to take advantage of global economies of scale. But these new opportunities are accompanied by new risks and new challenges. By outsourcing NPD, a firm may foster the development of strong new competitors. It may risk losing intellectual capital if it is not careful in how it handles technology development in some countries. On the other hand, there is the risk of being slower to capitalize on new opportunities than other firms. Although some NPD activities may be globalized on an incremental basis, e.g. a manager decides to outsource a small part of an NPD project, these activities may aggregate to have implications far beyond any single project. These must be thought through from a strategic perspective. A theme in this book is that NPD should be part of the overall strategies and objectives of the firm. This is especially true in the globalization of NPD.

5
Creating a New Product Concept

New product success depends heavily on the compatibility of the product with corporate strategy, and on the formulation of a new product concept that meets market needs. Information on the market must be collected and evaluated. At the same time the NPD team must not be so constrained by current market demands that it overlooks opportunities in new markets. This chapter takes up these aspects of the creation of a new product concept.

Corporate strategy and ideas for new products

Successful new product development starts from and is a part of corporate strategy. The classic SWOT analysis (an analysis of the company's Strengths, Weaknesses, Opportunities and the Threats facing it) is used by many firms to create an overall strategy. Table 5.1 shows how Taisei Corporation, one of Japan's largest construction and contracting firms, uses a SWOT analysis to formulate corporate strategy, including strategies on new business creation.

Using a SWOT analysis, Taisei has group discussions of: 1. How the company can mobilize its strengths to take advantage of new opportunities; 2. How it can overcome the weaknesses that keep it from seizing the opportunities; 3. How it can bolster its strengths to cope with possible threats; 4. How it can overcome its weaknesses to withstand the threats. Through these analyses, strategic initiatives, including the possible entry into new businesses, are proposed.

Aside from SWOT, other models of strategy formation that are widely used include the PPM (product portfolio matrix, also called the BCG matrix method) and benchmarking against competitors. Some firms have specific criteria to guide actions, such as requiring that each

Table 5.1   SWOT analysis at Taisei Construction

Opportunity and threat analysis

Opportunities	Threats
Expanding domestic demand	Diversifying construction demand
Industrial reorganization	Market entry by foreign companies
Urbanization	Increased construction labor costs

Strength and weakness analysis

Strengths	Weaknesses
Excellent performance in all construction fields	Overemphasis on short-term profit
Extensive technology	Overemphasis on in-house development
Outstanding problem-solving skills	Poor cooperation within group

Strategy applying SWOT analysis

	Opportunities	Threats
Strength	Expand metropolitan market	Need to fully manifest organization's strengths
Weakness	Expand joint ventures with firms in other industries	Need to enhance distinctive technologies
		Need to enhance marketing function

of the company's businesses be either first or second in its market. A good example of how a firm uses criteria like these to form strategy is provided by Emerson Electric, which in 2004 was ranked as the second "best company" in the United States (GE was first). Several aspects of Emerson's strategy account for its success: (1) The company focuses on products in mature industries so as to take advantage of the stability of these markets. (2) The company requires that its products are either first or second in each of its markets – other product lines are divested. (3) The company concentrates on six areas where it has special strengths: power systems, sensors, air conditioning systems, motors, plumbing tools and plant automation (most of these areas are related to plant production systems). (4) To differentiate its products and give them a competitive edge, the company invests heavily in high level research and development (6% of its sales is spent on R&D). (5) To maintain its competitive strength, the company pays special attention to long-range planning. Top management spends about 60 days each year establishing long-range plans for the company's six groups and business units. These plans are revisited every month.

Within the general framework of its strategy, a firm has to find new ideas for products and collect the information needed to evaluate them.

Ideas for new products and sources of information. Sometimes an idea for a new product is presented after extensive information has been collected. Other times the idea comes out of daily operations, and is presented even before information has been systematically collected. Drawing on ideas that come out of daily operations is sometimes called an "emergent strategy,"[42] a "middle-up approach" or a "middle manager interaction approach." The differences between these approaches and developing a new product idea after extensive information collection is not as great as it might at first seem. In either case, the company needs information on the markets for the product and on the technology that will be used to create the product.

Table 5.2 presents the findings of our survey on the sources of ideas for new products. More than half the respondents listed the exploration of growth areas, the observation of trends with products from competitors, and the examination of patent information. While the Table lists 35 different sources of ideas, these can be grouped into four general categories: 1. Customer needs; 2. Product successes of other companies; 3. "Seeds" from technological possibilities; and 4. Special strengths of the company. Table 5.3 gives examples of successful new products that were developed based on the various information sources.

Among the hit products shown in Table 5.3 that were inspired by consumer needs, the Sony Walkman is perhaps the best known internationally. The concept for the Walkman originated in Sony's Development Department. In its studies of market trends, the Department found three things. A large and growing number of consumers wanted personal music players. They wanted the music to be in stereo. And, they preferred music on tape to music on records. This led to two breakthrough ideas. One was based on the observation that consumers were far more interested in using recorders to listen to music than in using them to record. So, why not eliminate the recording function from cassette tape recorders? This made it possible to reduce the size of the recorder by 40%. It also allowed Sony's engineers to concentrate on improving the stereo sound quality of the recorders. The other breakthrough idea was to combine the new light stereo recorders with very

Table 5.2   Sources of ideas for new products

	% selecting
Needs	
1. Exploration of growth areas	60.2
2. Long-term predictions on industry structure	15.5
3. Long-term predictions on technology	36.0
4. Special market surveys to find related products	40.3
5. Trends in the consumption of related products	30.4
6. Survey on the defects of present products	36.0
7. Information on new materials	36.0
8. Information on substitutes	8.7
9. Information on complaints, user information cards	16.1
10. Reports and suggestions of salesmen	29.8
11. Information from sales channels	32.9
12. Interviews with consumers and purchasers	21.7
13. Information from monitors	17.3
14. Information from industry trade journals	9.9
15. Information from suppliers	19.8
16. Newspapers, journals and government reports	4.3
Success of others	
17. Successful products in foreign countries and/or other companies	22.9
18. Trends of competitor products	59.3
19. Observation of related products in exhibitions and stores	25.4
Technological possibilities	
20. Patent information	53.4
21. Scientific journals	16.1
22. Scientific articles in trade journals	11.6
23. Articles in newspapers, journals and public printings	4.3
24. Presentations at academic conferences	10.5
25. Opinions of technology experts	24.2
Strengths and weaknesses of company	
26. Expert opinions on the use of related products	8.0
27. Trends in competitor R&D	44.1
28. Economic and political trends in foreign countries	2.4
29. General domestic economic trends	0.6
30. Trends of policies of the government	4.3
31. Trends of important resources	2.8
32. Strengths and weaknesses of company's R&D	44.1
33. Strengths and weaknesses of company's marketing	26.7
34. Strengths and weaknesses of company's production	18.6
35. Information from testing of the new product	25.4

Notes:
1. For details about the sample, see Table 1.4.
2. Respondents were asked to select the ten most important sources.

Table 5.3   Successful product ideas from various information sources

---

Customer Needs
  Shiseido "Yakuyo Furorin" hair growth stimulant
  Asahi "Super Dry" beer
  Nippon Sanso stainless steel vacuum bottle
  Aiwa mini television
  Yamaha "Silent Piano"
  Toto Washlet toilet
  Mobile telephone
  Fuji "Utsurundesu" (Quicksnap) camera
  Sony Walkman

Success of competitors
  Sony PlayStation
  Honda Odyssey Minivan

Technological seeds
  Seiko Crystal Quartz Chronometer
  Sony CD player
  Toray Exene artificial leather
  Matsushita Panasonic bulb type fluorescent light
  Toray soft contract lens
  Canon laser printer
  Toray carbon fiber
  Sharp LCD display camera
  Sony and Matsushita Panasonic car navigation systems
  Matsushita Panasonic magnetic heating cooking instrument

Company's strengths and weaknesses
  Honda automobile
  Casio digital watch
  Sony musical content

---

small and lightweight headphones. Fortunately, Sony had already developed lightweight headphones for its conventional tape recorders.

Development of the Walkman was not quite as straightforward as this description might make it sound, however. It took 3 years to come up with a Walkman. As it came time to launch the new product the price was set at well over $200, based on the cost of production. The marketing department opposed the launch at this price because other tape recorders on the market cost only about one-third as much. Akio Morita, then the president of Sony, and a music lover, was impressed by the Walkman's sound quality. Based on his instincts about young consumers, he ordered the product launch. Walkman, of course, went on to become a spectacular success around the world. This again shows the importance of strong strategic leadership from the top. One of the authors vividly recalls an enthusiastic Morita showing off the newly introduced Walkman to an audience of several hundred undergraduate engineering students at Carnegie-Mellon University in the 1980s. The students not only wanted to find out how they could get the new stereos, but many were also mobbing Morita to find out how they could get jobs with Sony. As was mentioned earlier, Masaru Ibuka, the co-founder with Morita of Sony, was also a key early-stage product champion for the Walkman.

Other highly successful new product concepts also came out of observations of consumer needs. Fuji Film developed the single use camera based on the observation that consumers sometimes forget to bring a camera on trips or to special occasions like birthday parties. The stainless steel vacuum bottle was invented by Nihon Sanso, a company that produced oxygen, because the product developers knew that consumers often broke the fragile glass thermos bottles that were then in use. Yamaha knew that some people were reluctant to play the piano because they did not want to disturb family members or neighbors. To solve this problem Yamaha invented the "silent piano" (The piano can be switched to a digital mode, so the player can hear it through an earphone, but no sound comes out of the piano itself.).

The success of other company's products can also inspire new products. While the "new" product may, in a sense, be an imitation, if a company successfully differentiates it, it can be a huge success. Sony's PlayStation, for example, was not the first game system on the market. Sony, however, differentiated the PlayStation by designing it use compact disks instead of tape. It also provided more content by developing a new relationship with game software producers. PlayStation became a huge success with sales of nearly $6 billion and profits of nearly $2 billion a year.

The most important source of innovative new products is technological innovation. Seiko's Crystal Quartz Chronometer and Toray's carbon fiber composite material are examples of technology seed based new products. Other new products originate from the special strengths or needs of the firm. In the 1960s Honda was a world leading motorcycle producer, but the company's top management wanted to diversify. Based on its strength in small displacement engines Honda introduced a front wheel drive mini-car with a 360cc displacement engine, the N360. The N360 was not really a "hit product," but it was successful enough to get Honda into the automobile market.

Implications from the survey. One conclusion that can be drawn from the survey results reported in Table 5.2, and in the cases we have described, is that a company needs systematically and regularly to collect information about consumer needs, successful products from other companies, new technological possibilities, etc. The corporate planning, marketing and R&D departments must be constantly alert to useful information from these sources. Even when information that may lead to new products comes out of daily operations, or from middle management, rather than from external sources of ideas, it must be systematically evaluated and refined by these departments.

Another important point that comes out of this analysis is that the combination of several different pieces of information can lead to successful ideas. One major consumer electronics company uses a matrix of needs and seeds to generate ideas for new products (see Table 5.4). One "need" identified on the matrix, for example, is: "Comfortable living." Related "seeds" are the company's strengths in control systems and air conditioning. A new product opportunity, then, might be programmed air conditioning.

By combining market needs and technological seeds (or the company's technological strengths), ideas for new products are produced. A matrix like this is widely used by companies. The matrix is similar to the PPM (product portfolio matrix) model which has two axes, attractiveness of market and strengths of the company. However, the

Table 5.4   Matrix of technical strengths and environmental needs

Technological strengths	Control systems	Information	Energy	Service
Needs				
Safety	Protection from crime			
Comfortable living	Programmed air conditioning		Air conditioning	
Labor saving				Robots
Health		Home medical exams		
Information systems		Working at home		

analysis of competitors is lacking in this matrix and competitor analysis should also be considered during the assessment process.

Concept creation. The "concept" for a new product outlines the new product's intended features. The concept indicates the basic strategy for how the product will be differentiated from other products. The concept is established at the beginning of the NPD process. As Figure 5.1 shows, the new product concept consists of three elements.[43]

The first element is the product's set of "core benefits." This includes identifying the intended customers and the needs the product is intended to satisfy. It also includes the new product's intended image, quality, function and price. The second element is the "formal description" of the new product. This includes the product's targeted design, packaging, advertising and technological features. The third element is "augmentation." This includes the planned sales channels, the after-sales service system and the distribution system.

Figure 5.1 uses the case of Ajinomoto Mayonnaise (discussed in Chapter 3) to show the first and second elements of a product concept. Another case presented in Chapter 3 was Canon's small copier. The concept of the Canon personal copier included four elements. The target customers were to be people working in small offices. The copier was to weigh less than 20 kilograms (44 pounds). The copier was to be sold for less than $1,000. The copiers were to be designed for easy maintenance through the use of replaceable modules. The product concept for Toyota's Lexus included that the new car would be a status symbol for high income professionals and that it would be a very high quality car in terms of quality, price, performance and safety. The guiding image held by the team that developed the Lexus was the renaissance genius Michelangelo. The elements of the concept for the Walkman defined the product as a stereo player for personal use. It was to be a product for the younger generation. It would be a stereo that played tapes, was small, used a personal earphone, and provided high fidelity music. A key concept element for the 8 millimeter video camera was that it would be "a passport sized video camera."

Many NPD experts say that the creation of the new product "concept" is the most important step in the NPD process. It provides detailed goals for the new product, and successful decision-making starts by defining the goals and policies that guide the decision.

Formation of the new product concept starts with an exploration of the needs of the market. Panels of inside and outside evaluators judge how well the concept meets these needs. This is called the concept test.

Figure 5.1   Elements of product "concept" (Functions and attributes of product)

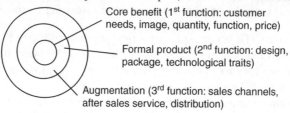

Core benefit (1st function: customer needs, image, quantity, function, price)

Formal product (2nd function: design, package, technological traits)

Augmentation (3rd function: sales channels, after sales service, distribution)

Example: Mayonnaise
1st function
(1) Quantity ... selection of oil
(2) Retail price
(3) Image ... rich taste, not oily
(4) Function ... delicious, healthy, deep taste
(5) Use ... for vegetable salad
(6) Target ... 40~50 year old users
(7) Profitability
2nd function
(8) Brand
(9) Kinds of product
(10) Quantity of a package
(11) Package style
(12) Design

Note: Items #(1) and (3) are points of departure
Source: Presentation by Mr K. Yasutake of Ajinomoto at a meeting of the Japan Productivity Center.

The new product image unifies the concept elements. It is used to appeal to the market, and to motivate the people engaged in development. In the development of the PC10 and PC20 at Canon, the previous success of Canon's AEI camera was taken as a success model, and "let's match the success of the AEI" was the slogan of the NPD team.

Cases of market research.   Regardless of the source of a new product idea, various kinds of market research are needed to formulate the detailed ideas or "concept" for the new product. As we have seen, Ajinomoto carries out extensive market surveys every 3 years on food consumption. Information from the surveys was used to formulate the concept for a new mayonnaise. Aishin Seiki, which produces automatic transmissions for Toyota, wanted to diversify into new products. So Aishin set up an office to explore opportunities in Tokyo's Akihabara district. Akihabara is well-known in Japan as a center for the sale of the latest high tech electronics products and components. Aishin's managers and engineers looked around Akihabara's stores, and carried out informal market surveys. In this way they came up with the idea of developing a car navigation system. This became an important new product for Aishin. Aishin's market surveys were very informal, but nonetheless they were highly successful.

Case: the Toyota Lexus

Early in the development of a concept for the Lexus, five Toyota designers were sent to Toyota's development center in California for 2 months. Their purpose was to study the American owners of luxury cars. They did this by going to shopping center parking lots to observe the drivers of luxury cars. They found that two types of Americans drove luxury cars. One group was older and often retired. Many members of this group were, or had been, high income blue collar workers. The members of this group liked traditional American luxury cars like the Cadillac or Lincoln. The other group was made up affluent baby boomers. These were often doctors or lawyers. They preferred German luxury cars such as Mercedes and BMW. The two groups differed with respect to education and occupation. Toyota decided to focus on the affluent baby boomers for its new Lexus.

This observation of California shopping center parking lots was part of an overall effort to identify the various dimensions of the luxury car market, including not only the status of luxury car owners, but also their preferences for image, quality, price, performance and safety. Once a product concept was decided on, Toyota's California development office proposed several designs, and made one-fifth scale models of them. The Japanese design center also made models of several other designs. Finally, a total of ten scale models was created. Three of these were selected for the production of full size mock ups. About 100 people from the marketing and other departments evaluated the models and selected a design for the Lexus.[44]

Limitations and advantages of market information. While the NPD process requires market information, there are limitations to the value of this information.

(1) Consumers know about the strong and weak points of existing products, but they obviously have no experience with innovative new products. When the first digital cameras were introduced, consumers could tell you what they liked and didn't like about film cameras, but they did not know what features they might want in a digital camera.

Would consumers use the capability of digital cameras to print pictures at home? Would battery life matter to them more than resolution? How important would the digital zoom prove to be?

(2) Ordinary consumers may not know their hidden, or even some of their real needs, so information from a random sample of consumers may be misleading. Researchers may need to ask experts on consumer behavior about unique new products.[45]

(3) Consumers are also not very useful in suggesting needs for high technology products. They don't know enough about what is technologically realistic, or what the latest technologies may make possible. High technology products generally have to be proposed by the manufacturers. Take the example of a medication used to treat ulcers. Peptic ulcers are caused by a bacterium called *H. Pylori*, which is found in the stomach lining. Most experts, however, did not believe that bacteria could be the cause of ulcers because they thought it was impossible for bacteria to survive the strong acids in the stomach. So, naturally there was no demand for a medicine that could kill the *H. Pylori* bacterium. It was generally assumed that stress and spicy foods were the main causes of ulcers. In 1982 two researchers discovered that the *H. Pylori* bacterium is in fact able to survive in the stomach because it can neutralize stomach acid. This led to the development of new stomach medicines (and a Nobel Prize for the researchers).

(4) Consumers may find it easy to explicitly state some aspects of what they want in a product. They might say, for example: "I like small cars." But sometimes they cannot or will not clearly express what they want. It may not occur to them to say, for example, that they are concerned about after-sales service for the car. They may be reluctant to say they are more interested in the prestige value of a car than its practicality. An understanding of these hidden needs can lead to successful products that are entirely new or that are differentiated from similar products.

There are several ways to discover hidden needs. One might observe the behavior of consumers (like the Toyota product developers who watched drivers of luxury cars). For some products it may be necessary to virtually live with consumers for several days to see how they use products. Another approach is to ask experts about problems people have with existing products. Pharmaceutical companies commonly form panels of doctors to systematically collect information about the experience patients have with medications. Some of these suggestions can be rather simple. The director of research at a European pharmaceutical company told us that panels of doctors had mentioned, for example, that older people were finding it difficult to swallow certain pills because the pills were too large. So, the company began making smaller pills.

A home appliance company found out that consumers were frustrated because their clothes tended to get entangled with each other in washing machines. This led to the development of a washing machine which is designed to prevent clothing from becoming entangled. Many consumers were unhappy because most washing machines are noisy, which is especially disturbing in apartments and smaller houses. Recognition that this was a problem led to the development of a silent washing machine. People often forget to bring cameras to special occasions, or on trips. Understanding this, as was mentioned above, a company developed an inexpensive single use camera. These are all examples in which new product developers conceived of new product concepts by seeing problems, and manipulating ideas to solve them.

Re-interpreting information and counter-intuitive thinking

How we understand and interpret information is critical. For example, consider the following alternative interpretations of information that led to the identification of new product or market opportunities.

- In Africa many people do not wear shoes. Conventional conclusion: … so we cannot expect to sell many shoes there. Alternative way of thinking: We can sell lots of shoes in Africa because many people there do not have shoes yet.
- In the Arctic it is very cold. Conventional conclusion: … so refrigerators are not needed there. Alternative way of thinking: Refrigerators are needed in the Arctic to keep foods from freezing.
- There are already many small stores in Japan. Conventional conclusion: … so Seven Eleven and other convenience stores will not succeed there. Alternative way of thinking: The fact that there are many small stores in Japan shows that there is a need for small stores, so Seven Eleven can succeed there.

Or, consider how overcoming the following preconceptions led to success.

- Only malt barley can be used to make beer. Sapporo developed "Draft One," a beer-like beverage, made from Canadian peas. Since the tax rate on beer-like beverages is much lower when the malt ratio is less than 67%, "Draft One" can be sold at a much lower price than conventional beer. It also has a good taste. As a result Sapporo sold 36 million bottles of "Draft One" in 2004.

- Once they get wet, swimming suits are wet and cold, so women would not want to keep them on as street wear after swimming. Toray developed "Sarahara" amphibian swimming suits that dry quickly, so women can comfortably wear them on the street with a skirt.
- Pianos have to be large, heavy, and expensive. Yamaha developed a hand roll-up piano keyboard, weighing just a few pounds (and powered by three batteries) and priced at just over $100.
- People who live in small apartments will not buy pianos because they don't want to disturb their neighbors. As we saw, Yamaha developed a piano that can be used with headphones so as not to disturb others.

These are just a few examples of counter-intuitive thinking. Re-interpreting information can also lead to new combinations and new products. For example:

- Liquid material in a bag explodes when heated in a microwave oven. A bag with small holes, however, can be filled with a gel and heated in a microwave to make a hand or bed warmer. About one million of these bags were sold for around $10 each.
- Generator operated head lights make bicycles harder to pedal. With "Magi-light," electricity is generated by a magnet on the spokes of the bicycle wheel and a coil in the light. This does not make it harder to pedal the bike. In 2004 some 40,000 of these lights were sold for nearly $50 each.
- Milk spoils after several days when it is kept in a refrigerator. The spoiling is caused by oxygen in the milk. Meiji Milk developed "Sweet Milk" with only 1.5 ppm of oxygen (compared to 10 ppm in ordinary milk). Even though Sweet Milk was priced about 50% more than conventional milk, sales reached over $300 million in 2004.

Of course, new products based on counter-intuitive thinking can fail. Consumers may not turn out to share the producer's view of what features are important. Some years ago Mazda failed with its rotary engine cars. These offered outstanding performance, but poor fuel economy. Consumers were unwilling to pay the added fuel costs to get the higher performance. One firm in Japan offered an extremely accurate watch for $3,000. Since even ordinary watches these days are highly accurate, consumers were unwilling to pay so much for a watch that was only a little more accurate.

Still, counter-intuitive thinking very often leads to break-through new products. How does one come up with concepts through counter-intuitive thinking? One technique is brain storming. Another is the use of "Osborn's checklist."

Osborn's Checklist.[46] New ideas are achieved by looking at things from new angles to create new combinations of existing knowledge. Many people in charge of development use the checklist shown in Table 5.5 to foster this kind of reverse thinking. Once a technology has been established and is being used for a product, one might ask, for example, if there might be any other uses for it. The table also gives some actual examples of new product ideas that came from using the checklist.

Table 5.5 Osborn's check list – questions to stimulate new ideas

Question	Examples
1. Other uses?	• Cutting metal by laser • Using optical fiber for diagnosis • Fertilizer from used sugar cane • Warm swimming pool by heat from burning garbage • Producing artificial meat from protein of soy beans
2. Can we borrow ideas?	• Cash card → telephone card • Reflex camera → automatic focus camera
3. Can we change something?	• Glass bottle → paper package • Communication by electricity → by light • Gasoline engine → hybrid car • Sound proof room → silent piano
4. Can we appeal to physical senses?	• Fountain pen whose ink can be seen • Sound of boiling • Sound of watch increases when not stopped
5. Can we substitute something?	• Tennis racket and golf club using reinforced carbon fiber • Metal bat ← wooden bat • Paper bag ← glass bottle • Shoes made from artificial leather • Power generation by wind

Table 5.5   Osborn's check list – questions to stimulate new ideas – *continued*

Question	Examples
6. Can we make it bigger?	• Large size tennis racket • Large size golf club head • Jumbo jet
7. Can we make it smaller	• Small camera • Walkman • Personal computer • Semiconductor tip • Mini auto bicycle
8. Can we take something out?	• Tubeless tire • Mobile phone (wireless) • Open car • Instant food
9. Can we replace something?	• Instant soup • Record → tape → CD → DVD
10. Can we reverse something?	• Reversible suits • Karaoke (from listening to singing)
11. Can we combine something?	• Mobile telephone with camera • Air conditioner (cooling and heating) • Dual focus glasses • Telephone with recorder

Source: Examples are by authors

Table 5.6   Phrases that kill creative thinking

(1) It is a good idea, but not practical
     It is too complex

(2) We are too busy now
     We'll do it later

(3) I tried it before, but did not succeed.

(4) Others will oppose it
     Who can carry it out?

Osborn also developed an effective approach to brainstorming. It's based on the idea that the brainstorming group should welcome unusual ideas. New ideas can be produced by combining one's own ideas with those of others. So, participants should not be too quick to criticize other people's ideas. Indeed, the group should present as many ideas as possible. During the first hour or more of a meeting, each member might present unique ideas. A leader will record them. Only then will the group begin to assess the ideas, and select those that seem most promising. This principle can be applied to every meeting, not just those concerned with new product development. The group must be careful not to kill new ideas by using such phrases as those shown in Table 5.6. It is all too easy to kill a new idea by dismissing it as impractical or too complex. Often postponing the consideration of an idea is tantamount to killing it.

Reconciling contradictory product features

In creating a new product, an NPD team may find that it has to develop one desired product characteristic without taking away from another desired product characteristic. The desired characteristics may seem to push product development in different directions. Examples include developing environmental friendly products that are also cheap to produce; combining high quality with low production costs; developing powerful engines that also offer low fuel consumption; developing tires that offer a good grip on icy roads, and yet are suited to driving at highway speeds. Reconciling product needs that apparently are inconsistent may be difficult, but often it proves to be possible. It may be necessary to make technological breakthroughs, or even to make apparent jumps in logic.

Toray developed a new soft contact lens by overcoming apparently contradictory factors. If a lens were designed so that it contained enough water to absorb oxygen, it would be too soft to manufacture. Moreover, it would be too soft to form a lens. Toray solved this dilemma by mixing three kinds of plastic. To find a way to do this they had to try more than 1,000 combinations of plastic.

In developing its best selling Yaris model, Toyota was faced with the problem of developing a small car with a large interior. How do you make a car larger on the inside, while making it smaller on the outside? Part of Toyota's solution was to raise the car's roof. This allowed them to raise the front seats so people in the back had more leg room. They also increased storage space in the car to give it the feel of having a large interior. The car was given a large trunk and a fold down rear seat, allowing it to accommodate two golf bags. They also increased the number of cup holders and storage area pockets. To increase the speed and fuel economy of the car's one liter engine, they reduced the weight of the engine, transmission, and body, and they improved the car's aerodynamics. Many models of components were developed to evaluate different ways of reducing the weight of the car, such as by using more aluminum. The developers also wanted a car that despite being small, would have a solid feel. To achieve this they increased the length of the wheelbase. They wanted a car that was small, but stylish. They created many clay models, and sent them to Paris to be evaluated. Over the past 5 years Toyota has sold two and a half million of these cars.

In brief, to solve the problem of mutually contradictory factors, the NPD team can look for technical breakthroughs and improved designs. They can also use segment maps, conjoint analysis and other methods to evaluate the relative importance to consumers of each factor. Two of these methods are described below.

Two methods for evaluating the importance of new product characteristics

Two relatively simple methods are widely used to collect information from consumers about their preferences for a product.

Segment maps. One way to identify a new market niche is to use a segment or product traits map. We gave an example of this in Figure 1.1 ("Market segmentation and the size of markets for different types of beer"). The product's most important traits are used as the axes of a segment map. In the case of Figure 1.1, these were the "thickness" and the "bitterness" of beer. The analyst determines the most important traits by asking consumers about the characteristics of products that are currently on the market. The consumers are asked to rank various products, or do an overall evaluation of them. Important factors can be identified by multiple regression analysis or conjoint analysis. Factor analysis is widely used to find the number of consumers with different preferences, which makes it possible to estimate the size and location of a market.

The following procedure was used to develop Figure 1.1.[47]

- A group was asked to discuss important factors in their beer preferences.
- Based on this discussion, the researchers developed 21 questions.
- About 200 consumers were asked in a questionnaire to locate eight brands along six different scales.

- The answers were analyzed by factor analysis, and the two most important factors were found. These were used as the axes in Figure 1.1.
- The eight brands were located on the map by factor loading.

Next the researchers computed factor scores for each respondent. A correlation of factors was used to find the clusters. Then the location and size of the circles in the figure were calculated.

Although segment maps can be very useful, they have two problems:

- An analysis using more than two product traits is hard to interpret. On the other hand, if we use a radar chart (like that shown in Figure 1.2) to incorporate more product traits, we cannot find the location of demand.
- This method can be used to estimate the market size for improved existing products, but it cannot be used to find ideas for completely new products. As we have seen, consumers don't know their preferences for such products.

Conjoint analysis. Conjoint analysis is a widely used technique to determine the relative importance of various product features. It assumes, of course, that the product is one where consumers can rank order their preferences for product traits. As we have seen, this would normally be truer for improved products than for totally new products. Once the researchers have determined what product traits are most important to consumers, they can use this information to develop a new product.

Table 5.7 gives an example of a conjoint analysis for ladies hair conditioners. Participants in the study were asked to rank their preferences for six groups of hair conditioner traits. The results were analyzed by multiple correlation analysis, and the utilities of each trait were found. The contribution rates were measured by the differences between the maximum and minimum values. This particular analysis looked separately at middle-aged and young women. Table 5.7 shows that for this product there is a large difference between these two groups. Middle aged women, for example, give a positive utility value to the highest priced conditioners (those at 800 yen, about \$8), while young women assign a negative utility value to the most expensive conditioners. Middle aged women assigned by far the largest contribution ratio to the maker of the conditioner, while younger women gave the largest contribution ratio to conditioners that distinguish between types of hair. In other words, middle aged women liked higher-priced conditioners with

Table 5.7 Conjoint analysis – women's hair conditioner

Middle aged women (17%)

Category	Level	Utility value	Contribution ratio (%)
		–3 –2 –1 0 +1 +2 +3	10 20 30 40 50 60 70 80 90 100
Maker	Specialized firm Cosmetics firm Foreign firm Super brand		62.14
Price	800 yen 500 yen 300 yen 200 yen		12.94
Prevention of dandruff and itching	No Yes		0.93
Different kinds of hair	Different Same		17.94
Tenderness to hair	Yes No		6.05
Scent	Yes No		0.00

Young women (23%)

Category	Level	Utility value	Contribution ratio (%)
		–3 –2 –1 0 +1 +2 +3	10 20 30 40 50 60 70 80 90 100
Maker	Specialized firm Cosmetics firm Foreign firm Super brand		1.62
Price	800 yen 500 yen 300 yen 200 yen		1.34
Prevention of dandruff and itching	No Yes		7.87
Different kinds of hair	Different Same		66.42
Tenderness to hair	Yes No		21.87
Scent	Yes No		0.87

Source: T. Ueda (1987).

prestigious brands, while younger women liked less expensive conditioners that were formulated to different types of hair.

Many companies have used conjoint analysis to find out what product traits are most important to potential consumers. Ricoh Company used it in developing a new copier. A construction company used this method in develop housing (evaluating the utility value and contribution ratios to potential buyers of commuting distance, size of the house, and price). As we have seen, Marriot Hotels used conjoint analysis to develop the medium-priced hotel chain "Courtyard by Marriot." Here the relevant utilities were hotel location, size of the hotel, size of rooms, shapes of room, size of desks in the room, type of door locks and room rates. Several years were spent doing the analysis. In 1985 30 to 40 Courtyard by Marriot hotels were opened, and in 1991, another 185 were opened.[48]

Conjoint analysis requires that three assumptions be made. 1. That the participants in the study are very familiar with the features (utilities) being studied. 2. That the participants in the study evaluate utilities in the same way as the population they represent. And 3. That it is possible for participants to rank the utilities in a meaningful way.[49]

6
Organizing for Effective New Product Development

Some companies, alliances of companies, and project teams are more effective than others at NPD, even though they do not necessarily have staff members who are any smarter or more creative. In this chapter we draw on our own research and on our observations of a large number of companies, as well as the research and observations of others, to describe some of the characteristics that make some companies, alliances and project teams particularly effective at NPD.

Organizational sources of ideas for new products

Table 6.1 shows the responses managers gave when asked where the ideas for their recent successful new products had come from. As the table shows, many of the new ideas came from top management and departments supporting top management. What is particularly striking, however, is that high performance companies were much more likely to get ideas for successful new products from these sources than low performance companies. At high performance companies 41% of managers mentioned top management as a source of successful new product ideas, compared to only 25% of the managers at low performance companies. Development departments at the head office were sources of ideas far more often at high performance than was the case at low performance companies. Companies that did not perform as well depended more heavily on ideas from marketing departments and customers. These findings cast doubt on the advice given by Henry Mintzberg[50] and other prominent management theorists that firms should follow emergent or "middle up" strategies.

Our research suggests that the role of the strategic planning groups should be reinforced. While it is the operating departments that pro-

Table 6.1   Sources of ideas for successful new products

	Low performers % mentioning	High performers % mentioning
1. Top management	25	41*
2. Planning department	23	26
3. Project team exploring new products	21	37*
4. Development department for exploration at head office	27	37
5. Development department for research management at head office	17	33*
6. Research laboratory under the head office	37	33
7. Development department at product division	63	81*
8. R&D laboratory at product division	15	26
9. Manufacturing and production technology department	13	15
10. Marketing department	58	52
11. Sales people	8	11
12. Sales channel	19	22
13. Employees in general	4	0
14. Customers	50	44
15. Overseas offices	2	4
16. University research laboratories	10	7
17. Other research organizations	2	4

*P < 0.1

Notes: 1. Respondents were asked to identify sources of their successful new product ideas.
2. For details on the survey respondents, see Table 1.4.
3. For how company performance was measured, see notes to Table 1.3.

duce today's profits, the strategic planning groups play vital roles in creating future profits and growth. Table 6.2 lists the various departments involved in NPD in the firms that were surveyed. Again, we see the importance of the strategic planning groups at high performance firms. It is also interesting to note that for all eleven of the departments we asked about, a higher percentage of managers at high performance companies reported that these departments were involved in NPD. Successful firms include more departments in their development of new products.

Centralized authority and strong strategic planning groups. Firms are structured based on function, product, or group. Most textbooks

Table 6.2 Departments involved in NPD

	Low Performers % mentioning	High performers % mentioning
Planning department	62	74**
Development department at head office (looking for new opportunities)	42	74**
Development department at head office (planning and controlling research)	62	70
Marketing department in charge of NPD	13	15
Incubator department	19	26*
Research laboratories under head office	40	44
Division development department	35	56**
Division development department (mostly design)	42	67**
Division research laboratory	23	30
Committee to evaluate technical aspect of new products	31	37
Committee to evaluate economic aspect of new products	15	26*

*P < 0.1,
**P < 0.05.
Note: See Table 1.3 and Table 1.4 for details on new products.

describe how as organizations grow, they move from function-based to product-based structures. We argue that changes in the environment now make it necessary for firms to move to a more centralized authority structure. Centralization is necessary to achieve dynamic changes in resource allocation and product mix. That's why successful companies such as Canon have moved to structures based on function. Canon has a strong corporate planning staff, strong centralized research laboratories, and a centralized marketing company.

Some successful firms use the product group or product "company" system, but even so these firms are still highly centralized. At these firms the laboratories and marketing departments are centered at the group level, rather than being scattered across the various product divisions. A few years ago Matsushita Panasonic consolidated its product divisions into three groups, integrating activities that had been scattered, and reducing the overlap of activities among the product divisions. This greatly increased Matsushita Panasonic's success in NPD. The company's financial performance also dramatically improved after the change was made.

The authors looked at the organizational charts of more than 25 Japanese manufacturing companies, and found that most of them have a functional organization structure. Strong R&D laboratories are centralized under the head office. The marketing department is also under the head office, and local offices are organized by district, rather than by product. This means that R&D and marketing costs are not assigned to production departments (which, naturally enough, would want to minimize their non-production costs). Another relatively common type of organization for these firms is the group or "company" structure. In this type of organization there is a functional structure. The research, marketing, and production departments are under the group/company. Here there is a medium level concentration of authority. Few of the firms we looked at were using a product division structure.

There are several reasons for this concentration of authority in successful firms. Higher levels of technology are increasingly needed. It is easier for large, centralized laboratories than small laboratories scattered amongst product division, to come up with the resources and capabilities needed to invest in and carry out high technology research. The speed and scale of change in the environment has also increased, so strategic decisions are becoming more important relative to operational decisions. Specialization is increasingly being emphasized over diversification. Many successful companies have aggressively divested their weaker products. To be sure, Table 6.1 shows that development departments in product divisions are important sources of new product ideas, but often these ideas are for improved products, rather than completely new products.

Core competencies

As we briefly discussed in Chapter 1, core competencies play an important role in developing new products and in maintaining competitive strength. Core competencies have the following features:[51]

1. They provide a common capability that can be applied across various products. For instance, Canon has technologies for precision mechanical engineering, optics and electronics and systems. Canon has applied these core technologies to cameras, copiers, printers and other successful new products.
2. The capabilities embedded in the company must be needed by existing customers, and they must be capable of producing high-growth new products. Sony's competency in producing small electronic

devices led to the creation of the Walkman, the CD player, and many other successful new products.

3. The competencies must be difficult to imitate. Manufacturers in Japan's Tsubame and Sanjo regions were once famous throughout the world for their cutlery. Later, however, they lost market share to lower-cost Korean producers making similar cutlery. In response the Japanese manufacturers developed new product lines that are much harder to copy. One company, for example, switched to much higher technology products, such as titanium head golf clubs, components for space vehicles, and high-quality kitchen goods. These products built on the company's strong competencies in metallurgy, plating, casting and other metal processing technologies, but they could not be easily imitated by others. The multiple skills of Seven Eleven Japan in sourcing, inventory control, and other areas proved to be difficult to imitate when others sought to enter this market. Conversely, Yaohan, a large-scale supermarket operator, rapidly expanded its business around the world, opening stores from New Jersey to Shanghai. But there was not much coherence in the expansion. Yaohan acquisitions ranged, for example, from a high-end department store in Beijing to middle market supermarkets in Japan. Yaohan's expansion was not based on core competencies, and in 1998 the company went bankrupt. Table 6.3 gives examples of the core competencies of some leading firms from different countries and in different industries.

Creation of core competencies. In Chapter 2, we discussed how some companies failed because they did not create core competencies. We also discussed how core competencies can be developed by recruiting new resources and by learning through success. Now we will take up the strategic aspects of creating and changing core competencies.

In order to create new core competencies, a company needs to discover new opportunities by finding an intersection between new market needs and company strengths. The company can draw a picture of its planned future product mix, overall strategies and visions, and then identify the competencies that will be needed to support this strategy. At Canon the corporate planning department proposed entering the copier business because the camera and the copier use many technologies in common. Once the strategy was decided on, research and development started. To achieve the new strategy Canon created new competencies in electronics, chemistry, computer programming, communications, new materials and even biology. The new competencies were needed to create new products, and work on the new products

Table 6.3 Examples of core competencies

Anheuser Bush (US). More than 40% of U.S. market for 40+ years.
- Twelve large plants give it strength in large volume production
- Ensure supply of fresh beer with 100 large trucks at each plant
- Uses "fortress strategy" by supplying full range of beers
- Obtains high quality barley and hops through control of 2,500 farms

Alcan (Canada). Leading producer of aluminum and packaging materials.
- Effective management skills to operate 173 plants in the world
- Plants near sources of raw materials
- Plants near customer

Bombardier (Canada). Largest manufacturer of medium sized airplanes
- Designs and produces experimental airplanes spending $10 billion for each
- Global network of component suppliers, e.g. jet engines from GE, airframes from Mitsubishi Heavy Industry
- Sells airplanes and provides services worldwide
- Trains pilots

Benetton (Italy). Leading supplier of fashionable clothing.
- Strong design capability
- Dyes and produces apparel at central plant in Italy
- Global chain of stores

Canon (Japan). Leading producer of copiers, digital cameras, etc.
- Complementary set of technical competencies including optical, mechanical, electronics and systems
- Ability to use technological breakthroughs to take lead in markets where it is second entrant (e.g. copiers)
- Outstanding strategic planning capability

---

resulted in the development of new competencies for the company. Nintendo's main product was once playing cards. Nintendo reinvented itself by developing video games and family computers. During the change in its product mix, it built new core competencies in electronics technology and software.

Project teams and incubator departments

Three special organization forms are often used by companies to lead the development of new products: project teams, incubator departments, and internal ventures.

Project teams. Project teams may be formed at the corporate, product division, or R&D department level. The teams work on strategic projects, new product development, and other problems or opportunities that come along. The team members bring their various capabilities to work towards clear goals, with set schedules and within a predetermined budget. When they complete their project, they hand it off to the relevant department, and the team is dissolved. Companies use both full- and part-time project teams. Full-time teams are more powerful, and are usually set up to deal with large, important projects. They tend to be more effective because the responsibilities of the individual members of a full-time team are clearly defined, their work is not interrupted by their home department needs, and good teamwork and communication can be demanded of the team members. A problem is that sometimes department managers resist sending their best people to work full-time on project teams because they want to keep these people to work on department activities.

Project teams are used far more often in Japan than in the U.S. or U.K. There are two reasons for this. First, Japanese corporations tend to have a relatively centralized authority structure. The profit responsibilities of product divisions and line departments are generally not as strict as those in the U.S. and U.K. As a result, department managers are less concerned about losing some of their best people to a project team. Second, because most employees of major companies in Japan spend their entire career at a single company, they are more willing to be moved around. There is less of a career risk because employment is assured, and indeed promotion can be expected as a result of serving on a team. In the U.S. or U.K. there is always a risk that a transfer to a project team will turn out to be a career dead-end at the company.

What's the ideal size for a project team? A lot, of course, depends on the project. Six or seven members can make a good working group, but in large projects such as the development of a new car, a successful project team may have to have more than a hundred members. When Nihon Sanso developed the stainless vacuum bottle, the company used a ten-person project team. Four members were from the development department, one was from marketing, one was from production, and one was an outside designer. Three female employees were brought into the team to add a female perspective to the development of the new vacuum bottle. The team worked together for 1 year. When Toray developed the soft contact lens it used a project team made up of five members (four chemists and a technician) during the first stage, and eight members (seven chemists and a technician) during the final stage. The engineering and testing departments worked with the team. The mass production and mass marketing of the new lens were handled by a new product division. As was mentioned in Chapter 2, when Canon developed the PC10/PC20 small copiers it needed a much larger project team. The Canon team included some 200 people.

Project team success factors. Our survey asked respondents about the factors contributing to the success of their project teams. A successful project team was defined as one where the team members worked hard, looked at problems from new angles, and created successful new products and/or production systems. The development of the crystal quartz watch at Seiko, the Walkman at Sony and the small copiers at Canon are all examples of successful new product development by project teams. Table 6.4 lists factors that our respondents reported were important to new product success.

First of all, the support of top management is needed to facilitate cooperation between the relevant departments. Without top management support the departments are inclined to go their separate ways, concentrating on their operational missions. Secondly, the teams' goals, responsibilities and schedules need to be clearly defined – clear goals are necessary to motivate team members. Third, it is important to have outstanding project leaders and high-quality team members with

Table 6.4   Project team NPD success factors

	Responses, %
1. Understanding and encouragement of top management	71.4
2. Clear goals, clear subjects, and clear responsibility	86.3
3. Operates like inside venture, delegation of authority to leader	24.8
4. Outstanding team leader (aggressive, confident, clear understanding of program, acquisition of resources)	62.7
5. Quality of team members	44.7
6. Team work of the members, with passion and tenacity	47.8
7. Full-time engagement	34.7
8. Capability and technological knowledge of members	30.4
9. Information collection on needs and competitors	48.4
10. Coordination and cooperation with related departments (particularly with production and marketing) (concurrent engineering)	49.0
11. Consensus within the company	36.8
12. Adequate investment of resources (sufficient budget)	34.1

Notes: 1. For details on sample, see Table 1.4.
   2. No significant differences between low and high performers, except for item #5.

complementary capabilities and knowledge. An example of this is provided by Sharp, which has launched many successful new products, including LCDs (liquid crystal displays), an 8mm video camera, and a portable electronic notebook. These products were all created by what Sharp calls "Kinpro," ("emergency project") teams over a period of 6 to 18 months. The teams were under the direct control of the company's president, and were composed of some of the firm's best people. Team members were entitled to wear golden badges, the same as those worn by company directors. Fourth, cooperation with related departments, such as production and marketing is essential. The project team can't do everything by itself. There may also be resistance to the new product by a department because the new product threatens to take sales or profits from existing products. Managers may be afraid that their own careers will suffer as older products become obsolete. To get the cooperation of related departments, the help of a product champion is needed. The product champion must be a high ranking person in the organization. It may be the CEO or senior executives in the development department. The product champion helps make sure the project has adequate resources, including personnel. He or she declares the importance of the project, helps facilitate communications between the departments, and resolves conflicts between the team and related departments.

Our survey indicates that the most important factors contributing to cooperation between the project team and related departments are: 1. A shared view of the goals and importance of the project; 2. Strong leadership by the project leader; and 3. Membership on the team of people from key related departments. In many instances, it is also important that researchers or other project team members be sent to the production and marketing department to help implement the project. The project champion plays a key role in creating these factors.

Incubation departments. At many companies "incubation departments" are responsible for taking the new product through its infancy stage. Canon's new business promotion department includes five centers that have helped support many new products during their early stages. Toray's new business development department fostered the early development of various medical products, penetration film (membrane), and contact lenses. An incubation department is useful because the priorities of the product divisions are to take care of current businesses as efficiently as possible, and to concentrate on short-term profits. Once a new product is profitable, it can be transferred to existing divisions.

It may even form the basis of a new independent division. Overhead expenses are not allocated to incubator departments. About 22% of the firms in our survey have incubator departments.

Internal venture system and spin offs. Some companies use internal venture systems. If a new product is successful, the division making it may be spun off to form another company. Take the case of Fujitsu, for example. Fujitsu is a company with sales of more than $4 billion, and a product line similar to IBM's. Decades ago Fujitsu itself was a spin off from Fuji Electric Company, a producer of electric motors. Some years ago Fujitsu spun off one of its divisions to form Fanuc, a leading producer of CNC (computer numerical controls) and industrial robots. In 1994 Fujitsu introduced a systematic new internal venture system. The company now has some 14 venture companies. These venture business are involved in a variety of different industries, including IC modules, network book sales, network tools, and software for mobile phones. Fujitsu's strategic planning department supports the internal ventures and serves as an incubation department for them. A staff member can write a proposal for the company to support a new venture. The proposal is given an initial review by a special committee and by Fujitsu's president. There are also interviews, which are even more important than the written application. If a proposal is approved by the president, the applicant's manager is informed, and the applicant can then apply directly to the committee. Approval of the applicant's department manager is not required.

Proposals are reviewed based on four criteria: Is the proposed product different from Fujitsu's current main products? Is the risk of failure large? Is the early-stage market for the product small? And: Is rapid development needed for the product to be successful? When the new business is established, the intrapraneur leaves Fujitsu, but if the new business fails, he or she can rejoin the company. Fujitsu gives technical support to the new venture through its planning department, provides up to 49% of its capital, lends it money without requiring security, allows it to use the Fujitsu name, and allows it to recruit staff from Fujitsu. Operations, however, are completely controlled by the intrapraneur, who also gets the profits from the new business. Fujitsu hopes this internal venture system will help the company discover new businesses, find new management styles, cultivate an innovative culture, and discover outstanding talent.[52]

An internal venture, like those at Fujitsu, is a kind of project team, but there are big differences. The internal venture is initiated by and organized by the person who proposes the idea, while a project team is organized by the company. Unlike the leader of a project team, the leader of the internal venture can receive profits as its owner. Unlike a project team, the internally generated venture can receive further support through an IPO (Initial Public Offering).

GE has established a set of guidelines to help it decide which businesses to spin off. A business is a good candidate for a spin off if it: (a) Is a niche product with a smaller market; (b) Has a person who is eager to run the new business; and (c) Is a "window product" for a new technology with uncertain future prospects. Also, if a product does not seem promising to senior management, the company will divest it. Fujitsu uses similar guidelines in deciding which businesses to divest.

NPD alliances

NPD alliances are increasingly important because the cost of development has exploded in many industries, and very rapid development has become a key success factor. There are several types of NPD alliances: (a) Groups of firms in the same or related industries that want to share the cost and risk of large, high-cost R&D projects; (b) Established firms undertaking highly uncertain and risky development projects with venture businesses; (c) Vertical alliances established to take advantage of the complementary skills and other assets of manufacturers and component suppliers (for example car assemblers and component suppliers); and (d) Alliances of firms in the same industry that construct dominant design or de facto standards for products.

An example of the first of these types of alliance is from the development of Toyota's hybrid car. Toyota worked with Matsushita Panasonic to develop the battery for the hybrid. Toyota shared this technology with its rival, Nissan, and both Toyota and Nissan are working together on a Japanese government sponsored project to further develop car batteries for hybrids. Later Toyota also licensed its hybrid technology to Ford. Takeda Pharmaceutical and Selera Genomics are jointly investing tens of millions of dollars analyzing DNA to discover the causes of (and some treatments for) various diseases. The cost and risk of undertaking this research would be too great for either of these companies to attempt independently.

Universities and venture capital firms often form alliances with each other, especially in the United States, but increasingly in other countries as well. Much of the U.S. biotechnology industry is based on firms that were started by university professors with financing from venture capitalists. Large numbers of U.S. and Japanese universities have established TLOs (technology licensing organizations) to increase the amount of technology transferred to the economy from universities, and to bring some of the economic rewards from these technologies back to the universities. Whereas in the U.S. this is often done via start up venture firms, in Japan many existing small and medium sized enterprises play this role. In the U.S., Japan and Europe, a number of universities and regions have established "incubators" to support new technology-based businesses. The incubators provide offices, IT equipment, laboratories, as well as general technical and business support for the infant firms.

A lot has been written about vertical cooperation in the automobile industry, but vertical alliances are also commonplace in the electronics industry. For example, in the case of personal computers the design may be done by the company that brands the PC, but manufacturing is usually outsourced to EMS (electronics manufacturing service) companies. This division of labor is especially common when a product's components are modular. With the recent dramatic improvements in communications capabilities and reductions in transportation cost, joint product development by firms working at sites distributed around the world has become increasingly common. Software and design charts can be produced in India and sent to a company in California. Apple developed the basic concept, major functions and design of the I-pod, but the MP-3 was developed by a venture company in California using Indian engineers, and is manufactured in China by a Taiwanese company.

The last type of NPD alliance develops de facto standards or industry designs. Philips, for example, developed the CD, but it cooperated with Sony to develop CD players, and then shared the technology with other companies. As a result Philips was able to establish the 3.5 inch CD as the worldwide standard. Whether to seek such alliances or not is a strategic decision. Sony chose not to use Nintendo's technology in developing the PlayStation. This would have given Nintendo control over the worldwide standard. Instead Sony used a different technology based on CDs rather than tapes. Sony then organized content providers for its PlayStation. Sony took the risk that it could independently develop the new technology, and also that it could entice content suppliers to provide a rich range of games for the PlayStation.

Some new products, like CD and DVD players, must be supported by software. Others, like cellular telephones, depend on network standards. In either case, the developer has to establish de facto standards for the product. A company might do this by simply giving the technology to rivals, or by licensing it to them on attractive terms. This will ensure the availability of the software, network access, and other complementary products or services needed to make the product successful. The strategic issue is whether or not the company has enough competitive strength by virtue of its technology or brand strength to keep enough of the market for its new product to recover the costs of development. The risk of sharing is that others will take away market share. There are also risks in going it alone.

Sony's Betamax initially dominated the market for video cassette players. Sony sought to maintain its dominance by restricting access to the Betamax technology. A Matsushita Panasonic plant producing large commercial video players was losing money, and was about to be closed. The plant manger proposed that the company develop a home video player so the plant could remain open. Given Sony's tight control over the technology, production of a Betamax was not a serious possibility. The plant manager initially had a difficult time getting support for his proposal. One problem was that the division making video players was losing money, and so could not support development. As a result, the proposal to develop a home video recorder started as an informal and confidential project. There were four project members. A senior manager from the finance department informally supported the project. One of the project members conducted a market survey. He found that consumers wanted a recorder with a recording time of two and half hours or more so they would not have to change cassettes in the middle of a movie or sporting event. The Betamax at that time offered a recording time of only one hour. This unsatisfied consumer need convinced management to proceed with the project. Matsushita Panasonic and Japan Victor (a Matsushita Panasonic affiliate) developed VHS with the longer recording time. Since producers of prerecorded videotape did not want to make tapes in two different formats, the challenge for Matsushita Panasonic was to make sure there were more VHS than Betamax machines. So, Matsushita Panasonic shared the VHS technology with other consumer electronics firms such as Sharp, Mitsubishi Electric and Hitachi. These firms not only helped make sure there would be more VHS than Betamax machines in homes, but also helped improve the VHS technology. In time far more programming was available in the VHS than the Betamax forms and Sony had to discontinue production of the Betamax.

Success factors in NPD alliances. Several factors have been found to affect the success of on-going NPD alliances.

First of all, it helps if the members of the alliance complement each others' strengths. A component supplier might design a transmission, for example, for a new car. The supplier sends the design through the extranet to the assembler. The assembler reviews the design and authorizes it. This "authorizing system" is different from past practices where the automobile assembler would develop its own design for components, and then send the design to suppliers. By giving some of the design work to suppliers, an automaker can often avoid unnecessary overhead and cut costs. Long-term alliances also allow concurrent engineering involving multiple firms, speeding up the development of a new car. Alliances of this sort are possible when firms have a long-term relationship. The firms feel they can trust each other with proprietary information. When an alliance partner does not have special capabilities to contribute to the relationship, however, the alliance will most likely fail. A few years ago the international pharmaceutical company Pfizer had an alliance with Japan's Taito sugar company. This alliance failed because Taito had little to offer beyond its distribution system. In time Pfizer no longer needed Taito's distribution system. Sometimes the partner with less to contribute will come under the control of the partner that has more to offer. Toyota and GM established NUMMI, a joint venture producing cars in California. Toyota offered its production system and personnel management system. GM contributed a plant that had been closed. Because of the disparity in contributions, Toyota tends to dominate the joint venture.

Secondly, there must be mutual trust. Trust means that one partner can predict the behavior of the other partner, and can expect cooperation even in vulnerable situations. There is a trust relationship between Ford and Mazda, for example, and between Philips and Sony. On the other hand, the trust relationship between Nintendo and its content suppliers seems to be weak because of the strong position Nintendo has. Nintendo can refuse to bear the risk of failure. As a consequence, many suppliers would rather supply content for the Sony PlayStation.

Third, it helps if the alliance members continuously learn from each other. In Japan the firms that supplied telephones and other equipment to NTT, when NTT was a government owned telephone monopoly in Japan, enjoyed a stable business that did not require them to learn. They neglected product development. Later, NTT was privatized and relied on the market to procure its equipment. Firms like Sony and Matsushita Panasonic became suppliers, and the original suppliers lost market share. On the other hand, Toshiba Silicon is a successful joint venture between GE and Toshiba. These companies frequently exchange engineers and learn from each other.[53]

Innovative organizations

Innovative organizations aggressively create new products, while conservative organizations do not. The innovative organization invests heavily in R&D and NPD. Innovative organizations not only aggressively develop new products, but they also invest multinationally. They take quick action against competitors' strategies, and they frequently make acquisitions and divestitures. A model of the innovative organization is shown in Table 6.5.[54] As the table shows, innovative organizations differ from conservative organizations in the structure of their top management team, in their approach to setting goals, in their product market strategy, in their organization, and in how they introduce new products.

Table 6.5 Features of innovative organizations

	Innovative organizations	Conservative organizations
Top management	Small (3–5 members) Members identify with company as a whole Meets frequently Supported by strong strategic departments Know who their rivals are, but don't blindly imitate Sense of crisis Welcome ideas for change	Large (>10 members) Members represent divisions
Goals		Sense of complacency Imitative
Product-market strategy	Selection and concentration	
Organization	Construct core competences Strong strategic planning departments	No new projects
Implementation	Many project teams Construct entry barriers	Delegate authority Ignore rivals

Small top management team. Innovative companies have relatively small top management teams under the board of directors. And, these teams meet frequently. This is the case at such innovative companies as Emerson Electric, where the five top executives meet regularly to make strategic decisions. When Sony and Honda were dazzling the world with their new product innovation, decision-making at these companies was made by the two top managers at each of these companies (Morita and Ibuka at Sony, and Honda and Fujisawa at Honda). These leaders constantly met to discuss company strategy. Innovative companies typically have top management teams with only three to five members, compared to ten or more at more conservative companies. At the more conservative companies members of the top management teams are typically division managers. It should not be surprising that these managers work hard to represent the interests of their divisions. In contrast, at innovative companies the small top management teams meet frequently and take the perspective of the company as a whole.

At Alcan, the executive committee is a little larger than is the case at most innovative companies, with seven or eight members, but the executive committee is not made up of the heads of Alcan's six products groups. Rather the committee members are managers in charge of general management or managers with functional responsibilities. They make decisions on the company's goals, product-market strategy, and resource allocation. They evaluate the performance of groups and units, and they recruit and develop talent.

The top management teams of innovative companies are supported by powerful planning staffs. They collect strategic information and propose new strategies. They explicitly do not represent the interests of product divisions. Canon and Sony in particular are noted for their strong strategic planning departments. The top management teams of less innovative companies represent the individual interests of their divisions. Members tend to adopt a "live and let live" attitude, seldom criticizing the plans of other divisions. These teams emphasize consensus, so they rarely discuss divesting or closing unnecessary plants.

Know their goals and know their rivals. Innovative companies know who their rivals are, and work hard to surpass them. Komatsu drove itself to surpass Caterpillar, doing whatever it could to improve the quality of its earth moving equipment. When Toyota was developing as a major automaker it saw Nissan as its main rival. Whenever Nissan launched a new car, Toyota immediately developed a competing car. Recently Seiko Epson has recognized Canon as its key rival, Asahi Brewery looks at Kirin Brewery, Pepsi sees Coca Cola, and Miller looks at Bush.

One reason it is healthy to constantly monitor what rivals are doing is that this can create an on-going sense of crisis – an insecurity that competitors are about to come up with a break though new product. A sense of crisis combined with clear goals breeds an innovative corporate culture. Less innovative organization do not have a sense of crisis. They do not recognize the power of competitors, and are satisfied with the present situation. They allow product divisions to work for their self interest, rather than the overall good of the firm. Major companies that have fallen into this situation at one time or another include Asahi Beer (which in the years before it introduced Super Dry beer had let its share of the Japanese market slowly drop to the point that the future of the company was threatened) and Nissan Motors (which once produced about as many cars each year at Toyota). Both Asahi Beer and Nissan lacked a healthy sense of crisis, and as a result lost market share and profitability. The problem of complacency in the face of strong competition can happen at the division level as well as the company level. Matsushita Panasonic, for example, had product divisions that were too independent, and that lacked any sense of urgency. These complacent companies and divisions managed to recover when their top managements took on more authority and instilled a sense of crisis.[55]

While it is important for firms to pay attention to what the competition is doing, this is not enough. In the 1980s managers from around the world flocked to Japan to learn about "lean manufacturing."[56] Japanese firms seemed unbeatable. A decade later many Japanese firms no longer seemed so formidable. A reason is that many Japanese firms tended to be "me-too followers." For example, all the Japanese integrated steelmakers decided to produce steel in the U.S. at about the same time, and following the same approach. Nippon Steel collaborated with Inland Steel, NKK with National Steel, Kawasaki with Armco, Sumitomo Metals with LTV, Kobe Steel with US Steel. They all constructed new steel plants or invested heavily in the modernization of old plants. But, because they were all following the same strategy, the result was a huge excess in production capacity. Eventually most of these projects to produce steel in the U.S. failed. The costs were extremely high for the Japanese firms. Rather than simply do what respected competitors were doing, the Japanese steelmakers should have independently developed their own strategies. It's one thing to pay attention to what the competition is doing, and quite another to blindly imitate them.

Product-market strategy. Successful innovative companies concentrate on products where the company has strengths, where the products reinforce each other, and where the products are based on core competencies. These companies try to have products which have either the largest or second largest share of each market. Canon has concentrated on office equipment, where it has high share of the markets for copiers and printers. As we have seen, it dropped out of the markets for semi-conductors, personal computers and word processors. There seemed little prospect that it could become strong in the markets for these products. Since 1990, many US companies have divested product lines. Kodak got out of the business of making drugs and home appliances in the mid-1990s, decreasing its sales from $20 billion to $12 billion. Sears divested its insurance, security and real estate businesses. The radical (and highly successful) restructuring of ICI's product mix was described in Chapter 2.

It is not easy to carry out a solid product market strategy. A company may have to invest in R&D for a new product, even though its current products are still profitable. There may be no obvious need to take immediate action. On-going success makes many companies lazy. Innovative companies like Canon and Emerson maintain a sense of crisis, even when things seem to be going well. They have strong planning departments and long-range strategies. The company often has to close plants when products are not successful. Labor unions and employees, naturally, will resist this, but it may be necessary for the survival of the company as a whole – and the protection of even more jobs than those that would be lost due to a plant closing. The division that does not fit the company strategy might be sold. GE has frequently done this – often with the result that employees found themselves more valued by their new company than they had been at GE.

Organizational structure. Innovative companies have strong head offices, and frequently use project teams or cross functional teams to create and implement innovative strategies. Nissan has recently used many cross functional teams to strengthen the company. Less innovative companies have decentralized organizational structures, and put the emphasis on daily operations, not on strategic change.

Implementation. An innovative organization is quick to move. After launching a new product, it moves quickly to increase the barriers to entry for competitors. It may do this by making product improvements, as Sony did with the Walkman, providing differential product services, reinforcing sales channels, or using competitive pricing policies. As we saw in Chapter 2, EMI developed CT scanners, but did not improve the technology quickly enough. The result was that GE, Siemens and Philips took this market away from EMI.

7
Creativity in Research Organizations

In this chapter we explore creativity in research organizations. A major problem facing managers is how to structure organizations to conduct research that is effective for the company. Machine-like organizations with their rigid hierarchical structures, tightly specified roles, elaborate decision-making rules and standard operating procedures (SOPS) are highly efficient at performing standard tasks. But they do not do well when it comes to tasks like research, where inputs cannot be standardized, where processes require frequent adaptation, and where outputs must be dynamically tailored for acceptance in fast changing environments. Many researchers on organizations and the psychology of creativity conclude that the best organizational form to carry out non-routine objectives is one that allows maximum flexibility and gives almost unlimited discretion to organization members. Some scholars call this an "organic" form of organization and contrast it with the "mechanical" form associated with traditional bureaucracies.[57] In this chapter we draw on some of our own research to suggest that while the mechanical organizational form is not suited to research, the pure organic form also has its problems. We propose a third model.

Problems with "organic" structures for R&D

While the organic structure would intuitively seem highly conducive to creativity, many business firms have encountered serious problem trying to use organic organizational forms for R&D. As was mentioned above, a well-known example is that of PARC, the Palo Alto Research Center of Xerox. This organization was unstructured, emphasizing the encouragement and support of individual initiative by researchers. One of PARC's major technological successes was a new computer operating system. The technological success, however, did not help Xerox, which was unable to exploit it as part of its corporate strategy. Later this operating system was used by Apple in Mackintosh computers. Now research at PARC is more tightly constrained to follow corporate strategy.[58] In the 1990s Eizai, a major Japanese pharmaceutical company, established a research facility in London. In an effort to maximize creativity Eizai hired top researchers from the U.S., UK and other countries. As at PARC, the researchers were encouraged to pursue their own research interests with little regard for corporate strategy. Nothing useful to Eizai came out of this organization, and it was dissolved.

The challenge of finding ways to harness the creativity of research organizations is widespread. Each year the Industrial Research Institute in the U.S. sends out a survey asking company representatives about problems facing technology leaders. For several years running the "biggest" problem has been "Managing R&D for business growth."[59] Competitive success today requires a focus on generating technologies in the lab that can rapidly be commercialized.[60]

Based on our surveys of R&D managers, as well as numerous company visits and published case studies of technological development, we believe that successful organizations are moving to a new model of organization for R&D, a model that is very different from the mechanical form, yet also differs in significant ways from the organic organization.

A survey of R&D managers

In 2004 we sent a survey to senior R&D managers at 461 Japanese companies in a wide range of industries.[61] To identify the factors important to success, we compared the responses of R&D managers from highly successful with those from less successful companies. Our measure of success included both financial and new product development indicators. Table 7.1 reports our findings on the characteristics of high-performing companies. Table 7.2 gives information about our sample.

Five points stood out. We found that in the more successful companies:

1. Top management exercises strong control over research. It sets clear long-term strategies and strives to encourage researchers.
2. Researchers are encouraged to communicate freely with academic researchers and to attend academic conferences.
3. There is a freer atmosphere for researchers.

Table 7.1   Characteristics of R&D organization at high-performing companies

	High performance companies (n = 39)	Low performance companies (n = 62)
(% of managers mentioning)		
Long-term strategy and vision	82*	68
Researchers participate in deciding research subjects	36	31
Free to do research within specified research subjects	28	31
Understanding/encouragement of top management	56*	45
Understanding/encouragement of immediate superiors	28	29
Free communications among researchers	26	
Communications with academics	64**	58
Successful researcher exemplars	3	13
Successful research exemplars	10	35
Atmosphere respecting free imagination	51*	43
Cooperation within team and good interface among research, production and marketing	59	60
Evaluations based on contributions to academic field and originality, as well as contributions to company	5	11
Evaluations based on performance, not seniority	67*	52
Evaluations based on outside reputation	3	10
Respect motivation from the job itself	26	29
Evaluate not only results, but also process	41*	27
Separate urgent projects from long-term projects	41*	32
Allow sufficient time	8	8

*P < 0.05 **P < 0.25

Notes: 1. Performance = ROS × 10 + equity ratio + new products ÷ sales (2000–2003).
2. Average performance for the sample was 113.1. In the table high performance companies are those with values above 113.1, while low performance companies are those below 113.1.
3. ROS is median value for return on sales during the years 2000–2003.
4. Equity ratio is for the year 2003.
5. New product percentage is for 1999–2004.
6. For details on sample, see Table 7.2.

Table 7.2 R&D survey sample

Industry	Number of companies
Construction	9
Food	8
Textiles	4
Pulp & paper	2
Chemical and drugs	25
Petroleum, rubber	1
Glass and stone	4
Iron, steel & nonferrous metals	1
Machinery	8
Electrical appliances	13
Precision instruments	3
Transportation equipment & machinery	10
Other manufacturing	4
Transportation & communications	3
Electicity & gas service	8
Services	1
Total	104

Notes:
1. Questionnaires were sent to 461 research laboratories in 2004. One hundred and four responses were received for a response rate of 22.6%.
2. A questionnaire was sent to one laboratory at each company.

4. Researchers are evaluated based on performance, rather than length of service. Different systems of project time goals are used depending on the type of project.
5. There is a clear distinction made between long-term projects and those that need to be addressed more immediately. A good example of this is provided below in our discussion of Nitto Denko.

One standard definition of "creativity" is "the ability to produce work that is both novel (i.e. original, unexpected) and appropriate (i.e. useful, adaptive concerning task constraints)."[62] Several models of the creative process have been developed (One can think in terms of the "components" of creativity, or the stages by which the creative process unfolds.[63] In our analysis we use both approaches.

Teresa Amabile, a leading scholar on team creativity and innovation in organizations, sees creativity as consisting of three major components: domain relevant skills, creativity-related skills and task motivation. Domain-relevant skills comprise the set of response possibilities from which the new response is to be synthesized and the knowledge by which the new response is to be evaluated. Creative individuals (and organizations) have what has been described as "T-shaped knowledge," broad general knowledge combined with very deep knowledge in some area. Creativity skills include the ability to understand complexity, but also to break out of perceptual and cognitive sets that might limit the generation of possibilities. In a classic work Alex Osborn, who is sometimes identified as having invented "brain storming," defines seven stages of the creative process: orientation (identifying the problem); preparation (gathering pertinent data); analysis (breaking down relevant material); ideation (finding alternatives); incubation (inviting illumination); synthesis (putting the pieces together); evaluation (judging the resulting ideas).[64] Although others use different terms, most offer conceptually similar models of the creative process.

In our survey, respondents were asked to identify characteristics of creative organizations. The responses were broadly grouped under the components and stages of the creative process as defined in the literature. As Table 7.3 shows, among the most often mentioned characteristics were having clear goals and policies (73%), encouraging communications with academics and researchers researchers (60%) and rewarding performance more than seniority (58%). These points will be discussed further below.

We also used factor analysis to identify the key elements of creative organizations. Table 7.4 shows our results. The factors identified were:

1. Intrinsic motivation. Researchers are motivated by the job itself, independently of other rewards. Their schedules are reasonably flexible. Although the speed and timing of research are important, they separate urgent projects from long-term research so that an appropriate amount of time is allowed to carry out the research.
2. Encouragement by top management.
3. Participation and communications. Participation of the researchers in deciding the subject and goals of research is important. This does not mean, however, that researchers freely select research topics. Research topics are selected based on corporate strategy, but the researchers participate in the selection process. There is also free communications among researchers. This enriches the knowledge of researchers and inspires new ideas.
4. Long-term vision. The firm has a long-term strategy and vision. This, of course, links to encouragement by top management.
5. Exemplars. Exemplars of past success can orient the approach of the researchers and encourage them to overcome difficulties. Thus, at

Table 7.3 Characteristics of creative organizations

Creative process/ component	Creative organizations provide	% mentioning
Identifying problems/ opportunities	Unity between corporate goals and researcher interests	
	*Clear goals and policies	73
	*Researchers participate in deciding research subjects	33
	*Understanding/encouragement of top management	48
Domain relevant knowledge and heuristic skills	Rich information resources	(self-evident)
	*Outstanding facilities and abundant funds....	
	*Many competent researchers with wide knowledge	
Idea generation Looking at things from new angles Trying many combinations	Contact with multiple sources of ideas	
	*Free communications among researchers	33
	*Communications with academics, universities and foreign researchers	60
	*Freedom of research within specified research subjects	30
Development Avoid premature judgment	Free atmosphere for researchers	
Do not follow others' opinions, be independent	*Respect free imagination	46
Experiment and consolidate	Long-term horizon where appropriate	
	*Separate long-term projects from urgent projects	35
Intrinsic motivation	Motivated by the job	
	*Respect intrinsic motivations	27
	*Evaluate process as well as outcomes	33
	*Evaluate based on performance, not seniority	58

Note: This table is based on the same data as that reported in Table 7.1. The values are the averages for all responses.

Table 7.4 Factor analysis, creative organizational settings

Questions	Intrinsic motivation	Top management encourage	Participation/ Communications	Long-term vision	Exemplars
	Factor 1	Factor 2	Factor 3	Factor 4	Factor 5
Long-term strategy and vision	0.02	−0.12	−0.51	0.15	−0.49
Researchers participate in selection of research subjects	0.09	0.02	0.68	0.00	0.05
Freedom of research within specified research subject	0.22	0.30	−0.51	−0.17	0.13
Encouragement by top management	−0.03	0.54	0.09	0.28	−0.37
Encouragement by superiors	−0.06	−0.53	−0.07	0.16	0.04
Free communications among researchers	−0.54	0.12	0.38	−0.08	0.05
Communication with academics	−0.08	−0.48	−0.11	0.08	−0.03
Successful researcher exemplars	0.20	0.02	0.09	−0.65	−0.10
Successful research exemplars	−0.04	0.07	0.07	0.09	0.70
Atmosphere respecting free imagination	0.28	0.27	0.28	0.14	−0.42
Cooperation within the team good interface amongst research, production and marketing	−0.73	0.04	−0.15	0.07	0.16
Assess researchers not only by contributions to the company, but to field and by originality	−0.18	0.01	−0.41	−0.67	0.02
Evaluate by performance, not seniority	0.18	−0.69	0.10	0.03	−0.15
Evaluate outside reputation	0.10	−0.04	0.20	−0.62	0.12
Respect intrinsic motivation	0.66	−0.05	−0.02	−0.06	0.24
Evaluate process as well as results	−0.12	0.04	0.00	−0.01	−0.60
Separate urgent projects from long-term projects	−0.02	−0.19	−0.27	0.40	0.23
Allow enough time	0.41	0.31	−0.12	0.08	0.04
% of variance explained	0.09	0.09	0.09	0.09	0.09

Note: The data reported in this data are the same as those reported in Tables 7.1 and 7.3.

the Dupont research center in Wilmington, Delaware there is a monument to W.H. Carothers, who discovered nylon, and at the Battelle Research Center in Columbus, Ohio, there is a monument commemorating the development of the copying machine. As we have seen, at Canon the development of the highly successful AE-1 single lens reflex camera was used as an exemplar for those developing the best-selling "PC10" and "PC20" small copiers.

The creative organization makes good use of intrinsic motivation, but is strongly guided by corporate strategy.

Sources of information – formal and informal

A variety of formal and informal sources of information are used to develop ideas for research topics. Formal sources include patents, scientific journals and books. Often access to these is provided through corporate research libraries or the internet. Informal sources include friends of researchers, attendance at academic meetings, etc. We asked our survey respondents which sources they used. Table 7.5 reports their responses about the use of formal sources.

The table shows that 80% of our respondents get ideas from customers and marketing departments. 69% get ideas from competitors. More than half get ideas from company researchers. Interestingly,

Table 7.5 Formal sources of research topic ideas

Source	Responses (%)
1. Needs from customers/marketing	80
2. Trends in other companies' new products and R&D	69
3. Presentations at academic conferences	25
4. Academic journals	26
5. Publication on patents	17
6. On line information	14
7. Ideas from company researchers	64
8. Company suggestion system	9
9. Corporate long-term strategy and vision	54
10. Conference on corporate research strategy	27
11. Matrix of corporate core technology and long-term market needs	62
12. Classification of technology	2
13. Other	3

62% get ideas from an analysis of the intersection between corporate technology capabilities and market needs, and 54% get ideas from the long-term strategy of the firm.

To stimulate thinking and improve communications many laboratories have meeting rooms. Some of these are even stocked with beer. In one company we visited, the meeting rooms had white board on three walls, so that members could write down their ideas or produce diagrams for all to see. At Canon's research center, the researchers work in a large room, but there are also many small rooms where a researcher can go to think without being disturbed. There are also rooms for small group discussions. At Honda, there are "idea rooms" where members can perform experiments. Honda has an "idea contest" where employees present unusual product ideas. New Honda employees are asked to keep diaries with ideas for improving operations.

Our respondents also use many informal sources of information. Table 7.6 shows the results concerning informal sources. Some companies have developed other ways to get ideas. At a laboratory to develop home electrical appliances, the director encourages researchers to take a commuter train to work instead of driving, so as to increase their opportunities to see new things. This director also sometimes asks researchers to go outside for a day to make observations on some specified subject. Once, for example, he asked them to observe as many kinds of buildings as possible, and to write a report on any ideas they got from their observations.

As the table shows, the most widely used informal source of information is university researchers (55%). Academic meetings, in particular, are a common source of information (46%). Friends of the researchers,

Table 7.6 Informal sources of research topic ideas

Source	Responses (%)
Friends of researcher	35
Attending academic meeting	46
University researchers	55
Communication with public research laboratory	29
Research at other home country companies	42
Research at foreign companies	20
Suppliers of parts and materials	19
Customers	30
Other	1

suppliers, public laboratories and other sources are also widely used. Consistent with the findings of Allen (1977), some 68% of our respondents report that there are "gatekeepers" in their R&D organizations – people who monitor the technological environment on behalf of the organization, and bring relevant information to the appropriate internal people. Sixteen per cent of our respondents reported that their organization has many "gatekeepers."

Given that so much important information comes directly or indirectly from customers, it is crucial that the interface between marketing and research be effective. Some researchers say that all too often there is a "Death Valley" between the research department and the market. In this Death Valley, research coming out of the R&D department dies before it reaches the market. To deal with this problem NTT created a post called "chief producer." The chief producer is expected to turn research generated technological "seeds" into profitable products for the company. NTT's small memory card with one giga bit of memory was developed by this method. On the other hand, ideas for research must be oriented to the market. At Hitachi, the researchers at the central research unit are expected to visit customers to learn about their needs. At Fujitsu researchers interact with customers as they develop information systems. Table 7.7 shows the mechanisms commonly used by our respondents' firms to facilitate the interface amongst R&D, marketing and production.

Information collection for R&D should not be a one shot process. There needs to be a constant feedback of information in what might be described as a spiral process.[65] We saw an example of this in the World case in Chapter 3. In the spiral process, new information is collected from internal experiments, from the market and from academics. Some 72% of our respondents emphasized the importance of frequent

Table 7.7   Methods used to improve the R&D, production and marketing interface

Method	% Using
Researcher moves to plant after development	26
Project leader is responsible for all processes from research to promotion and marketing	25
Project team includes members from all three departments	31
Frequent mutual communication. Development not linear, but follows U or spiral process	72

mutual communications. Thirty-one per cent mentioned the use of cross-functional teams and 26% said their company used transfers of personnel.

Selection and evaluation of projects

Successful firms were more likely to emphasize long-term strategy and vision as guiding ideas for research than less successful firms (61.5% vs 47.6%). Many put R&D directly under the control of the head office and many used committees of specialists to evaluate research plans and to control the progress of projects. It is not enough to rely on the ordinary organizational hierarchy.

But while it is necessary to ensure that R&D resources fully support corporate strategies, it is also necessary to allow researchers freedom in pursuing the authorized research subjects. Successful firms use various techniques to achieve this. At Honda, the development of a new compact car was delegated to young team members. The young team members came up with a boxy styled car that senior managers did not like, the Honda Fit. The senior managers reluctantly allowed the car to be launched because they wanted to motivate the young researchers. To their surprise, the Fit turned out to be a big hit with young people. Here, considerable freedom in the approach by the team was allowed, but the subject of development was decided by the corporate strategy.

Many R&D laboratories allow researchers to spend up to 15% of their time on projects of their own choice. It is expected that the gains from motivating the researchers will exceed the cost involved, but sometimes these bootleg projects result in very successful products. One example in Japan is Asahi Beer's "Honnama." This is a type of beer that uses two thirds less malt than other beers (it is cheaper than other beers, because it is subject to a much lower tax rate). Asahi's top management doubted that low malt beer could taste good. The researchers, however, used their "bootleg" time to develop a good-tasting low-malt beer that became a bestseller. Earlier, we gave the example of the Nissan Z as another successful bootleg project.

Research projects are typically evaluated at four points: when the project is being selected, midstream, when capital investment decisions are being made, and upon completion of the research. Early in the research process four criteria are commonly used in evaluating a project: external consistency (How large is the market? How new is the product? How differentiated is it from other products?), feasibility (Can the company develop and successfully launch it?), internal consistency

Figure 7.1   Selection of research themes

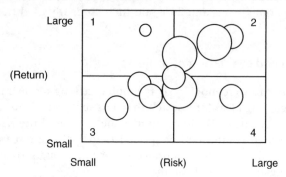

Notes:
(1) Quadrants
    1. Safe and profitable
    2. Invest for future technological competence
    3. Steady business
    4. Reconsider investment
(2) Size of circle indicates size of investment needed
Source: Information supplied by company to Kono.

Table 7.8   Criteria used in assessing research subjects

	% of Respondents Using		
	Basic research	Common basic technology	Product development and production technology
1. Fit with corporate strategy	65	65	75
2. Growth potential and market size	50	49	63
3. Reinforcement of core technology	68	80	15
4. Newness and creativity	85	58	31
5. Spreading effect	50	66	25
6. Feasibility	41	54	60
7. Overlap with other company R&D	18	29	59
8. Contribute product differentiation	54	61	54
9. Fit present production system	2	15	31
10. Fit present marketing system	1	4	27
11. Timing	23	25	36
12. Increase in sales	4	17	53
13. Increase in profit	9	15	56
14. Increase in profit divided by R&D expenditure	23	35	33
15. Limiting factors (other company's patents, etc.)	19	14	13

(How well does the product fit with corporate strategies and how compatible is it with the firm's core technologies? What are the potential spillover benefits?) and potential contribution to the goals of the organization (What are the potential increases in sales and profits?).

Some companies use a simple chart to evaluate research, particularly at the early stages of research. Figure 7.1 shows a chart used at one company to evaluate possible research themes.

The size of the circles represents the relative size of the investment required for the project. The four quadrants indicate the levels of anticipated risk and return. The small circle in quadrant 1, for example, represents a project requiring a relatively small investment, but that offers large potential returns with a fairly small risk.

Table 7.8, shows responses to our survey questions on the criteria used to assess research subjects.

In evaluating and selecting proposed research projects, our respondents emphasize corporate strategy, contribution to profit and spillover effects. They evaluate not just project success, but also researchers and research organizations. These computations are used in deciding the allocation of funds to the R&D organization.

Factors Affecting Speed of development. High technology R&D tends to require long lead times, yet rapid completion of a project is often a major aspect of success. Speed may be needed to establish patent rights, academic priority or other first mover advantages. We asked R&D managers what factors played important roles in the speed of development (See Table 7.9).

Table 7.9 Factors affecting the speed of development

Factor	Responses, %
Enthusiasm	69
Support by top management	34
Enthusiasm and leadership style of team leader	72
Control of schedule	60
Adequate funds and facilities	27
Use of computer	8
Parallel development	24
Alliances with other firms	47
Alliances with universities and research organizations	45
Cooperation between related departments	64

The most important factors were the enthusiasm and leadership style of the project leader (72%) and the enthusiasm of the researchers (69%). Also important was giving researchers some control over scheduling (60%). Interestingly, effective alliances with other companies, universities and research organizations were also important (47% for other organizations, 45% for universities and research organizations). Some 64% of our respondents mentioned the importance of effective cooperation between the research unit and other departments of the company in shortening the time interval between research and the launch of new products (as well, as in otherwise increasing effectiveness).

There was not much difference between successful and less successful companies in these areas. It may be that even the less successful companies in our sample are trying to apply best practices – all of these companies are relatively technology intensive.

Two successful R&D organizations

Nitto Denko Co. is a medium-sized Japanese manufacturer of high technology adhesive tapes. Its sales in 2003 were 452 billion yen (approximately 4.25 billion USD), with profits of 55.9 billion yen. In some respects the company is like a much smaller 3M. Nitto began by making relatively low technology adhesives, and moved into the production of high technology adhesive tapes used in medical applications, drug delivery systems and electronic components. The company spends about 3.5% of its sales on R&D, and has 500 research personnel.

Nitto's organizational structure for R&D is shown in Figure 7.2. This structure allows Nitto to maintain strong centralized control, yet allows considerable flexibility for R&D in its divisions. The Chief Technology Officer, who is also the company's CEO, maintains overall control of the research activities of the company. The company centralizes all research on technologies that are widely used across its product lines, while conducting research on current and related new products at the group or division level. There is a corporate technology strategy committee that includes the heads of all the R&D departments. This committee meets once a month. Recommended research themes are sent to the management committee for a final decision. An RD&E (research, development and engineering) conference meets monthly to select research subjects, and to follow up on research projects.[66]

Projects requiring the contributions of various laboratories are organized as "headquarters projects." These projects are selected by a survey team after extensive study. More than 10–15% of Nitto's researchers

Figure 7.2 Nitto Denko R&D organization

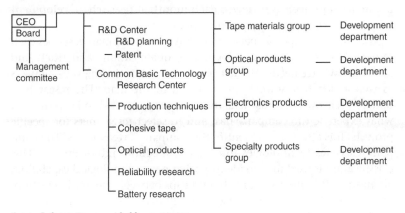

Source: Information provided by company.

are organized into headquarters project teams. There are three kinds of teams: S(strategic) teams, U(urgent) teams and Support teams. S teams do research in areas of strategic importance to the company. An example would be adhesiveness, a technology which is applicable to most of the company's products. These projects are given a time horizon of about 2 years. U teams work on "urgent projects." These are projects needed to deal with immediate competitive threats. Typically they must be completed within a year. Support teams carry out projects that have been tentatively suspended by other research teams. S projects are proposed by the headquarters research organizations, and U projects and support projects are proposed by the product groups. Most team members work full time on their project. They are separated from the departments that dispatch them. There are team leaders, team members and advisors. The leaders communicate with customers. The advisors are not team member, but have specialized knowledge and give advice.

Most of the research topics for the product group laboratories come from customers. The criteria by which topics are selected include marketability, profitability, ease of development, and limiting factors such as access to patents and market entry timing. Corporate research sector research subjects are generally chosen based on corporate strategy and the suggestions of researchers. Possible research topics for the corporate research sectors are assessed based on Nitto Denko's comparative strength in the research area, originality and marketability. The product groups review progress on new product development and product improvements each month at their strategy meetings. Progress on corporate level projects is reviewed each month at research, development and engineering technology conferences.

Nitto has developed a "personnel skills map." The map describes each researcher's career, technical expertise, qualifications and titles, and future knowledge needs. About 1,000 personnel, including key engineers as well as R&D personnel, are included in the map. The researchers update their own records. This inventory map is used to keep track of what expertise the company has, and to select researchers for specific projects. It is also used to identify the company's weaknesses. The company classifies technologies into major, medium, minor groups. This classification is used to help identify what new technological capabilities are needed. It is also used to help find gaps between the needed technological capabilities and the personnel skill inventory. This information can be used in deciding what training to give researchers. Nitto provides three career ladders for its researchers: a management ladder, a specialist ladder (with ranks going up to membership on the board of directors), and a status ladder (with five levels such as "chief researcher").

Sanyo Electric Company, a major Japanese manufacturer of electric products, has also been very successful at introducing new products.[67] Sanyo had sales of 2,699 billion yen in 2003 (about $25 billion) with profits of 96 billion yen (about $900 million). The company spent 125.2 billion yen on R&D (about $1.1 billion). It had 6,000 R&D personnel, including 800 at the corporate level. Sanyo's financial performance has been much better than that of such rivals as Hitachi, Toshiba, NEC and Fujitsu. The organizational structure for R&D management at Sanyo is shown in Figure 7.3. The top management committee makes strategic decisions. This committee has only four members, the chairman of the board, the chief executive officer, the chief financial officer and the chief operating officer. The small size of the committee is one reason Sanyo is able to make very quick decisions.

Sanyo's research activities, like Nitto's, are centralized. The corporate research center (with about 800 researchers) includes many laboratories which carry out "foundational research." There are two types of foundational research: (a) the development of technologies that are widely used in the company, such as new materials or mechatronics, and (b) the development of new businesses. The corporate research center also coordinates the research activities of the product divisions. It spends about 20% of the company's research funds. The corporate research center receives some 60% of its funding from the product

Figure 7.3 Sanyo Electric R&D organization

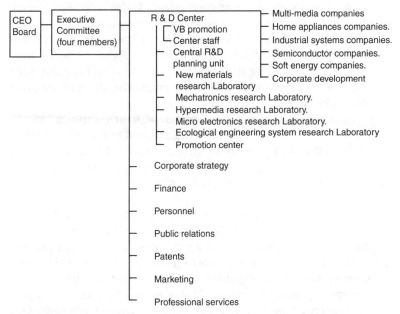

Source: Information provided by company.

divisions to perform research the divisions have commissioned. This concentration of research activities enables the company to carry out research activities that closely fit the corporate strategy. It also allows the company to change research directions as the strategy changes. Two organizations in the head office plan technology strategy for the company. One is the planning department, which has about 30 staff members. The planning department plans future corporate strategy including new product development and the future product mix. Plans for future strategy are the basis for research on common elementary technology. There is also a "central planning R&D unit" within the R&D center at the head office (the R&D center also has two staff departments and six other units). The central R&D planning unit has about 25 members and is responsible for using technological forecasting to plan technology strategies that fit the overall corporate strategy. The technology strategies the unit comes up with are reviewed and approved by the top management technology committee.

Sanyo has several meetings to select and evaluate research subjects. The meetings also encourage communications amongst the company's various R&D organizations. The most important meeting is that of the "corporate technology planning committee." At this meeting the heads of all the laboratories discuss the planning of research subjects. This committee also coordinates the activities of the company's various research organizations. Final plans are decided at the "corporate R&D meeting." At this meeting the corporate research center integrates the activities of the laboratories under the center with those at the other company laboratories.

The corporate R&D center does research on basic technology for the company, improves its core competencies related to present and future products, and creates new products. The research laboratories of the product companies (staffed by a total of more than 5,000 people) carry out research to improve current products and to develop new products. There are three kinds of projects. M projects are the most important. These include the development of digital cameras and related components, LSI, LSD (liquid crystal display) and batteries. The time horizon for these projects is from 1 to 3 years. S projects are strategic projects generally carried out by the corporate R&D center. One of these projects, for example, is the development of a fuel battery. The time horizon for these projects is typically 2 to 4 years. U projects are urgent projects to create new products or improve current products. One example is a project to develop a new type of washing machine that does not use soap. The time horizon for these projects is generally within 6 months.

The most important source of ideas for research topics is the company's long-range strategy as developed by the corporate strategic planning department. About 70% of the research subjects are determined by this "top down" approach. The subjects are linked to the corporate creed: "We preserve the earth and serve its people." Based on this creed, Sanyo invests heavily in research on solar cell reactors and new kinds of batteries. As in other companies, technological "seeds" are collected through academic publications and conferences. Customer needs are collected through the marketing department. There is an internal venture system. When a proposed idea is approved by top management, the researcher can work on the research subject for 2 years. A dilemma is that good researchers are already engaged in important projects, and have little time to try out their unique ideas. In order to collect new ideas from them, and to stimulate their creativity, "dream meetings" are held. At these meetings young researchers meet with the head of the corporate research unit to discuss their dreams and their present research subjects. Often new ideas come out of these meetings.

Other measures are also used to stimulate researchers. Researchers can directly request that the personnel department transfer them to other parts of the company through Sanyo's "free agent" system. As at many other companies that are strong in technology, Sanyo encourages researchers to get academic degrees, to attend academic conferences, and to study abroad. Research ideas are assessed during the idea stage, midway through the research project, and after the research is completed. The company uses both direct and indirect measures to assess the performance of research units. The direct measurements used are contribution to profit, the volume and quality of technology transferred to other departments, and the number and quality of patent applications. Two indirect measures are also used: presentations of papers at academic conferences, and technical exhibitions.

"Contribution to profits" is the contribution to sales multiplied by one-half the return on sales. One half of the return on sales is the assumed contribution ratio, which varies, depending on the project. The sales contribution value is decreased by 10% every year.

These assessments of the research units are expected to stimulate their creativity and productivity. The speedy completion of R&D projects is emphasized. The progress of projects is controlled through the intranet and through conferences. Alliances are frequently used to reduce development time.

Other companies are also moving to more centralized control of their R&D. In 2002, for example, Hitachi established an R&D strategy department reporting directly to the CEO. This department tries to find future product mixes which will connect Hitachi's strengths to the needs of the market. Hitachi's product divisions had previously been independent, and they tended to continue to emphasize improvement of old products rather than the development of new products.

Many companies still use a coordinating style of top management. The president tries to arrive at a consensus with the top management committee based on group discussions. This does not produce an aggressive strategy. When the top management committee is composed of directors of the product groups, aggressive decisions to change the product mix are difficult. Companies that have been strong at making dramatic and successful strategic changes in technological direction have tended to have strong top managements. Some are firms controlled by entrepreneur founders: Matsushita Panasonic, Sony and Honda in their earlier years, and Microsoft today. Other firms, such as GE, IBM, and Intel, have also been able to make dramatic shifts in their technology strategies. Dramatic changes could not have taken place if these companies had allowed their R&D units too much independence.

The incubation model of research organization

At the beginning of this chapter we discussed the common classification of organizational structures handling R&D into "mechanical" and "organic" organizations. Nitto Denko and Sanyo are clearly not mechanical organizations, but neither are they organic organizations. We believe that while the organic model may be suitable for some creative organizations, it does not provide adequate control for the organization of most corporate R&D. To be sure, strong bureaucratic top down controls can kill creativity. So the mechanical model does not provide a good alternative. We argue that the companies that are most successful at R&D use a third organizational model, "the incubation model" (for the incubation of new ideas). As will be seen, this model is closer to the organic model than it is to the mechanical model, but it also includes some features of the mechanical model. See Table 7.10 for a comparison of the incubation with the organic and mechanical models.

Selection of projects. R&D projects in the incubation model are more centrally controlled then in the organic model, though not as rigidly as in the mechanical model. The object of the control is not to enforce conformity with long-standing bureaucratic policies, but rather to ensure that the projects will contribute to corporate strategy. Researchers are given considerable input into the selection of projects, but they do not independently select the projects as they would under the organic model. Rather, their freedom is disciplined by corporate strategy.

Collection of information and ideas. In mechanical organizations the collection of information to get ideas for new products tends to be rule bound. Information from outside normal channels is not welcomed, and the organization has difficulty processing it. While incremental progress may be made in product refinement, there is little chance that new and original products will be developed. In organic organizations there is an extreme atmosphere of openness. Researchers are encouraged to seek stimulation from their fields. The environment inspires considerable creativity, but the creativity may be of little benefit to the company. With the incubation model information is systematically collected and new ideas are welcome from any source – but screens are

Table 7.10 Three organizational models

	Incubation	Organic	Mechanistic
Goal/Problem finding	Centrally controlled Fits corporate strategy Researchers help select Resource flexibility	Decentralized Fits researchers' interests Researchers select Resource flexibility	Centrally controlled Fits corporate tradition Hierarchy selects Tight cost controls
Information collection	Systematic on market needs and technology seeds Communications with outside sources Communication among Researchers	Informal domain relevant knowledge Coworkers skill diversity	Rules are sources of information Internal communication and cooperation constrained by bureaucracy
Idea generation	Welcome new ideas based on corporate strategy Strict evaluation and selection of research subjects	Exemplars Welcome new ideas Co-worker openness to new ideas	Many rules, hierarchy. conformity, competition with coworkers
Development & evaluation	Good interface R&D, marketing, production Separate long-term from urgent projects Support of top management and immediate upervisors Unsuccessful projects quickly stopped Assessment of projects, researchers R&D organization	Encouragement from high-level managers and immediate supervisors Competition with outside organizations	Critical evaluation through bureaucratic processes and hierarchies
Motivation of researchers	Both intrinsic and extrinsic Respect for academic achievement	Emphasis on intrinsic recognition/ rewards that confirm competence	Extrinsic critical evaluation failure punished
Applied to	All R&D in firm	Basic and common elementary research	Everything

in place to insure that the ideas are consistent with corporate strategies. This does not necessarily mean that a new idea will be rejected out of hand because it does not fit current strategies. Indeed, the new idea might be used to help systematically shape future strategies. The point is that there will be processes to ensure a congruence between the idea and company's strategy.

Evaluation, motivation and rewards. In mechanical organizations there is a critical evaluation of projects through bureaucratic processes. Evaluations are more likely to emphasis negative than positive aspects of a project. Successes are systematically rewarded according to bureaucratic policies, but the rewards tend to be rather small even when the successes are large. Failures are punished. Conversely, in organic organizations feedback tends to be disproportionately positive. Immediate supervisors encourage the researchers. Failure is not punished. Managers are generous with recognition and rewards, though researchers tend to be more strongly motivated by the intrinsic rewards of doing research. They are relatively free to work on topics of interest to them, and this freedom is the source of much of their satisfaction. The incubation model shares many characteristics with the organic model, but there are differences. The incubation model does not treat all projects in the same way. It separates long-term projects from urgent projects. It incorporates more systematic evaluations of projects to ensure that they are compatible with company strategies. Intrinsic rewards are important, but extrinsic rewards such as bonuses are used to a greater extent than in organic organizations. The incubation model is integrative, encompassing all R&D in the firm, while the organic model is confined more to basic and common elementary research. The incubation model includes measures to ensure the effective coordination of R&D with marketing, production and other functions of the company.

Mechanical organizations are rigid and rule-bound to the point that innovative projects have little chance of receiving support. A weakness of organic organizations is that they can waste company resources due to their slowness in stopping unsuccessful projects. They also do not provide effective coordination of research projects with corporate strategies and other functions of the company. They do not distinguish between long-term projects and those that must be successfully executed very quickly.

8
Evaluating New Products During the Development Process

So far we have looked at the various stages of the NPD process, why the process sometimes fails, and how organizations can be structured to increase the chance of success. In this chapter we will look at how new products can be evaluated during the various stages of the NPD process.

Kinds of assessments and who makes them

As was discussed in Chapter 3, different NPD processes are appropriate for different types of products. The most appropriate methods for assessing products during the NPD process also vary depending on the type of product. Recall, for example, how Five Fox and World (Chapter 3) developed fashionable apparel for women. The problem facing these companies was that fashions change quickly, and it can be disastrous for a company to be stuck with a large inventory of unfashionable apparel. We described how World got around this problem by effectively using a trial and error method of product assessment. The company would initially produce small lots of clothing in different combinations of color, length, and style. Based on which combinations sold best, they would quickly switch to the production of large lots of the apparel consumers wanted. In the case of new medicines, the evaluation process is very different. Here the evaluation of technical possibilities is the key element. Studies may be made to determine what sequence of DNA is related to a certain kind of disease. Large numbers of molecules may be screened to find those that show promise in the formulation of drugs. Unlike the case with clothing fashions, consumer needs/desires for medications are pretty well understood. What products are technically possible at a given time is much less clear.

Assessment is carried out at the various stages of the new product development process. As we saw in Chapter 3, Cooper recommends that five "stage gates," or assessment points, be established. Cooper's first four assessments points are: (1) during the concept stage, (2) at an early stage of development, such as during animal tests of a new drug, (3) at a later stage of development, such as human subject trials for a new drug, or, as we saw, in Canon's tests of the total functioning of a prototype copier, and (4) before capital investment. We would add an additional stage gate here (5), assessment just after launching. Finally, Cooper's final assessment point (6) is after the new product has established a sales record.

Where in the organization should assessments be made? Who should do the assessments? In the case of technology intensive projects or proposals for new research programs, it seems clear that a committee made up of people who understand the scientific issues should be involved. The more sophisticated the technology, the more difficult it is to assess, and the more important it is that the assessment be based on solid technical criteria. Table 8.1 shows how Sanyo Electric assesses proposed new R&D programs. The process is similar to that which many companies use in assessing technology intensive new products. At Sanyo the evaluation of proposed new R&D programs is carried out at meetings of top

Table 8.1 Meetings on R&D projects at Sanyo Electric

	Participants	Frequency	Responsibility
1. Corporate R&D meeting	Chairman, CEO, and other top managers	4/year	Decide on most important projects
2. Corporate R&D planning committee	Chief of corporate R&D center, all laboratory heads	8/year	Review major projects & R&D strategy, cooperation between labs and outside labs
3. Corporate R&D center management committee	Heads of corporate research center and corporate laboratories	1/month	Decide on corporate R&D
Liaison meeting	Managers of corporate laboratories	6/year	Mutual communications
Strategic meeting	Managers of corporate laboratories	1/month	Decide on strategic projects

management and the corporate R&D planning committee. Evaluations are also made at meetings of the management, liaison and strategy committees of the corporate R&D center.

When a project is risky, but requires a large investment, top management has to play the key role in deciding whether or not to go ahead. Of course, it is essential that the organization give top management the critical supporting information, but the final decision has to be made at the top. When Sony was considering whether or not to launch the Walkman, Akio Morita (then President of Sony) decided to go ahead with the launch, even though his marketing department had serious reservations. Morita, of course, proved to be right about the Walkman. But while top management has to provide leadership and strategic direction on what to develop, it has to avoid undue interference during the actual process of development. Two former presidents of Nissan Motors were notorious for interfering with design work, contributing to Nissan's steady loss of market share over the years to Toyota and Honda. Nissan's product planners felt they could not get final approval of their product unless they incorporated all the suggestions of the company president. An exception was the Nissan Z, one of Nissan's most successful cars. In the case of the Z the Nissan president did not interfere in the design process.

We have seen how panels of consumers were used to evaluate such new products as mayonnaise and home appliances. This was shown graphically in Figure 2.2 in Chapter Two. Sometimes, as we saw in the Ajinomoto Mayonnaise case, employees of the company participate in testing a new consumer product.

What to assess and how to assess it. Early in the NPD process the new product concept is formulated. Depending on the type of product, various *concept tests* might be employed. There may be an evaluation of a written or verbal description of the concept. Often the description will include pictures or models of the proposed product. Conjoint analysis (described in Chapter 3) is a kind of concept analysis. As we have seen, this method was used by Marriot to analyze the operations of several hotels, and then to develop a concept for a hotel that satisfied unmet consumer desires. The result was the Marriot Courtyards chain of hotels. When Toyota was developing the first generation Vitz, the globally popular small car, the company produced clay models of several possible designs. These were sent to Paris where designers were asked to judge which model they thought had the best style to succeed as a world car. Similarly, as we have seen, Ajinomoto made several models

Table 8.2 New product evaluation (% of managers using criteria at each stage)

Development stage / Criterion	Beginning (Concept development)	Middle (Development to final product.)	Last (Before launch)
	%	%	%
Attractiveness of market			
Market size	88.6	40.9	39.1
Position in product life cycle	25.9	15.5	14.1
Competitive situation	67.0	48.0	50.0
Stability of demand	26.5	16.2	25.6
Social responsibility value	15.1	8.4	7.4
Feasibility			
Access to technology	56.3	20.1	6.7
Required R&D expenditures	33.5	29.8	6.7
Required capital investment	39.2	53.9	31.7
Access to key resources	17.7	31.8	10.8
Competitive synergies			
R&D capability	61.3	24.0	5.4
Production technology	26.5	56.4	15.54
Cost of production	36.0	69.4	56.0
Sales capacity	22.1	24.0	57.4
Contribution to current products			
Impact on present products	36.0	18.1	18.2
Strengthen present sales channels?	10.1	23.3	56.0
Increase present research capability	24.0	22.0	6.0
Enhance current production technologies	9.4	27.9	22.3
Smooths seasonal/business cycles by	1.2	1.3	8.1
providing diversified customer base?	0.0	1.9	6.7
Profitability/Financial Risk			
Sales volume	46.2	38.3	56.0
Decrease of sales of other products	8.2	11.0	18.2
Profit over sales	32.9	50.0	70.2
Profit over investment	28.4	42.8	40.5
Years to break even	27.2	29.8	39.1
Loss in the worst case scenario	8.8	18.1	30.4
(after investment)			

Note: For details on sample, see Table 1.4.

of possible containers for its new mayonnaise. These were shown to a panel of evaluators, and one of the models was selected.

What do leading companies assess during the NPD process? We surveyed managers to find out what items they evaluate at three stages of development. Table 8.2 shows the results.

We organized the criteria into five categories:

1. Attractiveness of the market. Some of the literature calls this "external consistency."[68] The criterion most often mentioned was market size. Nearly 90% of the managers in our survey said their company assessed market size at the beginning of the development stage. It may seem obvious that the bigger the potential market the better, but it should not be forgotten that products can also be successful if they win a large share of a medium-sized niche market. Toray has done well by adopting a strategy of entering medium sized markets. 3M has also done this. In order to estimate total demand, it is necessary to estimate the demand for each segment. In the case of cameras, for example, there would be the demand for digital cameras, film cameras, and single use cameras. Throughout the NPD process it is necessary to assess the competitive situation the company and its new product is likely to enjoy. Two thirds of the managers in our survey mentioned using this criterion during concept development – and about half said they use it at the later stages of the product development process. Another factor contributing to the attractiveness of the market is the position the new product will have in the overall product life cycle for its product category – how long is it likely to be able to contribute to the company's success. Still, other factors are stability of demand and the social responsibility expressed in the product. For example, is the new product environmentally friendly?

2. Feasibility. The managers in our survey take a hard look at the feasibility of successfully developing the new product. Does the company have the technology in house or the ability to obtain it? Omron, the well-known producer of medical electronic and industrial control equipment, invested some $50 million trying to enter the semiconductor market, but did not have the strength in this particular technology to succeed, and eventually had to divest this activity. More broadly, a company must ensure it has, or can get, the capital and other key resources needed to successfully launch the new product.

3. Competitive synergies. This is sometimes called "internal consistency." Most of the managers in our survey evaluate the R&D and production capabilities of their firm to see if these are consistent

with a successful launch of the proposed product. They look at the cost of production and the capabilities of the firm's sales channels. In brief they are determining how well the firm's present core competencies can support the new product. What market share can they realistically hope to attain? Depending on the firm and industry, firms may make these evaluations at different stages of the NPD process.

4. Contribution to the current product line. This is another aspect of "internal consistency. Many managers look explicitly at the broader potential impacts of the new product. Will it support current products? Can it be used as a stepping stone towards the future? If the new product uses the same sales channels as current products, it may reinforce their sales. There may be economies of scale. The new product might sell well at low points in the season or business cycle for existing products, stabilizing total sales and profits. This might allow a more efficient use of the company's capabilities. Companies sometimes introduce new products to learn new technologies or marketing skills. A leading tire manufacturer, for example, started producing surf boards as part of an effort to learn more about the behavioral patterns of young people.

5. Profitability and financial risk. The financial implications of the new product are crucial, but they are difficult to estimate. Estimated sales, net present value, net cash flow, and the number of years needed to recover the investment should all be computed. If investment in R&D is the limiting factor, the following formula can be applied:

$$P = (Pts \times Pbs \times (Pr - Cx) \times As \times Ym)/ \text{R\&D cost}$$

Where:

P = expected profitability
Pts = Probability of technical success
Pbs = Probability of business success
Pr = Price
Cx = Cost of sales
As = Expected annual sales
Ym = Expected number of years on market

The estimated value of P should be greater than one. If the number of researchers is the limiting factor, the number of researchers can be used instead of investment in R&D. Of course, this does not give an estimated return on investment for the project, but it may help guide a choice between two or more possible research programs. The company needs to make the best use of scare resources, including human resources.

The possibility that the new product might cannibalize the sales of present products must also be taken into account. For example the development of a digital camera may decrease a company's sale of film cameras and film. A concern about this made it difficult for companies like Kodak and Fuji to quickly enter the market for digital cameras. In such cases top management may have to make a bold decision to sacrifice existing products. The decision of whether to sacrifice current products for the sake of possible future products, however, should be based explicitly on strategy. All too often it is a decision that simply emerges as one division introduces a new product without regard to the rest of the company, or, even worse, another division kills a new product development process to protect its own short-term interests. It also should not be forgotten that a new product may contribute more to the company than simple projections of sales of the new product would indicate. The new product might, for example, increase the sales of complementary products, as when a new copier increases the sales of toner.

Sometimes the investment needed to develop a new product may be too large to justify pursuing it. The investments needed to develop new semiconductors, commercial aircraft, and drugs can be huge. Estimated maximum losses that are less than the net worth of the company may sometimes be tolerable. A higher level of risk would generally be difficult to justify, but firms such as Boeing sometimes have to "bet the company" – investing more than the value of the company in the development of a new generation commercial jetliner. The only alternative would be to withdraw from the industry.

Weighing assessment criteria. As Table 8.2 shows, the relative importance of the various assessment criteria changes as development progresses. In the beginning stage, "external consistency," i.e. the size and stability of the market are most important. These items were mentioned more often by our respondents at this stage. In the middle stage, feasibility and consistency become more important. In the last stage before launching, profitability becomes the most important item. Of course, potential profitability should also be considered in the first stage of the development process, but in most cases potential profitability will be much less clear at the beginning of the project than it will later on as more information is collected. Also, the amount of investment that must be committed generally increases sharply just before the product launch. The firm may need to build new production facilities, develop sales channels, and begin a marketing campaign for the new product.

Decision-makers need to discipline themselves to ignore sunk costs when deciding whether or not to go ahead with a project. Past investments cannot be recovered. The factors that matter are potential profitability and how much future investment is likely to be required.

Forecasting demand for a product where there is no past data

Planners have to estimate demand for the new product, but of course if the product is new, there is no history to form a basis for estimates. There are, however, several ways to get around this problem.

1. Data on similar products. Estimates can be based on data for similar products. To estimate a time series for the diffusion of dishwashers (when this was still a new product), for example, data on the diffusion of washing machines was used. One reason this analogy was reasonable was that both dishwashers and washing machines are household durable goods. In the case of durable goods, sales include both first-time and replacement purchases. Projected sales for the two types of purchase have to be computed separately to get a good estimate. Estimates based on analogies are well established in NPD, and of course have long been used in the natural sciences. Lord Ernest Rutherford, for example, was inspired to develop his "planetary model" of the atom based on the structure of the solar system. Of course the product chosen to be the basis for the analogy has to be similar to the new product in certain key respects. Most importantly, it should be a product that will be used in a similar way by similar consumers, and that will sell for a similar price. Thus, the VHS player was a good analogy product for the DVD player.

   When we examine diffusion patterns for electrical home appliances over the past 50 years we find two different patterns. Some products diffused very rapidly, with about half of all households owning them within 5 years. An example of a fast diffusing product is the video tape recorder. Other products took 10 to 15 years to reach 50% of all households. Examples of slow diffusing products include tape recorders, stereo players and microwave ovens. There were a number of reasons for the slow diffusion of these products. In the case of microwave ovens, for example, consumers waited for prices to drop and safety concerns to be satisfied. The first tape recorders were initially high-priced gadgets of rather limited use, primarily for voice recording and language instruction. Sales began to take off when tape recorders could increasingly be used for the high quality recording and playback of music. Planners have to decide whether their new product is likely to be a fast or slow diffusing product.

Analogies can also be used to predict the direction of demand. A designer of fashionable ladies apparel, for example, might look at sales trends for other products to gain an insight into the "looks" consumers are beginning to favor. If antiques are selling well, for example, there might also be a good market for classic styles in clothing. In the 1950s the public fascination with space travel and airplanes translated into the popularity of cars that had extreme tail fins. In the early 2000s there was a general nostalgia for pre World War II styles in the United States, and Chrysler PT Cruisers and other cars reflecting the styles of the 1930s and 1940s became popular.

2. Logical estimation. As we have seen, in estimating the likely demand for its new small copiers, Canon started by estimating the number of small offices. To estimate the demand for rooftop solar heating systems, one company calculated the number of single-family houses in its market. It then subtracted the number of those houses that were in areas where the climate made solar heading impractical and those in districts where average family incomes were low. This information was used to estimate the maximum size of the market. Calculations can also be made of the rate at which an existing product will be replaced by the new product. Vinyl pipe for example is replacing metal pipe because it does not rust and is easy to fabricate. Estimates can be made of how much metal piping is in place, how old it is, and what its expected remaining service life is. This can provide the basis for an estimate of the maximum market size for replacement vinyl pipe. An analysis can be based on demand for complementary or other related products. In estimating the demand for carbon fiber, for example, one can determine what amount is likely to be used in each application. Based on comparisons of cost and physical performance, an estimate can be made of total demand. Similar methods can be used for other materials where it is reasonable to assume that the demand for the end use is known. The

demand for car navigation systems can be estimated based on the volume of automobile production.

3. Surveys. Surveys can be used to find out whether consumers are likely to buy the new product. Potential consumers might be shown samples or pictures of the new product. They might be asked to react to descriptions that give the price and features of the product. For surveys like this to be useful, however, potential consumers must fully understand the features of the new product. If the product is completely new to their experience, they may not really know how they will react when the product actually comes out.

Perhaps the most familiar example of surveys of potential "buyers" of products is in the political area, where Gallup and other pollsters try to forecast election results. Those using surveys to determine the size of markets for new products should note that while political polls are generally accurate, they have been spectacularly wrong on occasion. In 1936 a leading U.S. magazine of the time, the *Literary Digest*, predicted that Senator Alf Landon would win 57% of the popular vote to defeat President Franklin Roosevelt in a landslide. *Literary Digest* had polled a sample that included one forth of all registered U.S. voters. Some two million people from this sample sent in postcards indicating who they intended to vote for. Because this was one of the largest number of responses ever received in a poll many people were convinced it would be accurate. The problem was that *Literary Digest* had developed its sample of people to poll from those whose names were in telephone directories and automobile registration lists. During the Depression year of 1936 the people who had cars and telephones were far more affluent, and far more likely to vote Republican, than the overall population of voters. Alf Landon not only lost the election, he lost in the biggest landslide in more than a century. President Roosevelt was re-elected with some 64% of the vote. In 1948 the Gallup Poll predicted that Thomas Dewey would be elected president over Harry Truman. Here sophisticated polling techniques were used, so the sample does not seem to have been biased. The problem with the estimated final vote was that many voters changed their minds between the time the poll was taken, some 3 weeks before the election, and the time people actually voted. Other polls have wrongly predicted how people would vote on a range of social issues related, for example, to civil rights and tax increases to support schools. Depending on the issue, people may be reluctant to give their true views to a stranger.

Those using surveys to assess the size of markets for new products have to be careful they are asking the right respondents, that the preferences being mentioned are stable, and that people are not just telling interviewers what they think the interviewers want to hear. Respondents may not want to admit, for example, that they cannot afford a product or are unwilling to pay extra for a product that would be good for the environment. Conversely, some respondents may have no interest in a product until they actually see it. Experts should be able to assess the amount of error these respondents are likely to introduce into their findings. Past experience can be a good guide.

4. Field tests. Sometimes companies field test products before giving them a full launch. The company might, for example, begin by selling the new product in a medium-sized city that seems representative of the overall market. By doing this the firm can learn who the potential buyers for the product are, and how many products are likely to be sold once the product is more broadly launched. Sometimes the firm might want to assess the promise of several versions of the new product. It can test market alternative versions in the field. USA Today is now the largest circulation newspaper in the U.S. When it was launched in the early 1980s *U.S.A. Today* was different from standard newspapers, and it was not clear the public would accept it. Rather than take the risk of launching the newspaper all over the United States at once, the publisher began by selling it in Washington, D.C. and in a few nearby states. It then expanded its sales to the rest of the United States.

Figure 8.1 shows an analysis one company used in projecting the demand for a new piece of medical equipment, a special ultrasonic scanner. The new product concept was for this to be a portable ultrasonic scanner that would cost less than those currently on the market. Based on the fact that in this company's market there were about 60,000 small hospitals and doctors who might use such a scanner, the NPD team estimated that the maximum demand for the scanner would be 30,000 units. (This is an example of #2, logical estimation). The team did an analysis for three patterns of diffusion, fast, medium and slow. With rapid diffusion, the company could expect to obtain about 30% of the market over the first several years. The product would be profitable. Under the slow diffusion scenario, however, more competing firms would be likely to enter the market, so the company's market share would be somewhat lower. The analysts

Figure 8.1 A demand forecasting case

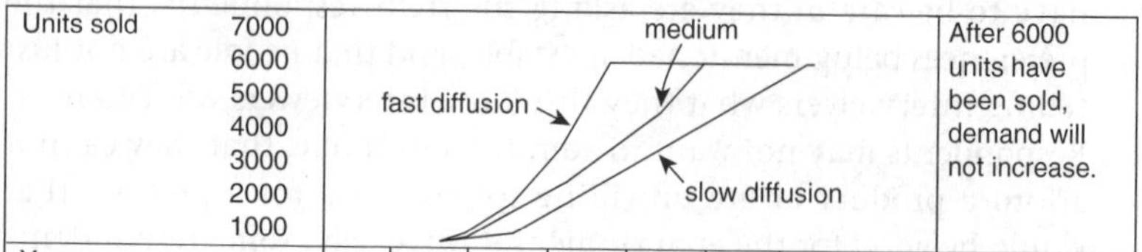

| Units sold | 7000 6000 5000 4000 3000 2000 1000 | medium — fast diffusion — slow diffusion | After 6000 units have been sold, demand will not increase. |

Year		1	2	3	4	5	6	7	8	
Fast	Total units	300	1500	3300	6000	6000	"	"	"	If demand grows quickly, our market share will not decrease.
	Our company's market share	←	1500	→	1500	1500	"	"	"	
		←	30%	→	30%	30%				
Medium	Total units	200	1100	2000	3300	4500	6000	"	"	
	Our company's market share	←	1000	→	1000	1000	1200	"	"	
		←	30%	→	30%	25%	20%	"	"	
Slow	Total units	100	500	1500	2400	3300	4200	5100	6000	If diffusion is slow, many new entrants will appear and our market share will decline.
	Our company's market share	←	600	→	700	800	800	900	1000	
		←	30%	→	30%	25%	20%	18%	16%	

Source: Presentation by T. Narasawa at meeting of Japan Productivity Center.

estimated their company's market share would fall to 25% during the 5th year, and then decline to about 16% in the 8th year. The initial retail price for the scanners would be around $60,000 (yielding a wholesale price of about $45,000), but after a few years the retail price would drop to around $35,000. Based on this analysis, it was estimated that under the slow diffusion scenario, the company could not make a profit. The problem facing managers in the company was deciding which diffusion scenario was most likely.

Technical evaluations

Technical evaluations are made to determine whether or not the standards set for the new product's components result in a product that meets the goals for the product. In the case of a copier, technical criteria for components might be aimed at making sure that paper in the copier moves smoothly and that the printing is clear. It may also be necessary to make tests to make sure that the technical criteria really meet consumer desires. In the case of Toto's "washlet toilet" technical criteria included the angle of the nozzle and temperature of the water. The real point, however, was to make sure the toilet was comfortable for most users. Comfort levels associated with different angles and temperatures were tested by both male and female employees of various sizes and shapes.

The HOQ (house of quality) is a model of the structure of quality that was originally developed by Toyota.[69] It is used to initiate a Quality Function Deployment (QFD) process. Figure 8.2 shows the "HOQ" for a PC printer. The functions consumers want, the "whats," are listed on the left side of the figure. The technological elements needed to realize these functions, "the hows," are listed in the middle.

The HOQ represents the technological process of development. The upper roof shows the relationships amongst the technological characteristics. Complementary or positive relationships are indicated by circles conflicting or negative relations are indicated by "×" or "◊". To overcome negative relationships, there would have to be either a technological breakthrough, or a rebalancing of characteristics.

The right side of the figure gives an evaluation by consumers of a new product compared to competing products. In Figure 8.2, A and B are competing products, and C is the company's new product. The consumers' evaluations are based on trial uses of the new product. Unfortunately for the team developing it, the chart shows that the new product in the diagram is inferior to rival products in every respect. The lower part of the chart gives the company's self-assessment of the new product based on its own testing. Even though consumers did not rate the product very highly, we can see that the company's self-assessment gave the product a good rating. The chart shows us a number of things. It shows how the product characteristics consumers want are transformed to technological factors. It clarifies the complementary and negative relationships that might exist. It highlights the negative relationships, to ensure that efforts are made to resolve them. It makes it clear when the assessments of consumers are different from those of the company.

Figure 8.2 QFD and the "house of quality"

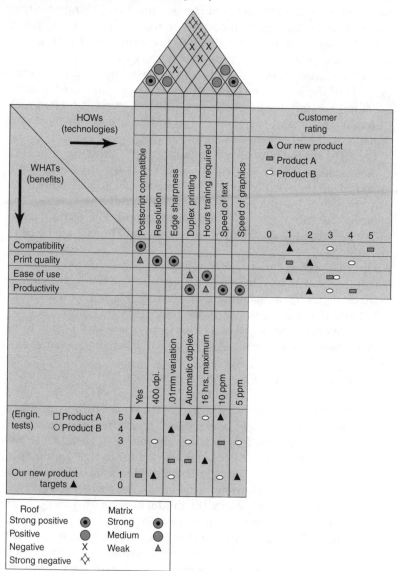

Note: This example shows how the results of a product use test, upon completion, can be compared with what was intended. Under "Customer Rating," intended users say the firm did not achieve its objectives.
Source: D. Rosenau and J. Moran, *Managing the Development of New Products* (New York: Van Nostand, Reingold (1993), p. 231 as modified by Crawford and Di Benedetto, New Products Management (2003), New York: McGraw-Hill.

Strategic and political considerations

A number of strategic and political considerations, beyond immediate customer satisfaction and market size, should also be taken into account in evaluating potential new products. Here are three examples of such considerations:

1. Is this a "bridgehead product?" Some new products may not make a large profit for the firm, but they may serve as part of a broader strategy for the future. For example a certain tire maker developed a new golf ball based on its competencies in rubber and related materials. The tire company's purpose was not to make a profit on the golf ball, but rather to use it to learn about the sporting goods industry, and to create a new competency in that industry. It is vital that a company do this when it is thinking about moving into a new industry. Such moves can be very risky. Nippon Steel, for example, failed in its effort to enter the semiconductor business. Even a company as generally successful as Toyota failed when it tried to enter the housing industry – its successes in the automobile industry kept it from devoting adequate attention and resources to this new industry. The introduction of bridgehead products raises issues similar to those in planning related or unrelated diversifications. Experience with the bridgehead product can make it clear what the problems facing the company in the new industry are likely to be.
2. What is the best pricing policy? One strategy is to set a low price for the new product, even if this means profits must be sacrificed. This "penetration price" policy might be used because there are competitors already in the market, and offering the product at a low price is the only way to gain market share. A low price may also be used to discourage competitors from entering the market. Sometimes a new product will have to be launched at a low price because it is a product with high price elasticity. Another pricing strategy goes in the other direction, putting a high price on the new product. This policy might be used for a luxury product, where price elasticity is low. A high price policy is generally used for new drugs that are protected by patents. The high price allows the pharmaceutical company to recover its development costs quickly. Once the patents expire, others will enter the market with generic medications using a penetration price policy. The "generic medications" may cost as little as one tenth as much as the original medication. One reason the producers of generic medications can offer such low prices is that their costs are low – in part because they do not spend much on R&D.

3. Are company "politics" an issue? It is naïve to assume that just because the success of a new product would be good for the company, the NPD process will automatically be supported by managers in all parts of the company. Other departments may withhold cooperation, or even actively oppose the proposed new product. Managers of other departments may be afraid that the new product will cannibalize the products for which they are responsible. Another concern may be that the success of the new product will result in members of the NPD team being promoted ahead of others in the company. The spectacular new product successes of Sony Music Entertainment, for example, led to the head of this division passing other senior executives to become president of Sony. Finally, success of the new product is likely to have lower priority for department managers than their day to day activities. After all, their operational performance is likely to determine their pay and career prospects.

In order to promote the development of a new product, the NPD team leader needs to be cognizant of these possible sources of resistance. Of course, every effort should be made to win over those who might oppose the new product. The leader of the NPD team, however, may also need to mobilize the support of high ranking product champions in the company and of other managers who will benefit from the success of the new product. As was mentioned above, the launch of the Walkman was initially opposed by Sony's marketing department. Fortunately, in this case the product champion was Akio Morita, then the president of the company, so the project went forward. At JVC (Japan Victor Corporation) the department in charge of making commercial video recorders was losing money, and resisted development of the home VHS. The director of finance at the company's head office served as a product champion during the early stages of development of the home VHS. This kept the project alive. Later, Konnosuke Matsushita, founder and president of Matsushita Panasonic (parent company of JVC) became the product champion, ensuring the launch of the new product.

9

Launching a New Product

As we saw in Chapter 1, a company can be the first to market a new product, only to have other companies quickly move in and take the market away from them. EMI invented the CT scanner, and Konica was the first to come out with an auto-focus camera, but both EMI and Konica were soon eclipsed by other firms that entered the market with improved versions of the new products. In Chapter 1 we described how Sony avoided this problem by continually making improvements after launching the Walkman.

Succeeding after the launch of a new product

In our survey on new product development we asked managers to identify the seven factors they considered to be most important in promoting the sale of a new product after launching it. Our findings are shown in Table 9.1. In this chapter we will discuss the items the managers identified as being important. We will begin with three that were among those most often mentioned: using a sequential strategy (22.5%), constructing sales/distribution channels (65.63%), making improvements (70.63%), and constructing barriers to entry for other firms (41.88%).

Using a Sequential strategy. At the time *USA Today* was introduced this newspaper was so different from existing "national newspapers" like the *New York Times* and *Wall Street Journal*, that no one could be sure how well readers would accept it. The risk of failure was huge. To reduce the magnitude of the risk, the publishers of *USA Today* used a sequential strategy in launching this new product (see the case describing the launch of *USA Today* below). Rather than launching

Table 9.1   What is important in promoting the post-launch sale of a new product?

Items	%
1. Use sequential strategy (Launch in one area, then decide whether to expand to other areas)	22.50
2. Collect and respond to complaints	48.13
3. Continuously improve product	70.63
4. Construct entry barriers (e.g. through control of raw materials, differentiation)	41.88
5. Decrease price to ward off competition	20.63
6. File for patents	72.50
7. Challenge weaknesses of competitors (e.g. package delivery company points out weaknesses of postal service; maker of a new drug attacks side effects of existing drug.)	23.13
8. Construct and reinforce distribution channels	65.63
9. Cooperate with and reinforce suppliers of complementary products (e.g. video game makers supports software suppliers)	15.63
10. Use internet for sales and promotion	2.50
11. High quality training of sales force and others in sales channels	45.00
12. Getting required permission from public authorities	9.38
13. Other	3.75

Notes: 1. For details about the sample, see Table 1.4.
2. Respondents were asked to select the seven most important items.

the paper nationally, they first sold it only in the Washington, D.C. area. When they found it was successful there, they made a few changes in response to initial reader reactions, than sold the newspaper in other parts of the United States. Initially launching a product in a small market can be a good strategy whenever there is a lot of uncertainty about the market. The risk, of course, is that a sequential strategy takes time, and rivals may enter the market. Those who launched *USA Today*, however, were pretty sure that no one else would enter the market, at least for the time being.

Construction of sales channels. Generally speaking, a product's market share is a result of how well it compares with competitors in terms of quality, price, the effectiveness of its sales promotion efforts, and the size and strengths of its sales channels. It is possible to collect data in order to estimate values for quality and price. The estimated values can be used to help select or construct sales channels. Research has shown that this can even be done when sales are to be carried out on the internet.

Firms can follow (a) an exclusive distribution channel policy, (b) a selective distribution policy, or (c) an extensive distribution policy.

Benetton, Gap, The Body Shop, *USA Today*, and most car manufacturers follow an exclusive distribution policy. They sell their product at outlets that do not handle their competitors (in some respects this system is breaking down in the U.S automobile industry as large dealerships acquire franchises for competing brands – even in these cases, however, the showrooms, repair facilities, etc. are typically kept separate). One might think that a company using an exclusive channel policy would want as many channels as possible, but this is not always the case. Matsushita Panasonic, for example is decreasing the number of its channels. The company found it was too expensive to maintain a large number of channels. The problem was that Matsushita Panasonic had to provide a full range of products to each of the stores that were its exclusive distributors, even when those products might not be profitable. Matsushita Panasonic also had to train a large number of sales people in the often highly technical aspects of the company's products. Matsushita Panasonic found it more economical to sell new products through large scale stores that already have technically savvy sales people. However, exclusive distribution channels do have advantages for certain types of products. They can be used as a source of quick and rich market information feedback. Sony has a relatively small number of exclusive "Sony Style" shops, partly to provide this kind of feedback. Similarly, most makers of fashionable women's apparel have several exclusive sales channels. This helps them stay close to their customers.

With a selective distribution policy the company picks out the channels it wants to use, but its product is sold with other brands. A firm may want, for example, to have its product sold only in prestigious stores, or only in stores that can provide strong technical support for the product. When Toyota developed the Lexus as a high status car competing with Mercedes and BMW, it established a new sales channel instead of using Toyota dealers. Lexus showrooms provide a more luxurious atmosphere than Toyota showrooms, and give customers the sense that they are receiving the high class treatment they feel entitled to.

Of course a company can use more than one distribution policy. Shiseido uses a selective distribution policy for its cosmetics, and an extensive distribution policy for its soaps and detergents. Matsushita Panasonic uses all three distribution policies – exclusive, selective, and extensive – depending on the product and the market. The Lexus policy is both selective and exclusive.

Case: *USA Today*

USA Today now has a circulation of more than two and a half million, by far the largest of any newspaper in the United States. It is sold all over the United States, and in sixty other countries. The origins of *USA Today* go back to 1980 when four young staff members at the Ganett Company were appointed to study possible concepts for a new newspaper. The team established a confidential research office in Cocoa Beach, Florida. The team spent about $1.4 million on market research. They asked some 8,000 people why they buy and read newspapers. Based on the responses the team established a product concept for a new kind of newspaper.

The newspaper would target a huge general-interest audience. It would cover news on national and international events, entertainment, financial news, and sports. Physically, the new paper would be compact (32–40 pages), feature lots of color (especially blue and red), and use easy to read fonts. Copy would be computer-set. Each *USA Today* article would be printed in entirety on one page, so people would not have to flip through the paper when reading. This would make it easier for people to read the paper on trains and airplanes. Advertising space would be limited. Articles in the newspaper would be concise and there would be many charts, graphs and pictures. Upbeat news would be given preference.

The new newspaper was launched in 1982. As was mentioned above, a sequential strategy was used for the launching. The paper was first sold only in the Washington, D.C. area. Some adjustments were made based on the response of the D.C. readers, and in 1983 sales were expanded to all 50 U.S. states. To produce newspapers for a national audience, Ganett used twelve satellites, and printing facilities in 35 different cities (the company already had most of these facilities because it was publishing 86 local newspapers around the United States), and installed 100,000 easy-to-recognize newsstands. After 1 year, the new paper's circulation passed half a million. By 1989 circulation had reached 1.3 million, second only to the *Wall Street Journal* in the United States. Advertising did not keep up with sales, so the newspaper did not make a profit for several years. Nonetheless, *USA Today* quickly became the cornerstone for the Gannett Company, which owns television broadcasting stations, magazines, news services and other enterprises. The group has operating revenues of well over $6 billion per year.

Case: Asahi Super Dry Beer

Asahi's Super Dry Beer was one of the biggest turnaround products ever. After the new beer was introduced in the mid-1980s, it quickly became the best selling beer in Japan. Asahi's share of the beer market, which had been stagnating at below 10% shot up to 40% by 1995.[70] In launching the new beer, Asahi's president took two aggressive actions. First of all, he had Asahi take substantial losses by recalling all the beer distributors had in stock, and discarding it. Because sales had been slow, Asahi Beer was being kept in inventory too long, and its taste deteriorated by the time it reached consumers. This was hurting Asahi's image. Secondly, in order to get as many people as possible to understand the distinctive quality of the new beer, the company initiated a campaign to get one million people to taste the beer. Hundreds of employees were mobilized to give out samples. These employees were not only from the marketing department, but also from R&D and production. By directly giving the beer to consumers on the street, the members of these departments gained a better understanding of consumers – which reinforced the company's efforts to give its corporate culture more of a customer orientation.

Construction of entry barriers. For a firm to fully benefit from a new product, it has to protect its market share from possible competitors. Several types of barriers to entry to the new market can be constructed. These include product differentiation, absolute cost advantage, economies of scale, organizational entry barriers, and exit barriers.

Of course, by definition a certain amount of product differentiation exists whenever a new product is launched. The challenge is to maintain it by continuous improvement. We have already described how EMI's CT scanner and Konica's auto focus camera quickly lost market share to technologically more aggressive competitors. The later entrants to these markets were faster than those that were first in the market to make improvements that were attractive to customers. Sony's Walkman was also in a strongly competitive environment, where a large number of strong rivals might have taken the market for portable music systems away from them. Firms such as Matsushita Panasonic, Sharp, and Toshiba were very efficient at the production and marketing of consumer electronic devices. Sony protected its market for the Walkman by continuously improving it. Within a short period of time Sony had made some 150 improvements in the original Walkman. Sony aggressively collected and analyzed complaints, comments and suggestions from consumers to come up with many of the ideas for these improvements.

Some new products can be protected by patents. Most new medicines, for example, are protected by patents. A common problem in many industries, however, is determining the appropriate scope of the patent application for the new product. The broader the scope of the patent, the more it costs to apply for the patent. On the other hand, if the scope of the patent is too narrow, the firm's intellectual property may not be adequately protected. Toray, a leading Japanese manufacturer of synthetic fiber, patented its production technology for nylon and polyesters – but the scope of its patents turned out to be too narrow. As a result, Chinese firms were able to use Toray's technology. The Chinese firms now dominate the markets for nylon and polyesters. On the other hand, Canon is especially noted for the strength of its patent office, and its ability to protect its intellectual property.

A firm can also protect the market for a new product if it enjoys "absolute cost advantage" in manufacturing the product. This means that the company's cost of production is lower than that of any other company, at any scale of production. A company may have absolute cost advantage because, for example, it has a monopoly on key raw materials, or owns key patents (so competitors have to pay royalties). Alcan, the Canadian aluminum producer, has an absolute cost advantage in producing aluminum because it has good bauxite mines in Canada and Australia. While a firm might seek out new products where it would have absolute cost advantage, the opportunities to do so are rare.

In some industries the investment needed to build a plant large enough to realize the necessary economies of scale can deter entry by other firms. In the semi-conductor industry, for example, the investment required to build a plant to produce at an economic scale is more than $3 billion. In such industries it may only make sense to enter a market for a firm that can get there first. Organizational barriers to entry include differences in organizational culture and a lack of management knowledge. Pharmaceutical companies find it difficult to enter markets for cosmetics, even though they may use similar technologies (there have been exceptions, Eizai successfully introduced a skin cream enriched with vitamin E). A company that produces artificial fiber might be tempted to enter the market for fashionable women's apparel or men's business suits, but will probably not have the appropriate corporate culture and specialized knowledge required to succeed. As we have seen, companies like Fox Five and World succeeded, not because of their strength in making clothing, but rather because they could quickly respond to fashion trends.

In some industries exit barriers can pose a barrier to market entry. A firm that wants to enter an industry like railroad construction, for example, would have to invest heavily in specialized equipment to do so, and would not be able to recover much of its investment if it later decided to leave this industry.

Competition and cooperation

One might think that a firm would want to keep the market for a new product all to itself. Often this is the case. There are, however, two situations where a firm launching a new product might welcome followers. One is where the followers might help the firm establish de facto business or technical standards. The other is where followers might help the firm expand the total market for the new product.

A new standard is needed when software has to be used with a new product. When video cassette recorders were introduced, for example, a standard had to be established so that producers of video cassettes would know what types of cassettes to make. Sony made the mistake of trying to keep monopoly control over its Betamax VCR technology. Its main rival, JVC, gladly shared its VHS technology with other producers of video recorders. The result was that before long there were far more VHS than Betamax recorders, so naturally producers of cassettes made more VHS than Betamax tapes. Since there were more VHS than Betamax cassettes available the VHS machines were more attractive to consumers. This, in turn, increased the relative appeal of the VHS machines. After a while Sony had to withdraw its Betamax from the market.

Followers can also help expand the total market for a product, increasing the profits the first mover can make. Fuji Film was first to introduce the single use camera, but Kodak soon came out with its own single use camera. The fact that customers in the U.S., and some other countries where Fuji Film was less well-known, trusted the quality of Kodak products gave added legitimacy to the single use camera, making more customers willing to try it. As a result Fuji was able to sell more single use cameras than if it had been able to monopolize this market.

What sort of firm do you want to enter the market for your new product? The famous management strategy theorist Michael Porter lists twelve different characteristics of desirable followers, but these can be combined into three general areas.[71] First of all, desirable entrants to the market for a new product will not seek to compete on the basis of price. Clearly, it would be disastrous if the price for your new product were to be driven down to a point where you cannot recover the costs of development. Secondly, desirable competitors avoid risk taking. You would not want a competitor that disrupts the market by making radical innovations in the product design or means of marketing it. And, third, desirable followers do not erect exit barriers. If a follower over-invests, it may need to lower its prices and compete vigorously just to survive. If the firm cannot easily sell off the specialized assets it has invested in, it may be forced to stay in the market and sell its products at a loss.

Strong brands

Brand construction should start during the concept formation stage. We saw in Chapter 1 how Shiseido did this when it developed its Tactics hair dressing for men. The brand image should instill trust, inspire dreams, and generate a sense of happiness.[72] The brand name guarantees quality, so the product can be sold at a higher price. A good brand image is essential if the firm is to avoid price competition.

A strong brand image is created when the following factors are in place:

(1) Purchasers have a good experience with the product, and this experience is based on the product's distinctive features and its consistently high quality. At one time Sony products could be sold at a 20% price premium because of the brand's quality image. As Sony's major products, such as television sets, became commodities there were fewer quality differences between brands and it became more difficult to come up with meaningful distinctive features. As a result, Sony began to suffer from price competition.

(2) Product images that create attractive associations. Some brands have been able to effectively create and exploit images that capture the imagination of consumers. When the sex goddess Marilyn Monroe was asked what she wore to bed, she answered: "I wear nothing but Chanel Number 5." This established the brand's identity as glamorous and sexy. Honda tries to associate its cars with young people. Honda's company creed is "dreams and youthfulness."

(3) Loyal customer base. Some brands have extremely loyal customers. How else does one explain why people not only want to own Harley-Davidson motorcycles, but also to wear clothing with a Harley-Davidson logo, and to eat in Harley Davidson restaurants? Loyal customers may come to identify themselves as a driver of a certain brand of car, and buy

that car even in years when most people regard competing cars as being more stylish or technically advanced. Sometimes a brand enjoys the advantage of loyal customers in some markets, but not in others. Matsushita Panasonic has loyal customers in Japan and in many other countries. In these countries it does not have to compete based on price. In China, however, Matsushita Panasonic does not have a large number of loyal customers, so its air conditioners and some other products are coming under strong price competition. This shows the importance of building customer loyalty.

(4) The "first fifteen seconds." Research suggests that most of us form a deep impression of a person within the first fifteen seconds of meeting him or her. These impressions are difficult to change. Similarly, customer images of a firm are often created in the first "fifteen seconds" of their dealings with the firm's employees. This means employees and sales staff should always be customer-oriented. Nordstrom is famous for building relationship with its customers. On one occasion a customer went to a Nordstrom store in Seattle to buy slacks. The store did not have the right size, so the sales person called five other Nordstrom stores. She still could not find slacks in the right size. So she went to a rival department store to get slacks for the customer. On another occasion, a customer stopped in a Nordstrom to make a purchase on her way to the airport. She inadvertently left her airline ticket on the store counter, as she rushed off to the airport. The sales person took a taxi to the airport to give the ticket to the customer.[73]

(5) Respect for employees. In order to cultivate a customer oriented attitude not just in marketing, but all through the value chain, the firm needs to respect its employees and give them training to foster a customer-oriented culture. Employees must be given enough knowledge to improve the product, to explain the product, and to give appropriate service after sales.

As Starbucks has expanded throughout the world, it has worked hard to make sure its employees are given uniformly high quality training. They learn all about coffee. Starbucks is also noted for treating its employees well (for example, by giving far more generous healthcare benefits than other firms in the food industry). This helps create an atmosphere where the employees will also treat customers well. The employees of The Body Shop are trained to understand and explain the idealistic environmental and social responsibility missions of The Body Shop. Disneyland trains its employees to be oriented to customer satisfaction, rather than just to the jobs they are assigned. A ticket seller's job is not just to sell tickets, but also to serve as a guide to Disneyland. A visitor may ask a ticket seller how to get to Magic Mountain or the Haunted Mansion, or what time the park will close. No matter what they are asked, employees should never just say "I don't know." They should tell the visitor what they do know, and then find out from a colleague whatever else the visitor needs to know. Members of Disneyland's cleaning staff are even told that they should find ways to pick up trash without bending over. Children (and others) who are looking at all the things around them might stumble over an employee who has bent over to pick something up. These expected behaviors are explained in detailed manuals. Employees are considered to be part of the "cast" on the Disneyland stage.

(6) Effective damage control, immediate recall of defective products. A few years ago Ford Explorer SUVs equipped with Firestone tires were involved in many accidents where the tread peeled off the tires, causing the SUVs to roll over. It has been estimated that around the world more than 250 people were killed and 3,000 were seriously injured in these accidents. Ford and Bridgestone (the parent of Firestone) blamed each other for the tire failures. Bridgestone said the problem was that Ford required the tires to be grossly under-inflated (possibly to make the ride more comfortable, or perhaps to compensate for design problems in the SUV). Ford argued that the problem was in the tires. They said similar problems had not occurred in Explorers equipped with tires made by other companies. While it is still not clear what part of the blame was due to the Explorer's design, and what part was due to faults in the Firestone tires, Bridgestone quickly sent new tires from Japan to the U.S. and other countries by air freight to replace the tires that were thought to be defective. Compensation was immediately paid to accident victims and their families, regardless of the amounts involved. By taking quick actions, even when it was not clear the tire maker had done anything wrong, Bridgestone was able to save the Bridgestone and Firestone brand images, and the company's world-wide consolidated sales and profits were sustained.

In contrast another prominent company severely damaged its reputation by covering up problems with its products. Beginning in 2000, and continuing for the next few years, a stream of reports suggested that Mitsubishi Motors had been covering up defects in its cars and trucks since the 1980s. Some 800,000 vehicles were affected, and people were seriously injured and even killed as a result of the defective cars and trucks. Some of Mitsubishi's former senior managers were eventually arrested for having been involved in covering up the defects. In 2004 the sale of Mitsubishi vehicles dropped 37% from the previous year. The company will find it very difficult, if not impossible, to rebuild its brand equity.

Many companies have established corporate brand management offices to maintain their brand equity. The major responsibility of these offices is to protect brand equity by setting rules for the use of corporate logos, and by controlling the use of corporate logos for products and services. These offices are also responsible for monitoring and coordinating the corporate creed and corporate culture, corporate financial performance (e.g. the growth rate, return on investment, return on equity, and economic value added), the company's performance in the creation of new markets and technological innovations, and corporate management systems that influence the company or brand image (e.g. human resource management, and corporate communications and disclosures). Some brand management offices are located at the head office, though this is not always the case.

Contingency plans

Even the best companies may find they have launched new products that have defects or other problems. By preparing in advance for this possibility, companies can avoid or minimize their losses. One thing pharmaceutical companies do to limit the damage that might be done due to serious side effects in a new medicine is to carefully collect complaints and reports of unexpected outcomes from doctors and patients. The earlier they respond to a problem, the less harm that will be done. Of course while ethical managers are concerned about the possibility of damage to the firm, their first concern is to prevent possible injuries to customers. In the case of companies making foods, as with those making drugs, product defects may result in the sickness or even death of consumers. Japan's largest dairy products company, Snow Brand Milk Products Co., Ltd., caused widespread suffering and was effectively destroyed as a major independent company because it could not mount a rapid response to a defective dairy product it had put on the market. Bacteria in Snow Brand milk caused more than 14,000 people to become sick. If the company had taken immediate action, fewer people would have been affected. Unfortunately, company managers tried to limit how much product they recalled, and they withheld information about the problem. Snow Brand's market share in Japan dropped from 45% into the single digits, and the company reported losses of over $400 million during the year of the incident.

Still another example of a brand being badly hurt by poor damage control is Perrier. In 1989 Perrier was the leading imported bottled water in the fast growing U.S. market. The brand had a strong connotation of sophistication because of its French origins. It also had an image of being pure and natural. In 1990 an environmental testing laboratory in North Carolina found traces of benzene in a bottle of Perrier – ironically, the laboratory had been using Perrier as a test standard in checking the purity of the local water supply. Perrier officials said the benzene must have entered the water because an employee in North America had made an error in cleaning some of the bottling equipment. A few days later benzene was also found in Perrier bottles in Europe. It turned out that Perrier water was not naturally carbonated, despite claims on the bottles, and that the benzene had contaminated the water during the process of carbonation. There was a worldwide recall of Perrier water. Meanwhile, the U.S. Food and Drug Administration made Perrier stop putting the words "Naturally Sparkling" on its bottles. As a result of all its bad publicity, Perrier sales dropped drastically. In the mid-1990s the company was selling only half as much Perrier-branded water as it had in 1989.

Problems can be classified by where they occur: in the market; in the environment (for example, air or water pollution); or, at the company, for example when a production process is defective, as with Snow Brand and Perrier, or there is an accident or fire). Sometimes the probability of an accident, such as a fire or the financial failure of a business partner, can be estimated. This sort of risk can be covered by insurance or by maintaining a certain level of reserves. Some events, however, such as catastrophic earthquakes or terrorist attacks, cannot be assigned a probability. Finally, there are events that fall between these extremes. With these events it is possible to make partial estimates of probabilities. Figure 9.1 shows a way of thinking about different possible problems.

Opportunities and threats can be classified by the probability that an event will occur, and by the potential magnitude of the event's effects. In Figure 9.1, area A represents events which have a high probability of occurring, and which would have a medium to large impact on the company. These events are subject to regular planning because the probability of the event can be estimated. The company can use insurance or maintain special reserves to cope with the risk. Area B encompasses medium to large impact events that have a small to medium probability of occurring. Contingency plans should also be developed for these events, because the impacts would be fairly large, and the probability of the event occurring is fairly high. Events falling in other

Figure 9.1 Where contingency plans are needed

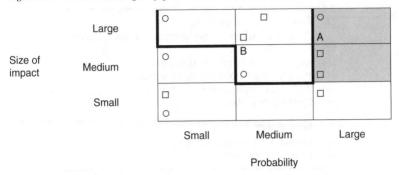

Notes: (1) ◯ = Opportunity ☐ = Threat
    (2) A = Areas appropriate for regular planning
       B = Areas appropriate for contingency planning

Table 9.2 Possible impacts of events

Event	Size of impact	Probability of occurrence (high, medium, low)	Probability of positive effects	Probability of negative effects
(Examples) 1. Development of new technology 2. Serious side effects from new medicine 3. Serious complaints about new product 4. Appearance of rival products 5. Export limitations 6. Rise in price of raw materials				

areas of the figure, that is those that are unlikely to occur and/or would have little impact on the company can be dealt with as they occur.

Table 9.2 shows how, in the case of major events, the size of the effects and the probability that the event will occur can be estimated.

Table 9.3 shows the major elements of a contingency plan: the event, the probability it will occur, its likely impact on corporate performance (including not just the impact on sales or profits, but also impacts on such things as brand equity and the environment), possible triggers for the event (just as an earthquake may lead to a tsunami, there may be

Table 9.3   Contingency plan outline

(1) Assumptions about event Possible event affects performance of the company (2) Probability (3) Impact on corporate performance (4) Warning signs, and timing of action (5) Personnel responsible for watching (6) Contingency plan In case of A In case of B (7) Impact of the plan when implemented (8) Remaining problems

Table 9.4   Identifying events that need to be taken into account

1. Events in past 10 years which had heavy impact on corporate performance

2. Possible events in next 10 years which may have heavy impact on corporate performance
1. General environment 2. Industry and competitors 3. Own product-market strategy 4. Organization, personnel and facilities 5. Operations and financial performance

observable events that would lead up to the event, and how these triggers relate to the size of the event), who is responsible for monitoring for the event and its triggers, and what actions the firm should take (who should do what?). Table 9.4 is another form that can be used to help identify events that could impact corporate performance.

Determining what events to plan for, and estimating their probability can be difficult, but planners say if contingency plans anticipate more than 20% of the events that occur, the plans should be considered successful. Some events, like changes in foreign exchange rates, are virtually certain to occur, and many companies routinely prepare for them. New medicines, unfortunately, are very likely to have side effects, so it is important to collect reports of problems as quickly as possible. It is also important to watch closely for the appearance of rival products after a new product is launched.

It is not enough simply to develop contingency plans, it is also important to keep improving the plans. Past events should be analyzed to identify events which might seriously affect the company's performance. Some events which will impact the future of many companies are already occurring. One example of this would be changes in the population age distribution. We can get a pretty good sense of how many 65-year-olds there will be in 20 years by knowing how many 45-year-olds there are today.

Other means to cope with uncertainty. Aside from developing contingency plans, there are several other ways for a company to cope with uncertainty. One is diversification of the product line. When one project fails, other projects or products can support the company. This assumes, of course, that each product has sufficient scale and is significantly different in demand features from the other products. Car makers may diversify by making various types of cars. Hybrids and compact cars may sell well when gasoline prices are high, SUVS may sell well when gasoline prices are low.

A company's net worth is its final protection against unforeseen events, so the risk associated with a new project should ordinarily be less than the net worth of the company (though there are very few industries, such as commercial aircraft, where the investment required for a new products often exceeds the net worth of even large companies like Boeing). If the investment required for the new product is beyond the amount a company can reasonably risk, it might consider alliances with other companies willing to share the risk.

A company can also hedge its bets, as we have seen, by making sequential decisions in introducing a new product. The new product might initially be sold in just one city, for example, as was done with *USA Today.* If sales are satisfactory then the product can be introduced in other markets. This approach allows the company both to test market acceptance for the product, and to identify problems that can be remedied before a full launch.

Of course, companies have to be highly alert to problems with their products, and respond quickly. As we have seen Snow Brand Dairy products, Mitsubishi Motors, and Perrier severely damaged their brand images because they were insensitive to problems their customers were experiencing.

10
Stopping an NPD Process and Changing Product Mixes

Managers sometimes face the painful necessity of having to stop an NPD process. On other occasions, they may have to divest or discontinue a current product that is no longer successful or that no longer fits the company's strategy. This chapter takes up these situations.

Stopping an NPD process

Sometimes barriers to the NPD process become intractable, or financial projections for the new product look increasingly bleak. This should not be surprising. As we saw in the case of the pharmaceutical industry, for example, the probability that any particular medicine will succeed is only about one in ten thousand. Sometimes market research shows there is less enthusiasm for the new product than had been expected. Those working on the new product have invested much of their time and talent in the new product, and naturally are anxious to see it through to completion. Eventually the process of development reaches a point where a substantial amount of additional money must be invested to continue. If the company is to go ahead with the product it may have to build new production facilities or develop new marketing channels. Managers may decide that further investment is not justified, and stop the process. Many managers find stopping an NPD process to be one of their hardest jobs. There will likely be disagreements between the NPD team and managers.

Researchers in one survey reported that managers differed from NPD team leaders in their assessments of the marketability of a new product 37% of the time. They differed from team leaders in their assessment of the prospects for the technical success of a new product 32% of the time. Managers had less faith in the competence of the researchers than the researchers themselves did 23% of the time. Some 17% of the time researchers said they were unhappy because the firm had decided to use technology from another firm.[74] Disagreements between managers and NPD teams about whether or not to continue investing in the development of a new product is a major source of frustration on both sides. It may be that the NPD team has done a good job, but the product still does not meet expectations. We noted earlier, how in cases like this, senior managers must be careful not to blame the team. If the product was a technical success, even though it failed in the market, it may be appropriate to reward the development team. Successful organizations tend to evaluate processes in NPD as well at outcomes.

Suspension of sales after launch

It is occasionally necessary to suspend sales after a new product has been launched. This happened in the well-publicized case of "New Coke" several years ago. A majority of coke drinkers preferred the old Coke. The traditional Coke was brought back. Even more seriously, a product may turn out to be dangerous. In the late 1980s Showa Denko developed a new process for producing triptofan, an amino acid used as a food supplement. Showa Denko's triptofan was approved by the relevant authorities and placed on the U.S. market in 1988. Unfortunately, the genetic engineering process used by Showa Denko produced a toxin in the triptofan. The toxin caused the deaths of 37 people, and permanently disabled more than 1,500 others. One reason so many people were poisoned was that the triptofan made by the genetic engineering process was not labelled differently from tryptophan produced by conventional methods. As a result it took longer to identify the problem.

Why was Showa Denko allowed to sell its genetically engineered tryptophan without testing its safety? Tryptophan produced by other methods had long been on the U.S. market, and the method by which it was produced was not thought to be a safety factor. Extra safety testing by Showa Denko, however, could have prevented numerous tragedies. It would also have saved the company tremendous damage to its image, not to mention some $2 billion in claims from the people injured and the survivors of those who died.

A similar failure to go beyond minimally required standards to ensure safety also caused widespread tragedy, and eventually bankrupted a respected company, Dow Corning. Dow Corning marketed silicone breast implants in the 1980s and 1990s. The company did not conduct clinical trials of the implants with human subjects because at the time it was not legally required to do so. At the time breast implants were defined as "medical devices," which did not require testing in humans. So the implants were put on the market. By the mid-1990s some 137,000 women claimed they were suffering adverse effects from the implants. Dow Corning was unable to handle all the legal suits against it. The company declared bankruptcy and re-organized. Settlements totaling more than $3 billion were offered to the women.

In 2005, at least two people died from carbon monoxide poisoning caused by defects in Matsushita Panasonic kerosene fan heaters. The company recalled the fan heaters, and repaired or replaced them. The defective fan heaters had all been manufactured between 1985 and 1992, so it was only after 15 to 20 years that the accidents occurred. Even so the company was held responsible. Aside from the cost of notifying people of the recall and paying damages (around $80 million in 2005), Matsushita Panasonic suffered damage to its brand name that hurt all of its products.

These cases suggest at least three points. 1. In addition to the tragedies inflicted on consumers, inadequate attention to safety in introducing a new product can be extraordinarily damaging to a company, destroying its brand image even for unrelated products and costing billions of dollars. 2. Simply following current laws and safety standards may not be enough to prevent these problems. 3. A failure to respond quickly can only make things worse.

A model for monitoring and preparing for post-launch accidents was described in Chapter 9. Damage caused by defective products can be minimized by: (1) Studying past cases of defective products. This can help a firm anticipate future problems. (2) Having a department, such as the claims department or the brand management office, carefully watch for any indications that a product may be defective. These monitors should be independent from the marketing and development departments to ensure objectivity. (3) Preparing an action plan that can be implemented as soon as a problem becomes apparent.

When problems are not corrected

Sometimes small problems are not corrected immediately, but are left to grow, or are repeated until they become extremely damaging for the company. Recent examples include Enron in the U.S. and, as we saw in Chapter 8, Snow Brand Dairy Products in Japan. Some wonder if Mitsubishi Motors can recover after its recurring failures to deal with an accumulation of relatively small problems over the years. Why do firms fail to correct problems right away? It is possible to gain some insights into this question from theories on the formation of attitudes and on corporate culture. The attitudes of managers about how to deal with product problems are formed by three factors (a) their general information or education about right and wrong, (b) the system of sanctions enforced in the company, (c) learning from experience.[75] A repeated failure to take action on defective products and unethical behavior generally starts from small events. When these failures are not discovered by higher levels of management or the monitoring department, and if they happen to increase the short-term profit or performance of those covering them up, they are likely to be repeated until eventually they cause large scale problems that can't be ignored. In the beginning those involved avoid sanctions by covering up the problem. The cover ups will continue as long as the people covering up the problems are not caught and punished by senior management, the claims department, auditors, or outside directors. Unethical behavior expands as small unethical actions are positively reinforced. We discussed failures due to "group think" in Chapter 1. Group think applies to major decision-making events. Here we see decision failures that incrementally grow through repetition, and spread like a cancer in the company.

Eliminating products from the product mix

Obviously a company has to take action when a product is a clear failure or poses hazards to the public. A less straightforward issue is what to do when there is nothing wrong with a product, but the product does not fit in with the current or future strategy of the company. The product may even be modestly profitable. In a situation like this some companies will continue offering the product. This approach tends to be followed by Hitachi and Toshiba. These companies produce everything from nuclear power generators to automated washing machines. They define their contribution to society as providing high quality products embodying the latest technology to consumers and offering attractive and stable jobs to their employees. While they seek profits, this is not their highest goal. They seldom divest.

A larger number of major companies, however, take a more strategic approach to their product mix. These companies find that it sometimes makes sense to eliminate a product, even when there is nothing wrong with the product, and it is not losing money. More and more companies began a strategic reshuffling of their product mixes in the early 2000s, as the world economy entered a period of slow economic growth. Pruning and simplifying their product mix allowed these companies to focus on what they could do most efficiently. The dramatic reshuffling of the product line at ICI was described in Chapter 1, and the case of GE under Jack Welch is well known. IBM sold its PC division to Lenovo, and Dupont discontinued the production of Nylon. Many companies have established basic policies to help them carry out a consistent and successful reshuffling of their product mixes.

Strategic models to guide product mix changes

1. Be first or second in market share. Some firms, notably General Electric and Emerson Electric, have a policy of divesting businesses where they can not be first or second in market share. Other huge firms such as Microsoft and Intel also follow this strategy, but even smaller and medium sized companies can follow this strategy, as long as their products are sufficiently differentiated. Examples include Mabuchi Motor (which make small electric motors) and Minebea (which makes miniature ball bearings).

2. Follow the "smile curve" principle. According to the smile curve principle, the largest profits are at the two ends of the value chain. Profits can be maximized by specializing on these ends. IBM, for example, was initially an integrated producer of PCs and PC operating systems. Later IBM outsourced the two ends of the smile curve. Production of semiconductors went to Intel and the development of operating systems went to Microsoft. IBM stuck to the design, production and marketing of the PC. As it turned out, IBM made the wrong bet in this industry. The PCs became low-margin commodities. Chips and software became high margin differentiated products. IBM eventually sold its PC business to a Chinese company. Now IBM is primarily a service company. It designs the software for mobile phones and digital cameras; designs total computer systems for banks, and operates the computer systems for delivery companies and some other businesses. It is still a huge company, with annual sales of well over $100 billion.

3. Determine if your product is based on a modular architecture or an integral architecture. With a modular architecture product the interface of components is standardized, so production or assembly is relatively easy. The product tends to be a commodity, where price is the most important basis for competition. The personal computer is a typical example of a modular product. Large production volume leads to lower costs, and so is the key to competitiveness. As a result, production is outsourced to electric manufacturing services companies (EMS). While these companies do not have well-known brand names, they can be quite large. Celestica, for example, had sales of $8.8 billion, and 46,000 employees in 2004.

Integral architecture products do not have standardized component interfaces. Special and high performance components are designed by the assemblers and by component suppliers. The production of the final product requires specialized competencies. Automobile production is a typical case. Competition is shielded to some extent from price competition because the product is differentiated. Fords are seen as being different from Hyundais or Chryslers. Because of the differentiation, outstanding car companies like Toyota rarely have to discount the prices of their cars. High technology components also tend to have an integral architecture, so the suppliers can also gain high profits. If its production process is based on an integral architecture, and is highly sophisticated, a business can fully reap the advantages of integral architecture. Shinetsu Chemical is doing this in producing silicon wafers for semiconductors. Many chemical industries use integral architecture production processes.

To succeed in a modular type product industry, a company has either to produce on a large scale or else to specialize at both ends of the value chain, outsourcing production. To succeed in an integral architecture product industry, a company has to have (a) an accumulation of advanced technological knowledge, (b) a skilled and devoted labor force, (c) an accumulation of the shared knowledge required to produce sophisticated products, and (d) policies respecting employees and encouraging long time employment, so the company can retain the required high levels of manual skills. Toyota and Honda have these features.

A company should consider divesting products that do not fit its strengths whether those strengths are as a modular or as an integral producer.

4. Attacking the high end from the bottom.   Low-end products can sometimes take market share away from high-end products.[76] Often the firms that dominate an industry have little interest in competing against the upstart firms that begin selling low-status, low-profit products. The major producers of motorcycles like Triumph, BMW and Harley Davidson, were not too concerned when Honda began selling motor scooters and very small motorcycles to people who would not otherwise have bought motorcycles at all. Eventually, Honda acquired the expertise to challenge the other firms in the production and marketing of high-end motorcycles as well. Sony entered the market for home entertainment equipment with cheap transistor radios, but eventually became a major competitor for such established giants as RCA and GE. As mini computers gained in capacity, they came to replace mainframes. Discount airlines like Southwest Air and JetBlue took markets from the large established carriers like American and United Airlines.

The strategy of entering markets from the bottom is often made possible by technological innovation, including advances in information systems. Incumbent firms can sometimes cope with these attacks by divesting high-end products that seem to have declining prospects (e.g. as when Nikon stopped making film cameras), merging with other companies to gain market power (e.g. as when Konica and Minolta merged in 2003), or by quickly diversifying into low-end products (as when Fuji Film introduced the single use camera).

If a firm's longer-term strategy does not call for the eventual abandonment of high-end products, it may be a serious mistake to cut a low-end product in the same product line. The firm could be making itself vulnerable to competitors attacking from the bottom.

5. PPM strategy (also called BCG strategy, growth share matrix). This strategy, known by a variety of names, was especially popular two or three decades ago. The gist of the strategy was to categorize products based on their relative market share and market growth rate, and then use this categorization to decide where the company should invest. "Stars" are products that have a large relative market share (and thus are expected to generate a lot of cash) and also are experiencing rapid market growth. A diversified company should always have star products. "Cash cows" are products that generate a lot of cash, but are not experiencing rapid market growth. These products should be "milked" for all they are worth. Profits should be taken from them, but as little as possible should be invested in them. Of course, market shares and growth rates change over time, so stars eventually become cash cows. "Question marks" are products that are experiencing rapid market growth, but that have a relatively low market share. They consume a lot of money, but don't generate much profit. They may become stars (and thus later cash cows), but must be studied carefully to make sure they are worth the investment needed to grow market share. The risk is that they will become "dogs." The dogs may not consume a large amount of money, but they do tie up resources in a business with little growth potential. These businesses are good candidates for divestiture.

The PPM strategy can give planners some useful insights, but a risk with this strategy is that it may lead a company to neglect its cash cows, and lose them prematurely. Black & Decker used this strategy, and ended up losing market share to invading Japanese electric tool producers.[77]

6. Synergy.   Many companies make it a policy to divest businesses that lack synergy with the company's other business units. Aoki Construction Company divested Westin Hotels and Resorts, Kawai Musical Instruments Co. sold off its semiconductor business. From the standpoint of synergy, one can think of a product mix as being (a) technology related (TR), (b) marketing related (MR), marketing and technology related (MTR), or unrelated (U). Considerable research has been done on the performance of firms with product mixes falling into these categories. Generally, this research finds that MTR firms offer the best performance, while U firms offer the worst. This is particularly true during periods of slow growth, which is why there were so many divestitures in Japan during the 1990s, and in the U.S. a few years later. It appears that a technology or marketing related product mix offers the company economies of scale and enables the company to develop stronger core competencies. A similar logic can guide new product development and the divestiture of current products.

7. Decreasing the number of brands or products.   Even if none of strategies mentioned above is a policy of a company, the company may find it useful ito reduce the number of its brands or products. When a company has too many brands, its products occupy too much shelf space in retail stores, and also make it difficult for the customer to select the most appropriate brand. For this reason Shiseido went to considerable expense a few years ago to eliminate many of its cosmetics brands. Sometimes an old brand should be withdrawn when a new one is introduced. This is what Asahi Breweries did when it launched its new Super Dry beer.

Methods of withdrawing brands or products

Firms can use a number of different methods in addressing the problem of unprofitable brands or products: (1) Close the plants making the product, (2) Switch to other products, (3) Sell the business and plants to another company, (4) Form an alliance with other companies, (5) Merge with another company.

1. Closing plants. When Teijin decided to stop producing acetate fiber (a man-made silk) in 2002, it simply closed its acetate production plant, and abandoned the production equipment. Similarly, a couple of years later Sony closed down its color television plants in Wales, in Pittsburgh, and in San Diego. In cases like these, a critical problem is dealing with the employees. Usually the company tries to keep as many employees as possible by transferring them to other departments. But sometimes this is not possible. If the employees cannot be retained, allowances may have to be paid to them

2. Switching products at a plant. If the plants switch to the production of similar products, the employees can be kept. Sometimes, however, the new product (or new production methods) will require different skills. This happened at the General Motors-Toyota NUMMI plant in California, as will be discussed later. Often there will be a complete shift in the type of products made at a plant. This happened, for example, at NEC's Tochigi Plant in Japan. The Tochigi plant had been producing about ten sets of industrial machinery and medical equipment a month. Its employees were specialists in the software used in operating industrial machinery and in electrical engineering. They were involved in a very low volume production process. In 1997 the plant was converted, and began to produce about 100,000 lithium batteries for cellular telephones each month. The plant now required expertise in chemical materials and mass production technology. The skills of the plant's 280 employees were no longer needed. Out of the 280, 110 retired, 30 were transferred to other plants, and 140 applied for jobs at the new battery plant. The 140 applicants each received a year of training at an NEC plant in another city. Since the other city was rather distant, the applicants stayed there in groups of three or four at houses rented by the company. During the year, NEC paid their full salary, housing costs, and travel expenses for two trips home.

3. Divestiture. The plant, product, and related patents might be sold to another company, with the employees also going to the new company. In Chapter 1 we saw how this happened at ICI. Divestitures and acquisitions have frequently been used by GE to reshuffle its product mix. In the 1980s 37,000 people left GE along with businesses that were sold to other companies. Jack Welch divested divisions that made television sets, semiconductors, and aerospace equipment. On the other hand, GE's Japanese rivals, Hitachi and Toshiba, did not divest products in a major way. This would have been contrary to their basic corporate values.

Konica Minolta was forced to give up some of its major products because of strategic and operating failures. The company decided in 2006 to sell its digital camera business to Sony, and to discontinue the production of film and film cameras. This was despite a long and distinguished history in the photographic film and camera industries.[78] Konica, one of the firms that had merged to form Konica Minolta, had produced film and cameras for more than 100 years. The company was the first in Japan to sell an easy-to-use popular camera, the first to sell color film, and the first to produce an auto-focus camera. Minolta had marketed the world's first coated lens and the first double lens reflex camera. One of the events that damaged the brand was the production of defective color film. Users cannot judge the quality of film by looking at it. Often the pictures they take cannot be retaken, so they have to trust the quality of the film based on its brand image. After allowing defective film to go into the market, the company was never able to recover its market share – which dropped from about 50% of the Japanese market to about 20%. And, while Konica Minolta was the first to sell an auto-focus camera, its rival Canon soon entered the market with a better auto-focus camera. The Konica Minolta camera could not sense distances at night, the Canon version could. Konica Minolta had acquired a film developing network in the U.S. to strengthen its presence there, but was not able to compete effectively against other companies that provided much faster and cheaper services. In the fiscal year ending in March 2005 Konica Minolta lost more than $70 million in its camera business, and more than $10 million in its photo business. Konica Minolta's digital camera division, which had only a 5% market share, is being sold to Sony. Sony will handle the maintenance of the digital cameras, and other companies will take over the mini film development laboratories. Konica Minolta will lose about one third of its sales volume (about $2.5 billion in 2004, out of total sales of 1,000 billion yen). The number of its employees will drop from 33,000 worldwide to about 29,300. Many of them will take early retirement. The company now plans to concentrate on non-consumer businesses such as optics, display devices, and medical imaging.

In 2005 the German company Siemens went so far as to pay another company, BenQ of Taiwan, some $300 million to take over its mobile telephone division. This was better than continuing to sustain losses in this product line. The costs of simply closing down the division (primarily from meeting obligations to employees) would have been even higher.

4. Alliances. Two or more companies may work together to achieve economies of scale. Sony, for example, is cooperating with Samsung to produce television LCD panels. This has been advantageous to both companies, even though they are fierce rivals in many other markets. In semiconductor production, scale is especially important. Construction of a semiconductor foundry using next generation process technology requires an investment of a billion dollars or more. So Hitachi, Toshiba and Renesas Technology (itself a joint venture between Hitachi and Mitsubishi Electric Corporation) began in 2006 to consider establishing a jointly owned independent semiconductor foundry business to produce advanced system LSI products for all of the partner firms.

Case: NUMMI. A Joint venture revives a closed plant.   In the early 1980s General Motors employed about 7,000 workers to produce Buicks at its Fremont, California plant. In 1982, however, the plant was closed and all of its employees were laid off. In 1983 General Motors signed a "Memorandum of Understanding" with Toyota to form a joint venture to take over the plant, and in 1984 NUMMI (New United Motor Manufacturing, Inc.) was established. Some 2,500 of the former GM employees were hired, and in 1985 NUMMI began producing Chevrolet Novas and Toyota Corollas. Since then Fremont has produced more than five million vehicles, including Geo Prizms, Toyota compact pickup trucks, the Toyota Tacoma, the Pontiac Vibe and the Toyota Voltz (a right hand drive model made for export to Japan). It now has more than 5,000 employees.

GM provided the initial capital for NUMMI. It also provided skilled workers, basic knowledge and sales channels. Toyota brought key elements of the famous Toyota production system to the joint venture. Toyota installed 170 new industrial robots and invested 40 billion yen (about $380 million) to modernize the plant's equipment. Two hundred and fifty foremen and other key workers were sent in groups of 30 to Toyota plants to learn the Toyota production system. They learned, for example, how to continuously improve the production system by generating ideas through group discussions ("Kaizen" meetings). Two or three of these meetings are held each week. At GM making changes in the operating system had always been the job of engineers. This changed at NUMMI, and the engineers were re-educated to welcome input from blue collar workers. The "line stop" system was also introduced. With the line stop system workers have the authority to stop the assembly line if they see a problem. Before, if a worker stopped the line, he or she could be punished, or even fired. Job titles were abolished, and employees were now expected to do any job. At the management level, group decision-making was introduced.[79]

5. *Survival by merger or acquisition.* Many companies that are running into difficulty merge rather than shutting down operations. Two of Japanese largest steel companies, NKK and Kawasaki, for example, were both losing money at rate that would have been difficult to sustain. The two companies merged in 2002 to form the JFE Group. After the merger the companies were able to reduce their total number of employees through an early retirement system. They also eliminated unprofitable businesses. In 2005 JFE had a net income of nearly $3 billion. Similarly, major steelmakers in the U.S., Europe, and other countries have merged into Mittal Steel.

Eliminating products from a product mix

A systematic process that can be used in eliminating an existing product from a company's product mix is shown in Figure 10.1.

Some additional points on the elimination of a product should also be taken into account:

1. Usually there will be resistance to the decision. Dropping the product will decrease the power of some managers, and it may eliminate jobs. So, there has to be some political power behind the decision. The decision should be based on a clear strategic policy, such as one of those described in Section III of this chapter. The decision might be justified, for example, based on a company policy to drop all products that are not first or second in their market.
2. It is easier for companies that frequently introduce new products to eliminate older products. These companies can transfer employees who are no longer needed for the eliminated product to work on new products. This suggests a virtuous cycle: the more new products a company introduces, the better able it is to eliminate less profitable products. The company profits both from introducing the new products, and from eliminating the less successful older products.
3. A number of excuses are commonly used to avoid dropping products.[80] It might be argued, for example, that it is possible to revitalize the product, or that the company needs a full product line to attract customers to the company's stores. Some may point out that the product covers its overhead cost, and argue that if the product is dropped, overhead costs will be higher for other products.

   While there may be some truth to these arguments, they should be looked at very critically. Too often managers are just avoiding difficult

Figure 10.1 Product elimination process

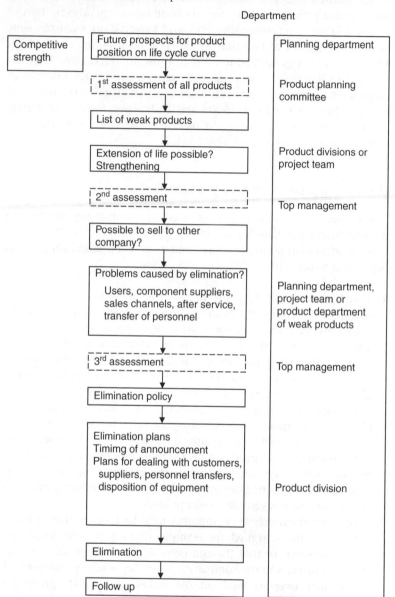

Note: Based on observations of many cases. Also draws on Baker and Hart (1999).

decisions in the vain hope that sales will increase in the future. No one likes to let people go or abandon parts of the company's tradition, but sometimes it is necessary for the health of the firm.

Product and brand elimination problems

Although a company should not allow possible problems to deter it from eliminating products or brands when this is in the best interest of the company, it does need to be prepared to deal with the problems that may result. We surveyed a large sample of managers about these problems. The results are shown in Table 10.1. The most important of

Table 10.1 Problems experienced in cutting products

Items	% mentioning
1) Relations with market	
1. Customer want continued supply	65.19
2. Need for after sales service	40.51
3. Relations with sales channels	29.11
4. Relations with suppliers	15.82
5. Competitors take over the market	22.15
2) Implications of changes in product mix	
6. Sales decrease	42.41
7. No product to replace the cut product	24.05
8. Product needed to support other products	20.89
9. Brand value of the company declines	17.72
10. Cut turns out to be premature response to routine fluctuations in demand	13.92
11. Cut premature, product could have been revitalized	16.46
3) Dealing with capacity that is no longer needed	
12. Opposition of other departments, especially marketing	22.15
13. Personnel management problems. Opposition by employees	18.99
14. Disposing of remaining inventory	25.32
15. Unused facilities	21.52
16. Investment in research becomes useless. Need to maintain related technology	15.82

Notes:
1. For details about the sample, see Table 1.4.
2. Respondents were asked: "What problems have you experienced when eliminating products. Please select the seven most important."

the problems mentioned concern relations with the market (including suppliers and customers), adjusting to the implications of changes in the product mix, and handling capacity within the company that is no longer needed.

1. Relationships with customers and vendors. Some customers may depend on the discontinued product to make their own products. In such cases the company should give the customer as much advance notification of the decision as possible. The company should also make every effort to help the customer switch to alternative components. If the product is a consumer good, consumers might have developed a special attachment to the product, as in the case of cosmetics and soft drinks. Special efforts should be made to transfer their loyalty to new products. In the case of durable goods such as automobiles and appliances, the company has to ensure that an inventory of parts is maintained for the expected life of the product. The company discontinuing a product should also be sensitive to the situation facing its suppliers.

Even after the product is dropped, the company will have to continue to support it. It will have to ensure that there is a supply of spare parts and service for the expected life of the product. If the product is found to be defective, the company may have to repair or replace it. As we saw, customers experienced serious problems with Matsushita Panasonic kerosene fan heaters more than 10 years after the product was sold, and Matsushita Panasonic had to take responsibility for these problem.

2. Product mix. When products or brands are eliminated there may be a temporary decrease in sales volume and the number of employees, though, as we saw with ICI, profits may be maintained. If the new products are successful, sales and profits will soon recover and increase, as was the case with Nissan and Asahi Brewery. In this sense, the elimination of old products and the development of new products are closely related. Eliminating the old products, rather than trying to salvage them, makes it easier to concentrate on more promising new products.

3. Dealing with excess capacity. After a product or brand is eliminated, the company will have to deal with the facilities and employees it no longer needs. When Nissan had to close two large plants in Japan to cut costs, the company was able to minimize the impact on employees by giving them time to decide whether they wanted to prepare for retirement or move to another plant. Perhaps the best outcome is when some or all of the capabilities used for the eliminated brand or product can be transferred to new products, or to a new company. Nissan was able to sell its missile production system to another company. Konica Minolta, as we saw above, sold its digital camera business to Sony. Jack Welch took General Electric out of the semiconductor, home appliance, air conditioner, television, coal mining and other businesses, and reduced the number of GE employees by 100,000. Most of these GE employees, however, were able to keep their jobs at the new companies that took over their businesses. Welch argues that it is cruel to bind employees to hopeless businesses. He believes it is far kinder to let the employees move to companies or activities where they will be valued. Welch sold and bought about 100 companies. In order to help maintain the morale and motivation of GE's remaining employees, he initiated the six sigma movement and trained several thousand employees at the company's training center.

11
Recent Trends

In Chapter 1 we described how current trends mean that successful NPD in today's environment requires companies to have more creative R&D organizations, use information technology (IT) more extensively, develop new products more quickly, base NPD on core competencies, develop products for global markets, ensure that their product mixes are in line with corporate strategies, and develop environmentally friendly products. We have already discussed creativity in R&D organizations (Chapter 7), core competency-based NPD (Chapter 6), developing products for global markets (Chapter 4), and the strategic restructuring of product mixes (Chapter 10). We also touched on ways to speed the NPD process in Chapter 3. In this chapter we will further discuss the need for faster development. Then we will take up the use of IT in NPD, and the development of environmentally friendly products.

Faster development

Speed is crucial in today's fast changing environments. The successful organization has to create many useful ideas, start to develop them quickly, move expeditiously through the development process to product launch, and then immediately follow up as needed after the launch. "Speed" in this sense is clearly not the premature introduction of new products pressed by autocratic senior managers or irresponsible public organizations. We saw in Chapter 1 how this sort of speed can be as devastating for a company as a failure to respond to changes in markets.

Miles and Snow categorize companies into four types, based on the strategic decision model the company uses:[81] (1) "Reactors" passively adapt to changes in the environment. They do not have a consistent strategy based on a clear vision. (2) "Defenders" emphasize improvements in efficiency within a definite domain. They do not explore new opportunities. (3) "Prospectors" explore new opportunities, are sensitive to changes in the market, introduce many new products and change their organizational structures and systems to meet new demands. (4) "Analyzers" engage in both aggressive strategic action and defensive activities. They enter new domains, but they also improve their efficiency and systems within their present domain. Although Miles and Snow don't say that the prospector and analyzer models are necessarily superior, these models entail faster NPD. And, it seems clear that in fast changing environments they are most likely to prevail. In the cases we described, GE and Emerson Electric were winners, and Westinghouse was a loser. Canon was a winner, and Konica Minolta was a loser. GE, Emerson, and Canon were all faster to *satisfy customers needs* with a new product – even when, as in the case of GE with the MRI and Canon with the auto-focus camera, they were not the first to put the new product on the market.

Five factors seem to be most important in making a firm a fast mover: (1) a top down (but not authoritarian) approach to decision-making, (2) a strong top management structure, (3) a strong head office and strong strategic planning departments, (4) an innovative corporate culture, and (5) core competencies that allow quick implementation. An innovative corporate culture encourages risk taking behavior. We will not go into detail on this here, since it is treated at length in another book by one of the authors.[82] We have already discussed the need for strong top down strategy formation and decision-making in Chapter 6 (see Table 6.1), but will elaborate a bit further on this here.

Top down process for making strategic decisions. Some management scholars advocate "bottom-up" or "middle-up" decision-making models. With these models strategic ideas come from the product divisions or middle management, and the role of top management is simply to integrate all the ideas that come up from below. We do not believe these models are well-suited to the effective management of NPD. One problem is that bottom or middle-up decision-making processes are not conducive to the elimination of unprofitable products. Division managers tend to fight desperately to avoid losing their products. Another problem is that these models make it difficult for a company to initiate risky new strategies. Coordinated action backed by strong company-resources has to be directed from above. As we have seen, Matsushita Panasonic experienced some of the problems caused by using a bottom up approach. As a result, the president of the company adopted a top down process in 2000. Company performance improved dramatically.[83] We argue that while the delegation of authority may be effective for operational decisions, it does not lead to innovative and quick strategic decisions.

Small top management team. Effective top management teams in charge of general management tend to be small, consisting of only four or five members. They meet frequently and make the strategic decisions for the company. The team members are experts in what the company does, but they are *not* representatives of the product divisions. This is in contrast to a style of top management where there is a management committee consisting of members from the company's product divisions. In committees made up of product division managers, decision-making tends to be based on consensus. Decision are often politically based – "help me get what I want for my department, and I will help you get what you want for your department." In contrast, effective top management teams are more likely to look to what is good for the company as a whole. A number of very successful companies use this form of management, including Emerson Electric and Alcan. This form of management was also used by Sony and Honda when those companies were still managed by their founders – and were still enjoying their greatest success.

Strong strategic planning department. Companies that are good at NPD tend to have strong strategic planning departments. Canon is a good example. Canon's strategic planning department collects strategic information, and advises top management on strategic issues. With the help of this department Canon has been able to take decisive action in response to a fast changing environment a number of times. We have seen how they developed copiers and personal copiers. We have also discussed how they were able to cut out unpromising product lines, such as personal computers, word processors, and liquid crystal displays, despite having invested huge amounts of money in developing these products. Several aspects of the NPD process are centralized at Canon. The company has centralized research laboratories, and a centralized marketing department.

Another very successful company, South Korea's Samsung Electronics, has strong strategic planning groups at its head office. One of these groups evaluates the company's product mix, making recommendations about which products should be eliminated or transferred to subsidiaries. A second group is made up of high caliber staff members who explore corporate strategies for the future, and examine opportunities in foreign countries. After 2 to 4 years, some members of this group are transferred to the groups implementing their recommendations. A third group collects market information, giving emphasis to the behavior of competitors. This group constructs global information networks. The three groups at Samsung provide strategic information to the top management team, making it possible for them to make well-informed aggressive decisions.

To be sure, we have seen examples of companies that made very quick NPD decisions, but where the decisions were misguided. The problem often was that these decisions were based on insufficient or inaccurate information. The decisions tended to be made by authoritarian CEOs or top-management groups afflicted with "group think." To avoid this, companies need competent staff members who collect as much relevant information as possible. A discussion of how to recruit, motivate, and retain the most competent people for strategic planning groups is beyond the scope of this book, but two points can quickly be made here.

(1) Outstanding companies have good reputations. This generates a virtuous cycle for them. The good reputation allows them to attract good employees. This gives them high quality human resources, which results in good performance. The good performance, in turn, enhances the company's reputation. Companies like Canon and Samsung are currently benefiting from this sort of virtuous cycle.

(2) Companies that are successful in NPD tend to be generous towards failure. As we saw in Chapter 2, Canon experienced a major failure in the development of its Syncroreader some years ago. This was the system that allowed audio recordings to be made on the back of letters. It was an interesting product, but few customers were willing to pay $1,000 for the machines needed to read and write such letters. Rather than punishing others for the failure of the product in the market, Canon's president himself took the blame for the failure. At Samsung, up to two failures are allowed (but not three).[84]

Core competencies and speed in implementation. One technique used to accelerate the development of a new product is concurrent engineering, as was discussed in Chapter 3. With concurrent engineering work on design, production, components and marketing, are done simultaneously, rather than sequentially. This, of course, requires close cooperation between various departments in the company, and also with suppliers and other associated companies.

To succeed with NPD in a fast-paced environment, firms have to develop competencies in concurrent engineering and in specific aspects of the products they are producing. Sometimes technological changes drastically change planning cycle times. In the case of film cameras the planning cycle was 2 years. For digital cameras it is only 3 months. Konica Minolta's century plus experience in producing film cameras did not help much in this new environment, and the company ended up turning over its camera business to Sony. Sony did not have much experience with cameras, but it did have competencies that allowed it to rapidly develop electronic products like the digital camera. As we have seen, Canon, another old film camera company, aggressively developed new core competencies that allowed it to have continued success with cameras, as it also moved into other industries.

Information technology (IT)

The literature on IT is very large, so here we will simply summarize its impact on various aspects of NPD.

Searching for new opportunities. IT provides a tremendous capacity to store and retrieve information. This information is broadly used by companies trying to identify the "seeds" and "needs" for new products. It is easy, for example, for firms to review claims listed in new patents, and to use these claims to come up with ideas for new products. Companies like Walmart and Seven-Eleven have thrived, in part, because of their effective use of POS (point of sales) information collected within their stores – this information tells them what the market wants. It also gives them rapid information about changes in demand. Of course, in-store POS information does not identify opportunities for products that are not currently sold. Because of this, Seven Eleven's head office takes responsibility for exploring opportunities in new areas, and then sends its recommendations to the stores.

New IT products. IT is big business, and so is the development of new IT products. Companies like IBM, NEC and Fujitsu have sales of over $100 billion each in this industry. In 2005 Google had sales of $4 billion and profits of $1 billion. Only 3 years earlier, Google's sales and profits were only one tenth these amounts. Growth continues, as Google constantly develops new products by which firms can advertise on the internet. This is not just a U.S. phenomenon. Rakuten in Japan had sales of $1.5 billion and profits of half a billion dollars in 2005.

Raketen's products include the provision of information on commerce, stock share trading, and travel. Other internet entrepreneurial firms are thriving in Europe, China and elsewhere.

Designing new products. Computers are frequently used for design and simulations. Simulations can be used, for example, to analyze the characteristics of materials. Many manufacturing companies, including very small ones, use CAD/CAM. Design information is also exchanged between component suppliers and assemblers through an extra-net system. This allows component suppliers to cooperate in the design of new products to a much greater extent than in the past.

IT has allowed remarkable advances in the design of production processes. Take the case of INCS Inc, for example. This is a Japanese venture company that was started in 1990, and now has about 300 employees, most of whom are engineers. INCS's main business is the design and production of molds used in making cellular telephones. An analysis showed that the production of a mold comprised about 1,000 processes. The company found that some 500 of these processes could be done by computer. Thanks to a process redesign INCS was able to reduce its production time from 45 days to about 6 days.

Internal communications. E-mail, teleconferencing, video conferencing, data sharing systems and other information technologies have drastically improved internal communications in companies. These technologies allow NPD teams to work together from different sites, sometimes at locations thousands of miles apart. It also makes it possible for researchers to solicit new ideas through the internet. As a result, YuzoYoshikuni, an NTT researcher, was able not only develop an important new technology, but also to win an academic prize in the process. Yoshikuni was stymied in his research on optical fiber connections. Through NTT's intranet he was given a breakthrough idea by a person working in another section of the company. With this input Yoshikuni was able to develop an important new optical fiber connection device. Takeda Pharmaceutical Company has 1,700 medical representatives in Japan. Thanks to IT, Takeda can instantly deliver information to the representative's personal computers. This includes information on new dugs, newly discovered effects of existing drugs, and case studies of sales successes and failures. This system has not only allowed the company to increase its sales, but has also helped it to become more efficient. Takeda was able to reduce the number of middle managers it needs. It also was able to increase the number of its sales offices, so they can be closer to doctors.

Advertising.　The internet is widely used for the advertising and direct sale of new products. When a team plans to use the internet to market and sell a new product, however, it does need to take careful account of the fact that consumers will be more systematically comparing prices with rival products than would be true with other means of distribution. The team also has to make sure that an appropriate distribution and transportation system has been established.

In our survey we asked managers several questions about how their company uses IT in new product development. The results are shown in Table 11.1.

The survey shows the importance of information obtained through the internet in identifying needs for new products. Nearly half of our respondents indicated that responses to home pages, e-marketing experiences, and virtual community information are important in

Table 11.1　IT and new product development

Item	% Selecting
Exploring opportunities	
1. Consumer needs suggested by responses to home page, e-marketing, virtual communities, etc.	45.39
2. E-mail orders and complaints	21.71
3. Analysis of POS data and customer data base	21.05
New products with IT content	(not in survey)
Improving internal exchange of information	
4. Improved communications through IT	71.05
5. Internet exchange of design charts with component suppliers and others	23.03
Simulations, etc.	
6. Use of CAD/CAM	61.84
7. Physical simulations (product designs, medical effects, etc.)	28.29
8. Economic and financial simulations	23.68
9. Use in factor analysis, conjoint analysis and other modeling	15.13

Notes:
1. For details about the sample, see Table 1.4.
2. Respondents were asked to select the five most important items.

identifying consumer needs. Around a fifth also mentioned e-mail orders and complaints, and about a fifth mentioned the analysis of POS data and computerized customer data bases. More than 70% said improved communications within the firm due to IT had been an important contributor to NPD. This may be especially true now that it is easier to protect confidentially through the use of new encryption technologies.

The use of IT in factor analysis and conjoint analysis was mentioned as important by about 15% of our respondents. CAD/CAM is widely (and effectively) used in the design of new products. Nearly a quarter of our respondents said that the electronic exchange of design diagrams between component suppliers and assemblers was important in their NPD processes. These electronic exchanges facilitate the use of "design-in," or concurrent engineering. Internet communications also makes it possible to have design centers in the fast-growing markets of India and China. Physical simulations can replace experiments, saving researchers both time and money.

Environmentally friendly products

Consumer attitudes are rapidly shifting to a preference for environmentally friendly products and sustainable growth. Care for the environment is seen as a social responsibility of business. This implies that companies should sacrifice short-range profits to respond to the needs of society. Three areas of social responsibility are shown in Table 11.2. The table indicates the degrees to which certain behaviors are seen as required, desirable, undesirable or entirely unacceptable.

Some things companies do are regarded as completely unacceptable. Indeed, they are against the law. Examples would include paying bribes, knowingly making dangerous products, or falsifying financial reports. Other things might be widely regarded by the public as undesirable, but nonetheless are legal. Examples might include laying off workers or causing pollution that is noticeable, but within legally allowable limits. A firm may be criticized for these actions, but arguments could be made that they are necessary for some greater good, such as the survival of the firm (and the economic benefits it provides) or to keep prices low for consumers. There are also actions that are regarded as desirable, though they are not mandatory. Examples would include making donations for community events or to non-profit organizations. These actions might be praised in the media, though some would question whether it is fair for shareholders to have some of their

Table 11.2 Areas of social responsibility

Area	Social acceptance	Examples of behavior	Who/what impacted	Related to business operations
Charitable contributions	Desirable	Aid to NPOs Community donations	Public	No
Social and environmental responsibility	Mandatory	Legally required recycling of products Employment of disabled	Physical and social environment	Yes
	Undesirable	Unregulated environmental pollution		Yes
Corporate ethics	Unacceptable	Bribery False financial reporting	Stake holders	No

wealth given away without their consent to causes espoused by company management. On the other hand these gifts may be regarded as good investments in public relations and employee morale. Laws and regulatory standards may require a firm to recycle or severely limit the generation of pollution. A question for managers is whether or not to spend more company resources than is necessary to meet legal requirements. As we have seen, adherence to legal requirements did not protect Showa Denko and Dow Corning from being held responsible for the harm done to consumers by their actions. Moreover, it seems likely that legal requirements and the public standards of acceptable behavior will become increasingly stringent. It may make sense for firms to be seen as being ahead of these trends, rather than being dragged along by them.

Setting standards for the environment. Any new product is likely to have an impact on the environment. The production and/or use of the product may emit CO_2 or other air pollutants. It may contaminate water supplies or do something else that hurts the environment. These effects have to be considered well before the product is launched.

To cover all the environmental impacts of a product it is necessary to make a life cycle assessment. Ways of doing this are discussed below.

Minimizing environmental impacts. A number of things can be done to minimize the environmental impact of a new product. During the design process attention should be paid to limiting the materials used for the new product. It may be possible to find ways to extend the life of the product by replacing some parts. The body of Fuji's single use camera, for example, can be re-used. There is nothing new about replacing parts to extend the life of a product. Cars and many other products have always been built so that they can be re-used, even after some of their original parts have failed. We simply replace the parts.

As we will see below, Fuji Xerox[85] designs some of the parts of its copiers so they are not only easy to assemble, but are also easy to remove when the copier has reached the end of its service life. This makes it easier to re-use the parts. Waste materials from the production process can sometimes be cleaned and recycled. Many companies use waste wood and paper as fuel to generate electricity for heating and air conditioning.

Case: Fuji's "film with a lens"

Fuji's "film with lens" was introduced in 1986 and quickly, to the great surprise of the leader of the team that developed it, became a best seller. The consumer "need" that Fuji wanted to address was the need people have for a camera to use when they have left their camera at home while traveling or attending a special event. A "seed" for the project was that Fuji wanted to find ways to sell its new high speed ISO 400 film. It took about a year for the six part-time members of the project team to come up with the new camera. The product requirements were that the camera could be dropped without being damaged (so a soft plastic body was used), that it would take clear pictures even when held by shaky hands (so the high speed ISO 400 film was used) and that it be able to focus at a wide range of distances (a combination two piece plastic lens with an F11 aperture was used to allow focal distances from one yard to infinity). None of these product requirements necessitated a techno-logical break-through. Indeed, almost all of them could be achieved by using Fuji's accumulated technology.

The "film with a lens" is a single use camera, which initially meant that it would be thrown away after the film was used up. Environment-alists complained about this, so the company redeveloped the camera and its support systems so that the camera body could be reused. Today, about 90% of the components in Fuji's "film with lens" cameras are reused. This was made possible by making some changes in the design of the camera and developing an automatic process to disassemble the cameras, select re-usable parts, and clean them.[86]

Environmental problems as new opportunities. Environmental problems can be taken as opportunities to develop new products. Ebara Company is expanding its sales by producing equipment and plants to burn and dispose of garbage and industrial waste. Organo Company and Kurita Company are making good profits by producing water purification chemicals and equipment.

Case: Toyota's hybrid car

Around 1992 Shoichiro Toyoda, Toyota's CEO, suggested that the company develop a new car for the 21st century. The goal was to develop an environmentally friendly car. A product development team was formed.

Concept formation. Electric cars may be clean from an environmental standpoint, but they have a number of drawbacks. It takes a long time to charge their batteries and they can only go a relatively short distance before they need to be charged again. Efforts to increase the mileage on a charge resulted in much heavier batteries. For these reasons Toyota's development team decided to try to develop a hybrid gasoline-electric car.

There are two types of hybrid car. One uses a series system: power is transmitted from a gasoline engine to a generator, then to a battery, then to an electric motor, and finally to the wheels of the car. This is a simple system, but it does not provide enough power for when the car has to go up hills. The other type of hybrid car uses a parallel system. With a parallel system power is transmitted by three modes: from a gasoline engine to the wheels, from a generator to an electric motor to the wheels, and from a battery to an electric motor to the wheels. At low speeds only the electric motor is used with this system. At high speeds both the electric motor and the gasoline engine are used. When the car is climbing hills, the engine, motor and generator are all used to provide maximum power. When the car is decelerating, or going downhill, the battery charges. An automatic control system starts and stops the engine. Toyota's project team used simulations to select the most suitable from among about 20 alternative power systems.

Reconciling contrary demands. The team faced a number of difficult technical problems. They needed a strong, long-lasting battery – but the battery also had to be small. Toyota had little expertise on batteries within the company, so it worked with Matsushita Battery Industrial Company (a subsidiary of Matsushita Panasonic). Matsushita Battery's 240 Nickel Hydrogen Batteries were to be connected in a series to generate 288 volts. Since this was a series combination, if one battery happened to fail the system would not work. Strict quality control was essential.

A second problem was that frequently charging and discharging the battery caused it to overheat. Overheating shortened its operating life. This problem was solved by finding ways to keep the battery from over-charging and over-discharging.

A third problem was that as the gasoline engine automatically started and stopped, there would be vibrations and annoying high pitched sounds. These were eliminated by reducing the air flow. The technology needed to do this had already been developed, so the solution to this problem was attained by applying existing knowledge.

A fourth problem was related to the fact that the gasoline engine is started by the electric motor. That means there is no need for an electric starter. But, the electric motor is driven by a 288 volt battery. Conventional cars typically have 12 volt batteries, so if the battery of the hybrid happened to fail it could not be jump started. To solve this problem, a transformer was attached to transform the 12 volts of a conventional car battery to 288 volts.

Still another problem was the small size of the car's interior. It was especially confining for those sitting in the backseat. This problem was solved by increasing the height of the roof and raising the height of the driver's seat. This allowed more leg room for backseat passengers.

Success factors. The Toyota hybrid has been a phenomenal success, far outselling hybrids put on the market by other companies. Several factors account for this success. One is that the car quickly acquired a reputation for being "stylish." Honda was a little earlier to put a hybrid car on the market, and the Honda hybrid was rated by the U.S. Environmental Protection Agency as having the best fuel efficiency of any car, but consumers did not like its appearance. Honda's first hybrid was taken off the market. To ensure that Toyota's hybrid would be attractive to consumers Toyota developed several design alternatives. These were evaluated in various countries. Ultimately a design from Toyota's California development center was adopted. The price for the car was set at about twenty thousand dollars. This was not enough to produce a profit over the first few years, but it seemed clear that this system would soon be applied to a range of other Toyota models. Toyota was able to develop this revolutionary car in only 4 years because so many departments and suppliers cooperated in its development. This was a major success of the large-scale use of concurrent engineering.

Case: The Body Shop

The Body Shop sells skin and hair care products that are famous for being environmentally friendly. The company was started in 1976 by Anita Roddick and her husband Gordon. The couple had owned a restaurant and a hotel in Little Hampton, England. Their goal for the new company was to produce skin and hair care products based on the following philosophy.

Naturally-based products. They would only use ingredients with a long history of safe human use. Natural materials would be used as much as possible, for example they would use oils from nuts rather than from petroleum by-products. The Body Shop would carry out research to find plants, herbs, fruits, flowers, seeds and nuts that could be used to create new products. This research would include the identification of ingredients that come from renewable sources. Careful studies would be done to ensure that The Body Shop's use of natural ingredients would not hurt the environment. However, their products would contain preservatives to keep the natural ingredients fresh.

No animal testing. Safe ingredients would be used in their products, but the safety would be assured by testing on human volunteers, not on animals.

Minimal waste from packaging. They would use as little packaging as possible, and whenever possible they would use packaging materials that could be recycled.

Franchise stores. The company would expand by using a franchising system. They would not sell their products in department stores and other outlets. With the franchise system they can control the image and marketing of their products. The stores are all decorated in green to show The Body Shop's environmental friendliness. The brand image is further controlled by the use of standard pamphlets and brochures. Members of the sales staff are recruited from those who understand and believe in the mission of the company. They are trained so that they can explain the importance of environmentally friendly products to customers.

No media advertising. The Body Shop would rely on reports in newspapers and other publications and mouth-to-mouth communications, rather than paid advertisements in the media.

By 2006 the Body Shop had more than 2,000 stores in 53 countries. That year it was bought out by the French cosmetics firm L'Oreal for over $1 billion (with more than $200 million going to the Roddicks). L'Oreal was hoping to maintain the ethical image of The Body Shop while further expanding the company.

Success factors, and problems. Although the Body Shop was highly profitable for its founders, it was starting to experience some problems in the years before the company was sold. It had built a niche for itself by focusing on environmentally-friendly products produced in an ethical manner. The problem was that the company could not construct the barriers to entry it needed to protect this market for itself, particularly in the United States. In the U.S. many companies entered the market, and similar products were soon being sold at department stores and at other stores.[87]

Coping with environmental regulations. Producers of durable goods are faced with growing demands that they recycle as much of their products as possible. This needs to be part of the planning for a new product during the design stage.

Case: Fuji Xerox

Fuji Xerox has the following general policies on new product development and recycling:

- New products should be designed so that they can easily be recycled.
- New products should have a minimal impact on the environment. Harmful materials should not be used. There should be a minimal need to dispose of components and a minimal use of energy in producing the product.
- The quality of new products that incorporate reused components should be equal to that of products using new components.

Based on these policies, Fuji Xerox established the following guidelines for NPD teams designing copiers:

1. Use durable materials so as to extend the life of components.
2. Make those components that have shorter life expectancies easily detachable.

3. Design the product for re-use. In one case, for example, a hole that had no current function was put into a case so that the case could be used in some future copier after recycling.
4. Select re-usable materials. Use materials which do not pollute the environment, for example use water-based paint instead of oil-based paint.
5. Strengthen components to lengthen their service life and allow them to be re-used.
6. Use simulations to predict how many, and what kinds of copiers will be returned. This minimizes over-production.

The closed loop system. Based on the above policies and principles, Fuji Xerox recycles its products in a "closed loop" system. This system is shown schematically in Figure 11.1. It includes the following steps:

1. Recovery of used copiers. Since Fuji Xerox copiers are leased to customers, collecting the copiers after they have reached the end of their service life is straightforward. Generally speaking, machines less than 10 years old can be used for recycling. On the other hand, components from machines more than 20 years old usually cannot be recycled.
2. Disassembly and cleaning. The old copiers are taken apart by hand. Components are cleaned carefully so they will not be damaged. Robots clean the components using thin alkaline water and ultrasonics.

Figure 11.1   Closed loop system at Fuji Xerox

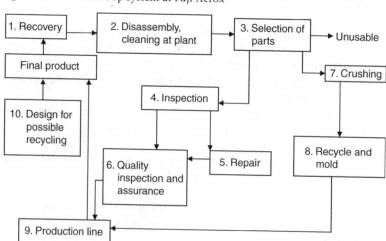

3. and 4. Sorting of parts/inspection. Components that can be re-used are separated out. Ultrasound inspectors that can detect sounds inaudible to human ears are used to check the motors.

5. Repairs. The most expensive electronic panels are repaired. Older semiconductors are replaced. When there has been a design change, new semiconductors and other parts are installed. After a strict inspection ensures that the used components have the same quality as new ones, they can be used in new machines.

In Figure 11.1 "re-use" refers to old components that have been selected as re-usable (box 3 in the figure), passed inspection (box 4), and can be used again. "Re-cycle" refers to components that did not pass the standards for re-use, but are suitable for recycling. These components are crushed (box 7), and are molded (box 8) into boxes or used as materials for plastic components. They can then be sent to the production line (box 9) for use in new parts. Metal frames and motors are disassembled. Components produced from recycled materials are inspected and used in new copiers. The design of the product (box 10) maximizes the possibilities for re-use and re-cycling.

Fuji Xerox has been very successful in achieving its environmental goals by using this system. About 25% of all of its new copiers include reused and recycled components. The performance of these copiers is as good as that of copiers made using all new components. About 50% of the used components from Fuji Xerox copiers are reused. About 97% of the materials used in the copiers are recycled. As a result there is little need to dispose of old materials. This environmental friendliness, however, is not free. The cost of production when recycled materials and components are used is higher by 10 to 20%.[88]

Three principles for deciding how much to invest in environmental protection

While we would all like to keep our environment pristine, activities that produce things we need or want almost inevitably have environmental impacts. There certainly are opportunities to reduce production costs while also reducing damage to the environment, but companies often have to manage trade-offs between efficient low-cost production and environmental friendliness. Three alternative principles might be used in making these tradeoffs: maximizing, dominating, and "satisficing."

Maximizing principle. With this principle, weights are given to multiple goals including environmental protection and other social responsibilities, profits and sales. The goal is to maximize the total points across all the goals. A problem with this system is that it is difficult to decide how to assign relative weights to the various goals. The failure of the socialist economies in the late 20th century suggests the difficulty of accomplishing this. These economies sought to maximize every goal, and as a result were notoriously inefficient in allocating resources. Efforts to use the maximizing principle in allocating resources have generally proved to be wasteful.

Dominating principle. Under this principle alternatives are sought that will improve the value of one goal, while simultaneously maintaining (or even enhancing) the value of other goals. For example, by locating a plant in a rural area, a company might simultaneously reduce unemployment in that area, and save on labor costs. By developing and producing a hybrid car, a company might help in the conservation of resources, while also making a profit. Some companies have adopted what they call PPP. This most often means the "pollution prevention principle." To 3M, however, it means "pollution prevention pays." While this is often true, and has stimulated environmentally friendly actions, companies still need guidance in cases where, in fact, pollution prevention costs money.

Satisficing principle.[89] Under this principle the company lists its goals. Instead of seeking to maximize the achievement of each of these goals, it seeks levels of achievement it can live with. It's as though instead of spending an hour to find the absolutely best parking space, we settle for the first parking space that is "good enough" that we come across in ten minutes or so. A company may seek "good enough" solutions to social responsibility problems, while trying to maximize profits and sales. Indeed, this is generally the most practical approach. Governments and non-profit organizations frequently use this approach. For example, a city government might set goals on how many parks to have, or how many playground facilities to build. More is better, but not if the cost of providing them does not leave enough money for the police and fire departments, or if it requires raising taxes to levels the public cannot afford. The problem here is how to find levels that satisfice.

There are several approaches to determining how much to invest in social benefits such as a clean environment, medical care, and product safety.

(a) Ratio of social benefits to economic costs. As the level of social benefits increases, the cost of providing these benefits also increases.

At some point the economic costs may increase sharply. This may be the point where further social investment in social benefits does not make sense. The social benefits ratio approach may seem reasonable from the standpoint of theory, but in practice it is difficult to measure social benefits.

(b) Maintenance of natural ecological systems. Environmental protection does not necessarily require that industrial plants purify the water they are discharging into a river to the levels required to make the water drinkable. Nor does it necessarily require that smoke stack effluents be cleaned of all particulates. Industrial pollution only becomes a problem when the amount of pollutants going into water or air exceeds the amount that can be cleaned by trees, rain and other natural cleansers. So, environmental standards could be set based on the recovery ability of the natural environment. The problem is that this may result in a reduction in the creation of wealth. People may gain a cleaner environment than they really need (or want) at the expense of other things they value more highly.

(c) Continuous improvement standards. Instead of setting rigid standards that require the elimination of all negative environment impacts, it is possible to set standards that just seek to improve the present situation. The standards might, for instance, require a decrease in the consumption of energy by 40% or a decrease in the consumption of electric power consumed to make a product by 50%. Unlike the social benefits ratio and maintenance of natural systems approaches, the use of continuous improvement standards is not based on any theory of a sustainable level of environmental protection. The decreases in pollution mandated may not be enough to ensure a healthy environment. The use of continuous improvement standards does, however, offer important advantages. It creates specific goals, making it easier for companies to make decisions. It rewards creative efforts to protect the environment while increasing profits and sales. Firms are free to find the cheapest possible way to achieve the goals.

(d) Social averages. When regulations are not the main constraint in determining what a firm will do in such things as environmental protection, product quality, employment of the disabled, and product safety, some firms seek to be average for their industry. This principle is based on the theory that the aspiration level of people is decided by the level of the reference group. There are advantages, however, to being seen as more socially responsible than other firms, and it may be that, in any case, increasingly stringent regulations will soon require all firms to meet a higher standard.

Systems and organizations for social responsibility

For a company to ensure that it is environmentally friendly, and more generally a good citizen, it needs to have special systems and structures in place. Companies that have such systems include Hewlett Packard, Texas Instruments, and General Electric.[90] Here are some examples of what these and other companies do:

Written standards of business conduct. Some companies have written standards of business conduct that define the proper relationship between the company and society, the environment, and interest groups. At IBM, and some other companies, all employees are asked to sign the standard of business conduct, affirming that they will observe it.

Committees on Corporate Ethics. The top managements of some companies have organized Committees on Corporate Ethics. The Committees review the ethical implications and consequences of corporate policies and strategies.

Corporate Ethics Departments. Some companies have Corporate Ethics Departments. These departments collect information on current developments in thinking and policies regarding corporate ethics, create networks within the company, and train managers and employees on corporate ethics.

Corporate ethics hot line. Some companies have set up corporate ethics hot lines so that employees can report ethical problems to the corporate ethics department. The hot lines may use e-mail, special telephone lines, special boxes or regular mail.

Management leadership. At many firms top management, department heads, and other managers regularly explain the importance of corporate ethics. They reaffirm their commitment to ethical behavior.

Corporate ethics audits. These are carried out by the auditing department. The results of the audits are reflected in the merit reviews of managers.

These systems are concerned with areas beyond the development of environmentally friendly products, but they certainly encompass environmental responsibility, and apply to responsible NPD. A new product may be sold globally, causing environmental problems around the world. That is why a new global standard on environmental management, the ISO 14000, was developed a few years ago.

ISO 14000 model. The ISO (International Organization for Standardization) is made up of the national standards institutes of more than 150 countries. ISO began developing voluntary technical standards in 1947. These defined narrow technical specifications for such items as screw threads and photographic film, making it easier to trade products between countries. In 1987 ISO introduced the well-known ISO 9000 standard for quality management. Under ISO 9000, quality management practices and methods of achieving continuous improvement are evaluated. Firms may be certified as having met ISO 9000 standards, and many companies and governments now require their suppliers to meet the ISO standards. In 1997 ISO 14000 was introduced to evaluate environmental management. ISO 14000 evaluates what the company does to minimize the harmful effects on the environment caused by its activities, and to continuously improve its environmental performance. Efficient and effective environmental management practices are defined as those that effectively ensure that the product will have the least harmful impact on the environment at every stage of the product's life cycle. The company must do what it can to minimize pollution and the depletion of natural resources. Increasingly firms must be certified as meeting these standards to sell their products internationally. ISO 14000 follows the system generally used in quality control management, separating processes into four stages: plan, do, check, and review.

- Plan (Environmental Planning). The company must define appropriate environmental policies. These policies must be documented and communicated to employees, and they must be made public. The policies should be specific and measurable. They should include a commitment to continual improvement.
- Do (Implementation and Operation). The company must appoint an executive to be responsible for environmental issues. This person must periodically report to top management on the environmental performance of the firm. The company is also required to determine what sort of training its employees need to meet the company's environment objectives, and to provide this training. The company is required to have documented procedures for informing the government and the public about environmental issues. The company must also have emergency response procedures in place.

- Check (Monitoring and corrective action). The company must have documented procedures for monitoring the environmental impacts of its operations. Equipment used to do this has to be calibrated and maintained according to established procedures. The company must periodically evaluate its compliance with environmental laws and regulations. The company must also have procedures for making sure environmental records are easily retrievable and traceable. The company also needs to regularly ensure that its systems continue to be in compliance with ISO 14000.
- Review (Management Review). In addition to regular systems for monitoring and checking its performance, the company is required to have regular reviews by top management of the environmental management system to ensure that the system continues to be suitable, adequate and effective. This review must be documented, and it must address any needs for change.

Life cycle assessments. As was mentioned above, ISO 14000 mandates that companies make life cycle assessments of their products. They must examine the effects on the environment of a product's components, of the materials used in making the product, of the production process, of the consumption process, and of recycling. How is this done? Figure 11.2 gives an example of how one company makes life cycle assessments of its home electrical appliances.

Obviously, things are not nearly as simple as they might appear in the schematic. Companies have to collect extensive information about possible impacts. Matsushita Panasonic, for example, has prepared a 250 item data base on materials. The data base indicates the effects of

Figure 11.2   Life cycle assessment of a product

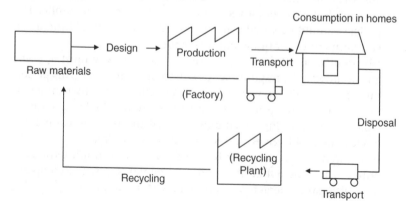

materials used in new products on the environment. It covers every stage of the life cycle, including production, use and disposal. It indicates the scale of environmental impacts and has information on how to minimize these impacts. This data base was created by Matsushita Panasonic's research laboratories in cooperation with universities.

12
Success Factors in New Product Development

Each new product is unique, and no two new products are developed in quite the same way. Part of the challenge for those involved in managing NPD is finding commonalities that make it possible to learn from their own experiences and those of others. In Chapter 3 we described how different processes should be used, depending on whether the new product is technology intensive, market intensive where consumer preferences are stable, or market intensive where consumer preferences are highly dynamic. The development of a new drug or copying

Figure 12.1 Success factors in new product development

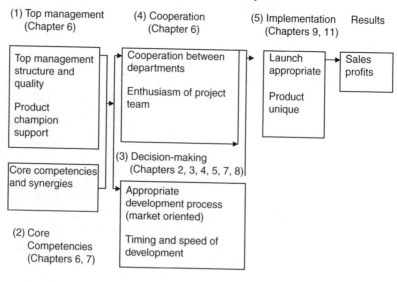

machine should be approached very differently from the development of a new mayonnaise or a new line of women's clothing. But, even though there are major differences in new product processes, certain success factors are generally applicable. These factors, and how they fit together, are shown schematically in Figure 12.1.

The most important organizational components determining NPD success are top management and the strategic planning departments. The relative importance of these components came out clearly in a

Table 12.1   New product key success factors

Success factor	% selecting
(1) Top management	
1. Decision-making and support of top management	50.31
2. Strong leader supports the project with long-term vision	44.65
3. Clear goals	46.54
(2) Core competencies	
4. R&D capability	46.54
5. Creativity, cooperation and enthusiasm of NPD team	36.48
6. Outstanding NPD team leader	16.35
7. Authorization of under the table research	00.63
8. Fit with production technology and facilities	35.22
9. Fit with marketing ability	16.35
10. Strength of sales channels	24.53
(3) Information to support decision-making	
11. Marketing research to find hidden needs	33.33
12. Fit with the needs of purchasers, or joint development with purchasers	45.28
13. Use of IT	4.40
(4) Cooperation	
14. Between R&D, production and marketing. Concurrent development in the company	23.90
15. With consumers in the company	6.92
(5) Launch and characteristics of products	
16. Strong advertising and sales promotion	12.68
17. Unique product, good product differentiation	56.60
18. High quality, high credibility, low cost	41.51
19. Segmentation (through analysis of rival products)	15.72
20. Timing (fast development)	27.67

Notes:
1. Respondents were asked to select seven key success factors for new products developed by their company in the past 5–10 years.
2. For details about the sample, see Table 1.4.

survey when we asked managers to identify the key success factors for the new products their company had developed in the past 5 to 10 years. The managers were asked to identify the seven most important success factors. Table 12.1 shows the results of this survey. Aside from top management leadership, the other key success factors can be grouped into four categories: linking the product to the company's core competencies, having well-designed decision-making parameters, achieving effective internal cooperation, and performing a well-executed product launch.

Top management

More than half of our respondents said that the quality of decision-making and the strength of support from top management were key NPD success factors. More than 40% also mentioned the importance of having strong leaders with long-term vision and clear goals.

NPD and the elimination of old products are change processes, and change processes, as we saw in Chapter 6, are ultimately the responsibility of top management. The dramatic changes that took place at GE and IBM, and reinvigorated those companies, were initiated by their CEOs, Jack Welch and Louis Gerstner. Conversely, the decline of Westinghouse, once a major rival of GE's, may have been caused by a top management that did not give sufficient attention to changing the company's product mix in a fast changing environment. The top management of Nippon Columbia (better known in the U.S. by the Denon brand name) concentrated on selecting which popular singers to promote, and spent little time thinking about the product mix the company would need to thrive in the 1990s. Both of these were venerable companies with long histories. Sadly, it did not take them long to fall into irreversible declines.

As we have seen, a number of things can cause the decision-making of top management to go astray. Top managers can become victims of "group think" and devote company resources to ill-conceived projects. This tends to happen when the top management group is too homogeneous, and when it does not actively seek all the information it needs. Top management needs to have strong staff support to collect information and challenge assumptions. We have seen how strong strategic planning sections help companies like Samsung move decisively into new markets. Another kind of decision-making pathology occurs when top management teams are made up of representatives of company divisions or other constituencies within the company, rather than members whose primary identity is with the company as a whole. It is all too easy for top management teams made up of division managers to get caught up in political pressures. A promising new product might be killed out of fear that it will cannibalize existing products or divert resources from the established divisions. Conversely, products that should be divested might be retained because of coalitions amongst product managers.

It is also crucial that members of the top management team be able to serve as "product champions," providing active support in the battle to overcome resistance to changes in the product mix, and to make sure the NPD team has all the resources it needs. We saw how Sony's Akio Morita did all of these things in the development and launching of the Walkman. Powerful product champions at JVC also made it possible for JVC to develop a video cassette recorder that ultimately destroyed Sony's Betamax.

Of course many great new ideas emerge from middle ranking employees. The generation of these ideas should be encouraged. But a company should only invest in the development of new products that fit the basic strategy of the company – and it is the job of top management to determine that strategy and to evaluate how well potential new products fit the strategy.

Strong core competencies and good organizational fit

The core competencies of the firm and the fit of the new product with company strengths were also mentioned as key success factors by many of our respondents. Some important core competencies relate to the firm's NPD capabilities. Nearly half of our respondents mentioned the firm's R&D capability, and more than a third mentioned the creativity, cooperation, and enthusiasm of the NPD team. The fit of the new product with other competencies of the firm is also important. More than a third of our respondents mentioned the importance of fit with the production technology and facilities of the firm, and a sixth mentioned the importance of the fit of the product with the firm's specific marketing abilities. The strength of the company's sales channels was rated as highly important by about a fourth of our respondents.

But, while the fit of a new product with existing competencies is important, a company should not be limited by a static conception of its capabilities. A company can create new capabilities by hiring key personnel, or by acquiring other companies. After it decided to develop the crystal quartz watch, Seiko Epson hired a number of electronics experts to work with its experts in watch design. Over the years, Emerson Electric has acquired many companies to expand its product mix to include related products. To be sure, acquisition strategies got something of a bad name during the merger and acquisition wave of the 1980s. Many of the firms that had rushed to make acquisitions were soon divesting the acquisitions. This simply suggests that firms must be strategic in their acquisitions. They must be guided by a good sense of their own ability to absorb and leverage the competencies they hope to acquire through an acquisition.

While transitions in product mix can be challenging, there are numerous examples of firms that have risen to the challenge. At IBM, hardware accounted for more than 60% of sales in 1990. By 2005, software and services accounted for about 75% of sales. This transition was possible because the company had so many competent software engineers and programmers. We have seen how Canon moved away from the film camera industry to digital cameras and copiers – and aggressively withdrew from industries where it did not have the right mix of competencies. Nintendo once was a manufacturer of playing cards, it acquired the necessary competencies to become a leader in video games.

Informed decision-making

Our respondents emphasized the importance of making sure that decisions on the development of new products are based on consumer needs. Nearly half mentioned this as a key success factor. About a third pointed to the importance of marketing research to identify hidden needs. Occasionally there are instances where a NPD process veers off and becomes excessively driven by a desire to overcome technological challenges, for example, rather than by information on what consumers want. Earlier we mentioned how the Japanese automobile maker Mazda was badly damaged by over investing in the development of the rotary engine – even though it was not clear that consumers placed very much value in the special features offered by rotary engines.

The process of developing a new product design that fits consumer needs varies from product to product. In the case of technology intensive products, such as copiers or automobiles, engineering decisions that take place after the marketing research has been completed, such as during the processes of mechanical engineering and testing, are important. It may be necessary to resolve contradictory design needs, such as making a car small, while also giving it a spacious interior.

In Chapter 5 we saw how this was done at Toyota. In the case of marketing intensive products where consumer preferences are dynamic, such as fashionable women's apparel, a trial and error approach can be useful. Here, as we have seen, it is essential that the NPD team get quick feedback from consumers, respond by rapidly adjusting designs, and quickly move into production

In the case of marketing intensive products where the costs of development, production, and marketing are large (recall the Tactics and *USA Today* cases), intensive marketing research is needed. In Chapter 1 we saw how Shiseido found it very useful to conduct in-depth interviews with consumers when it developed Tactics, its hair tonic for men. As we saw in Chapter 9, in developing *USA Today*, the Ganett Company formed a project team and carried out intensive marketing research. Consumers were asked what they did not like about newspapers. This led the team to design a newspaper that was, for example, easier to read on trains and airplanes because it did not carry articles over from one page to another. In the case of new medicines, tests of effectiveness and safety are made first on animals, then on healthy young volunteers, and finally on patients suffering from the disease. Computer simulations of the actions of drugs are also used, but testing on live human beings is essential to make sure a new drug is both effective and safe.

While market research is important for all types of products, it does have its limitations. It may give misleading results in the case of products that consumers are not yet familiar with. Consumers may not know they "need" these products until they experience using them. They may not know exactly how they would use them. When home video equipment was first introduced, RCA (then a leading producer of consumer electronic products), and some other companies, assumed that the video machines would primarily be used like phonographs, playing back pre-recorded content such as cooking lessons or video magazines. RCA developed a video disk player that had no recording function. The players were rejected in the market place. In the 1970s content providers were unsure whether people would primarily buy or rent pre-recorded video cassettes – and focus groups members didn't know either. Researchers may need to ask experts. They might look for analogous products.

Cooperation

Another key success factor in developing a new product is cooperation within the company. Nearly a quarter of our respondents highlighted the importance of cooperation between the R&D, production, and marketing functions. Although we did not ask specifically about it in our survey, cooperation with suppliers and customers is also important. Internal and external cooperation are essential in achieving speedy and successful new product development.

Several factors can contribute to poor cooperation amongst R&D, production and marketing. R&D staff members may be more likely to have advanced academic degrees, and feel that they should have greater status than people in production and marketing. This sense of pride may stand in the way of their ability to get crucial information about production and marketing issues. They may feel, for example, that they are being ordered around by a lower status person when a marketing manager tries to tell them how a new product could best meet consumer needs, or a production manager asks them to make changes that will allow more efficient manufacturing. Researchers may be inclined to seek elegant technical solutions to problems, even when these offer no advantages that are valued by consumers. Product development, even when it is technically outstanding, can also be problematic when it does not fit the company's strategic direction. We saw how this happened when Xerox's Palo Alto Research Center developed the first personal computer (discussed in Chapter 2). Production departments naturally prefer designs that allow for efficient manufacturability. Last minute design changes are anathema. Marketing wants designs that delight the customer, and may want to keep making design changes in response to new market information long after production feels it needs the design to be frozen. These conflicts in subunit goals can be aggravated when the different departments are at different sites, and the people in them seldom meet each other.

Companies use a variety of means to overcome NPD coordination issues. A powerful product champion can ensure that the various departments subordinate department goals to company goals. At Sharp, the giant consumer electronics company, members of important project teams are allowed to wear a gold lapel pin similar to that worn by the company's most senior executives. This gives project team members greater status within the company, and makes it easier for them to gain the cooperation of others. A variety of means of conferring status on the project team members might be considered, depending on the corporate culture. As we have mentioned before, another mechanism to improve cooperation is to transfer personnel. NPD teams can be made up of highly regarded people from the various departments, who then return to their original departments. Changes in performance evaluation procedures can also help. A common problem is that managers are evaluated based on the performance of their department, with much less attention paid to their overall contributions to the company. Managers should look carefully at their performance evaluation criteria. Incubation departments can also be used to facilitate coordination by eliminating the conflicting demands imposed by different functional areas.

Cooperation with suppliers and other companies can also be crucial to fast and effective new product development. In some industries this may require stable alliances. We have seen how one reason Toyota has been able to quickly develop new cars is its effective use of concurrent engineering, involving suppliers in the design process from the earliest stages. Toyota is able to rely on its suppliers because the suppliers can also rely on Toyota. Some years ago, for example, when Toyota changed some of its car models from rear wheel drive to front wheel drive, it no longer needed drive shafts from one of its suppliers. To minimize the damage done to the supplier Toyota gave it orders for other components.

Effective product launches

Perhaps not surprisingly, the factor most often mentioned by our respondents as contributing to a successful new product launch was having a good, well-differentiated product. More than 56% of our respondents listed this as a key success factor. High quality and low cost were other key success factors.

Aside from characteristics of the newly launched product itself, however, a number of other factors contribute to a successful launch.

Sales channels. A strong sales network is critical to the support of a new product launch, though the exact features that make a sales network strong may vary from product to product. For Matsushita Panasonic it's having thousands of exclusive and selective sales outlets. This allows the company to quickly get new products to market. The Body Shop has distinctive products targeted at customers who are particularly concerned about health and the environment. To reach these customers around the world, Body Shop built an exclusive sales network of about 2,000 stores all over the world by franchising. Its franchisees were carefully screened to make sure they shared the values of The Body Shop, and could reach its target markets. The Swedish furniture maker Ikea sells furniture that customers can assemble at home. Ikea's stores are set up with large parking lots so customers can easily load the unassembled furniture in their cars. When companies, like Amazon or Dell, sell most of their products via the internet, they need large well-situated distribution centers. Companies like Apple, Sony, and Nike have set up special stores where they can feature new products, and get rapid feedback from customers.

Mass launches and sequential strategies. When a movie company has an expensive, but not very promising, film it may choose to release the film all over the world at about the same time. There may be no preview screenings for critics. The hope is that the distributors will recover as much money as possible before word-of-mouth spreads the information that the movie is a bomb. If the movie company is not quite sure how audiences will respond to certain aspects of a movie, such as how it ends, they might show variants of the movie at "sneak previews" to find out what audiences prefer. Before a larger-scale release the film may be re-cut to better suit what audiences seem to like. If there is even greater uncertainty about a film, the movie company might have limited releases in certain markets that seem typical. Information from the limited releases may be used in decided how much to invest in promoting the film. Similar considerations may apply to other product launches. As we saw, *USA Today* was initially launched in Washington D.C., than gradually offered in other markets. There is the risk in using this type of sequential strategy, however, that aggressive competitors might notice the product's early successes, and move quickly into the market.

Frequent improvements. After a new product is successfully launched, aggressive competitors may enter the market. This can be especially problematic if the competitors have powerful sales networks or other strengths that give them the ability potentially to seize a major part of the market. One way a firm can maintain its market for a new product is to make frequent improvements. We have seen how Sony did this with the Walkman. On the other hand, Konica-Minolta (automatic focus camera) and EMI (CT scanner) did not make improvements fast enough to keep out powerful competitors. Konica-Minolta and EMI gained little from being the first to introduce these important new products.

A careful analysis of complaints can provide critical information for improving products. Of course it can also help in reducing possible injuries to customers. Mitsubishi Motors covered up problems customers were experiencing with Mitsubishi vehicles. When the problems became known, the company suffered severe damage to its brand equity and its market share.

Attracting desirable competitors. While it is often desirable to make sure there are barriers that keep competitors from quickly moving into the market for a new product, sometimes success may require having other firms put their versions of the new product in the market. We saw how Fuji Film's "single use camera" benefited from having Kodak introduce a rival single use camera. Kodak's entry into this market gave the product more legitimacy. JVC actively supported the entry of other firms into the market for VHS cassette recorders. There had to be a critical mass of firms making this product before content providers would commit to the VHS standard. Of course, even when a company wants to attract competitors into a market for its new product, the company has to make sure its product is differentiated enough to maintain first mover advantage. This may be done, as we saw in Chapter 9, by establishing a strong brand.

So, while each new NPD may be unique, there are basic principles that lead to successful new products. Some things, like the importance of a top-management that is structured to be well informed and decisive cut across most types of NPD. To be sure, other aspects of NPD, like how and when information about consumer needs/preferences should be collected, depend on such things as how different the product is from those already on the market and how complex the technology is. Even so, the underlying concepts and sub-processes do not vary greatly. We believe ongoing changes in the environment for new product development: pressures for faster development, the increasing use of IT, globalization and demands that firms meet higher levels of social responsibility will only reinforce the principles we have outlined here.

Notes

1 Ansoff (1965) and Pessemier (1982) use similar classification schemes.
2 See Sanderson and Uzumeri (1997) for examples.
3 See Tushman and Anderson (1986); Christensen (1997); Christensen and Raynor (2003); and Henderson (1993).
4 Conjoint analysis is a simple technique for measuring the trade off value of various product attributes. It is explained in more detail below, at the end of Chapter 5.
5 Teece (1986) provides the classic analysis of many of these cases.
6 For a description of this see Sanderson and Uzumeri (1997).
7 See Zahra (1996).
8 See Welch (2001). This is also the source of some of the other GE examples given in this book.
9 See the reference list at the end of this book for full citations.
10 See Baker and Hart, 1999.
11 See Kono, 1999.
12 See, for example, Dertouzos et al., 1989.
13 Nakajo and Kono, 1989.
14 On the three skills see Katz and Kahn, 1966.
15 See Uchihashi, 1978.
16 See Kawade, 1989 and Sull, 1999.
17 Full information on the works cited here is given in the "References" section at the end of the book.
18 This case is based on Yamanouchi, 1989.
19 Much of the general information on the pharmaceutical industry presented here draws on Economist, "Survey: Pharmaceuticals." June 16, 2005.
20 This section was written by Professor Akihiro Takeda of Kansai Kokusai University.
21 The two cases here are based on presentations by Ajinomoto managers at study group meetings of the Japan Productivity Center.
22 This section was written by Professor Fumiko Kurokawa of Dokkyo University.
23 This section was written by Associate Professor Tatsuhiko Inoue of Waseda University.
24 This discussion is based on a visit to Sony Motion Pictures by the first author.
25 For a discussion and theoretical interpretation see Christensen (1997) and Christensen and Raynor (2003).
26 See Cooper, 2001.
27 See Dertouzos et al., 1989.
28 See Thomas, 1995.
29 Much of this discussion is based on Lynn and Salzman (2005) and Lynn and Salzman (2006).
30 See United Nations Conference on Trade and Development (2003).

31 This number, like other estimates of the number of engineering graduates in China and India, has been disputed, and is likely inflated. Nonetheless, it seems hard to dispute the broader point that increasingly large numbers of engineers are being trained in these and other emerging economies.
32 See Hicks, 2004.
33 See Dalton, Serapio and Yoshida, 1999.
34 See McKendrick et al., 2000.
35 See Prahalad, 2006.
36 The literature in this area is growing fast as the technology develops. This section draws particularly on a special issue on "Research issues in knowledge management and virtual collaboration in new product development" in *Journal of Engineering and Technology Management* 20 Nos. 1–2, 2003.
37 See McDonough, Kahn and Griffin, 1999.
38 Some of this discussion draws on *Business Week On-line*, 2005.
39 See Roberts, 1999.
40 From Kimzey and Kurokawa, 2002.
41 See *Business Week On-Line*, 2005.
42 See Mintzberg and Waters 1985.
43 See Kotler, 2002; Nishikawa, 1990; Yasutake, 1997; Crawford and DiBenetto, 2003; etc.
44 See Kurokawa, 1997.
45 See Von Hippel, 1988.
46 See Osborn, 1953 and 1979.
47 Some of these ideas are from Urban and Hauser, 1987, Chapter 9.
48 See Thomas, 1995.
49 On conjoint analysis, see Muto and Asano, 1986; Ueda, 1987; Takahashi and Hara, 1987; Okamoto, 1998; Asano and Yamanaka, 2000; and Kanda, 2000.
50 See Mintzberg, 1973.
51 See Prahalad and Hamel, 1990; Hall, 1993; Hamel & Heene, 1994; Ansoff, 1965; and Penrose, 1959.
52 This section is largely based on a presentation by Naomi Tokunaga of Fujitsu at the Japan Productivity Center.
53 See, for example, Lorange and Ross, 1992 or Kono and Clegg, 2001.
54 This model is based in part on Hamel and Prahalad, 1994 and Pearson, 2002, but is more generally based on our observations of many successful companies.
55 On the importance of a sense of crisis, see Kono and Clegg, 1998 and Kotter and Heskett, 1992.
56 The classic English-language work on Japanese lean production is Womack, et al. (1991).
57 See, for example, Amabile, 1998; Arieti, 1976; Burns and Stalker, 1961; Kawakita, 1967; Kono, 2003; Osborn, 1953; Woodman, et al., 1993.
58 Based on Smith and Alexander, 1988 and interviews by the first author at PARC.
59 *Research-Technology Management*, various years.
60 See MacMillan and McGrath, 2004.
61 The companies had annual sales ranging from $300 million to over $20 billion. We received 104 usable responses. We asked respondents to

classify the type of R&D done at their organization based on the goals for the research, time horizon, evaluation method, organizational structure and mode of research. 15.7% of our respondents classified their primary activities as basic research, 28.6% as basic component research (research aimed at developing new core technologies to support the firm's long-range product-market strategy), 35.2% as new product development, 6.2% as production technology research, 10.3% as testing and safety research. 3.6% did not include their research in any of these categories. Table 7.10 gives information on the sample.

62 See Sternberg, 1999, page 3.
63 See Arieti, 1976, for a review of some of the classic models.
64 See Osborn, 1953.
65 On the spiral process, see Kono, 2003.
66 This description is largely based on a presentation given by Rokumuro at the Strategic Planning Study Group of the Japan Productivity Center in Tokyo in 2002.
67 This description is based on Horii, 2003 and on a visit to the company by the first author in 2003.
68 This classification follows Rumelt, 1984.
69 See Houser and Clausing, 1988 and Crawford and DiBenedetto, 2003.
70 For details, see Nakajo and Kono, 1989.
71 See Porter, 1985.
72 See Aaker, 1996 and Shimaguchi, 1998.
73 See Shimaguchi, 1999.
74 Sugimura, 1986, based on responses from 247 researchers.
75 For details on this theory, see general psychology texts and Kono and Clegg, 1998.
76 See Christensen and Raynor, 2003.
77 Based on the first author's discussions at Black and Decker.
78 Konica and Minolta merged in 2003 to form Konica Minolta. Konica was established in 1873, and at one time was the world's third largest producer of photographic film. It also made cameras and office equipment. Minolta was established in 1928, and had been a leading producer of cameras and office machinery.
79 This discussion is based on a detailed report by NHK, Japan's public broadcasting system.
80 See Baker and Hart, 1999.
81 See Miles and Snow, 1978.
82 On corporate culture, see Kono and Clegg, 1998.
83 Mankins and Steele, 2006 review some of the limitations of the bottom up approach.
84 The information on Samsung is from a presentation by Prof. Hamada at a study group meeting of the Japan Productivity Center in March, 2006.
85 Fuji Xerox and Fuji Film are separate companies.
86 This account is based on Ishii, 2005, and information gathered during the first author's visit to the plant.
87 See Thomas, 1995.
88 The account is based on information collected by the first author during a plant visit, and from Fuji Xerox company reports.

89 See Simon, 1960.
90 This is based on a report by Y. Oyama presented at the Conference of the Japanese Academy of Management in 1997.

References

English Language

Aaker, D.A. (1996) *Building Strong Brands*, New York: The Free Press.

Allen, T.J. (1984, 2nd ed.) *Managing the Flow of Technology*, Cambridge, MA: MIT Press.

Amabile, T.M. (1998) "How to kill creativity," *Harvard Business Review*, Sept–Oct. 1998.

Amabile, T.M., Hadley, C.N. and Kramen, S.J. (2002) "Creativity under the gun," *Harvard Business Review* 80 (August): 52–61.

Ansoff, H.I. (1965) *Corporate Strategy*, New York: McGraw-Hill.

Arieti, S. (1976) *Creativity, the Magic Synthesis*, New York: Basic Books.

Baden-Fuller, C. and Stopford, J.M. (1994) *Rejuvenating the Mature Business*, Boston: Harvard Business Press.

Baker, M. and Hart, S. (1999) *Product Strategy and Management*, New York: Prentice-Hall.

Baldwin, C.Y. and Clark, K.B. (1997) "Managing in an age of modularity," *Harvard Business Review* Sep–Oct.: 84–93.

Brown, S. and Eisenhardt, K. (1995) "Product development" past research, present findings, and future directions," *Academy of Management Review* 20: 343–378.

Burgelman, R.A. (1991) "Intraorganizational ecology of strategy making and organizational adaptation," *Organization Science* 2(3): 239–262.

Burgelman, R.A., Maidique, M.A. and Wheelwright, S.C. (2001, 3rd ed.) *Strategic Management of Technology and Innovation*, Boston: McGraw-Hill.

Burns, T. and Stalker, G.M. (1961) *The Management of Innovation*, London: Tavistock.

Business Week On Line (2005) "Outsourcing innovation," www.businessweek.com. March 21.

Chamberlin, E. (1933) *The Theory of Monopolistic Competition*, Boston: Harvard University Press.

Christensen, C.M. (1997) *The Innovator's Dilemma*, Boston: Harvard Business School Press.

Christensen, C.M. and Raynor, M. (2003) *The Innovator's Solution*, Boston: Harvard Business School Press.

Clark, K.B. and Fujimoto, T. (1991) *Product Development Performance*, Boston: Harvard Business School Press.

Clark, K.B. and Wheelwright, S.C. (1992) "Organizing and leading 'heavyweight' development teams," *California Management Review* 34: 9–28.

Collins, J.C. and Porras, J.I. (1994) *Built to Last – Successful Habits of Visionary Companies*, New York: Curtis Brown.

Cooper, R.G. (2001, 3rd ed.) *Winning at New Products*, Cambridge, MA: Perseus Publishing.

Crawford, M. and Di Benedetto, A. (2003, 7th ed.) *New Product Management*, Boston: McGraw-Hill.

Dalton, D., Serapio, M. and Yoshida, P. (1999) *Globalizing Industrial Research and Development*, Washington, D.C.: U.S. Department of Commerce.

Dertouzos, M.L, Lester, R.K., Solow, R.M. and the MIT Commission on Industrial Productivity (1989) *Made in America*, Cambridge, MA: MIT Press.

Drucker, P.F. (1954) *The Practice of Management*, New York: Harper.

Economist (2005) "Survey: Pharmaceuticals," June 16.

Gort, M. (1962) *Diversification and Integration in American Industry*, Princeton, NJ: Princeton.

Hall, R. (1993) *Organizations, Structure and Process*, Englewood Cliffs, NJ: Prentice-Hall.

Hamel, G. and Heene, A. (eds) (1994) *Competence Based Competition*, New York: John Wiley and Sons.

Hamel, G. and Prahalad, G.K. (1994) "Competing for the Future," *Harvard Business Review*, May–June: 63–76.

Harrison, N. and Samson, D. (2002) *Technology Management: Text and International Cases*, New York: McGraw-Hill.

Hayes, R.H., Wheelwright, S.C. and Clark, K.B. (1988) *Dynamic Manufacturing*, New York: Free Press.

Harrison, N. and Samson, D. (2002) *Technology Management*, New York: McGraw-Hill

Henderson, R. (1993) "Underinvestment and incompetence as responses to radical innovation: evidence from the photolithographic alignment equipment industry," *Rand Journal of Economics* 24 (Summer).

Hicks, Diana (2004) "Asian countries strengthen their research," *Issues in Science and Technology Online*, Summer.

Hofer, C.W. and Schendel, D. (1978) *Strategy Formulation, Analytical Concepts*, St Paul, Minnesota: West Publishing.

Houser, J.R. and Clausing, D. (1988) "The house of quality," *Harvard Business Review*, May–Jun: 63–73.

Janis, I. (1972) *Victims of Group Think*, Boston: Houghton-Mifflin.

Jonash, R.S. and Sommerlatte, T. (1999) *The Innovation Premium*, Cambridge, MA: Perseus.

Journal of Engineering-Technology Management (2003) Special issue on "Research Issues in knowledge management and virtual collaboration in new product development," 20.

Katz, D. and Kahn, R.L. (1966) *Social Psychology of Organizations*, New York: John Wiley.

Kimzey, C.H. and Kurokawa, S. (2002) "Technology outsourcing in the U.S. and Japan," *Research-Technology Management*: (July–August): 36–42.

Kono, T. (1984) *Strategy and Structure of Japanese Enterprises*, London, UK: Macmillan.

... (1996) "Strong head office creates strong companies," *Long Range Planning* (January): 1–12.

Kono. T. and Clegg, S. (1998) *Transformation of Corporate Culture*, Berlin: Walter de Gruyter.

Kono, T. and Clegg, S. (2001) *Trends in Japanese Management: Continuing Strength, Current Priorities and Changing Priorities*, Hampshire, UK: Palgrave.

Kotler, P. (Rev. ed., 2002) *Marketing Management*, New Jersey: Prentice-Hall.

Kotter, J.P. and Heskett, J.L. (1992) *Corporate Culture and Performance*, New York: The Free Press.

Kurokawa, A. (1997) "Global strategy of design and development by Japanese car makers," Paper presented at 1997 annual meetings of the Association of Japanese Business Studies, Washington, D.C.

Leonard-Barton, D. (1992) "Core capabilities and core rigidities," *Strategic Management Journal* 13: 111–125.

Leonard, D. (1995) *Wellsprings of Knowledge*, Boston: Harvard Business School Press.

Levitt, T. (1960) "Marketing myopia," *Harvard Business Review* (May–June): 72–83.

... (1963, 2002) "Creativity is not enough," *Harvard Business Review* (August, 2002): 137–144.

Lorange, P. and Ross, I. (1992) *Strategic Alliances*, Oxford, UK: Blackwell.

Lynn, L.H. (1982) *How Japan Innovates*, Boulder: Westview.

Lynn, L.H., Piehler, H. and Kieler, M. (1993) "Engineering careers, job rotation, and gatekeepers in Japan and the United States, " *Journal of Engineering and Technology Management* 10: 53–72.

Lynn, L.H. and Salzman, H. (2005) "Third generation globalization: the new international distribution of knowledge work," *International Journal of Knowledge, Culture and Change Management.* 4: 1511–1521.

... (2006) "Collaborative advantage," *Issues in Science and Technology*: (Winter): 74–82.

McDonough, E.F, Kahn, K.B. and Griffin, A. (1999). "Managing communications in global product development teams," *IEEE Transactions on Engineering Management* 46 (November): 375–386.

Macadoc, R. (1995) "Distinguishing and measuring six different forms of first-mover advantage for product innovations," *Annual Meetings of the Academy of Management*, Vancouver.

... (1998) "Can first-mover and early mover advantages be sustained in an industry with low barriers to entry/imitation?" *Strategic Management Journal* 19: 683–696.

MacMillan, I. and McGrath, R.G. (2004) "Nine new roles for technology managers," *Research-Technology Management* (May/June): 16–26.

McGrath, M.E. (2001) *Product Strategy for High-Technology Companies*, New York: McGraw-Hill.

McKendrick, D.G., Doner, R.F. and Haggard, S. (2000) *From Silicon Valley to Singapore*, Stanford, CA: Stanford University Press.

Mankins, M.C. and Steele, R. (2006) "Stop making plans, start making decisions," *Harvard Business Review* 84 (January): 76–84.

Miles, R.E. and Snow, C.C. (1978) *Organization Strategy, Structure and Process*, New York: McGraw-Hill.

Mintzberg, H. (1973) "Strategy-making in three modes," *California Management Review*, Winter.

... (1987) "Crafting strategy," *Harvard Business Review* 65 (Jul/Aug): 66–75.

Mintzberg, H. and Waters, J.A. (1985) "Of strategies, deliberate and emergent," *Strategic Management Journal* 6: 257–272.

Moschandreas, M. (1994) *Business Economics*, London: Routledge.

Nakajo, T. and Kono, T. (1989) "Success through culture change in a Japanese brewery," *Long Range Planning Journal* 22:6.

Nakajo, T. and Kono, T. (1989) "Success through culture change in a Japanese brewery," *Long Range Planning Journal* (November).

Narayanan, V.K. (2001) *Managing Technology and Innovation for Competitive Advantage*, Upper Saddle River, NJ: Prentice-Hall.

Nikkei (2004) *How Canon Got its Flash Back*, Singapore: John Wiley and Sons, Asia.

Nonaka, I. and Nishiguchi, T. (eds) (2001) *Knowledge Emergence: Social, Technical, and Evolutionary Dimensions of Knowledge Creation*, New York: Oxford University Press.

Nonaka, I. and Takeuchi, H. (1995) *The Knowledge-Creating Company*, New York: Oxford University Press.

Nutt, P.C. (1999) "Surprising but true: Half the decisions in organizations fail," *Academy of Management Executive*, 13: 75–90.

Nystrom, H. (1979) *Creativity & Innovation*, New York: Charles Scribers.

Osborn, A.F. (1953, 3rd ed. 1979) *Applied Imagination: Principals and Procedures of Creative Thinking*, New York: Charles Scribners.

Oster, S.M. (3rd ed., 1999) *Modern Competitive Analysis*, New York: Oxford University Press.

Pearson, A.E. (2002) "Tough-minded ways to get innovative," *Harvard Business Review*, Special Issue on the Innovative Enterprise (August): 117–124.

Pelz, D.D. and Andrews, F.M. (1966) *Scientists in Organizations*, New York: Wiley.

Penrose, E. (1959, 1966) *The Theory of the Growth of the Firm*, Oxford: Basil Blackwell.

Pessemier, E.A. (2nd ed., 1982) *Product Management Strategy and Organization*, New York: John Wiley.

Peter, T.J. and Waterman, R.H. (1982) *In Search of Excellence*, New York: Harper & Row.

Pinchot, G. (1985) *Intrapraneuring*, UK: Harper & Row.

Porter, L.W. and Lawler, E.E. (1968) *Managerial Attitude and Performance*, Illinois: Richard D. Irwin.

Porter, M.E. (1985) *Competitive Advantage: Creativity and Sustaining Superior Performance*, New York: The Free Press.

Prahalad, C.K. and Hamel, G. (1990) "The core competence of the corporation," *Harvard Business Review* 68 (May/June): 79–91.

Prahalad, C.K. (2006) *The Fortune at the Bottom of the Pyramid*, Upper Saddle River, NJ: Wharton School Publishing.

Quinn, J.B. (1978) "Strategic change – logical incrementalism," *Sloan Management Review* 20 (Fall): 7–21.

... (1985) "Managing innovation: controlled chaos," *Harvard Business Review* 63 (May/June): 73–84.

Roberts, E.B. and Berry, C.A. (1985) *Sloan Management Review* (Spring): 3–17.

Roberts, E.B. (1999) "Global benchmarking of the strategic management of technology," paper presented at the *MIT Symposium on the Strategic Management of Technology*, December. Cited in Kinzey and Kurokawa (2002).

Rogers, E.M. (5th ed., 1995) *Diffusion of Innovations*, New York: Free Press.

Rothchild, W.E. (1976) *Putting it all Together: a Guide to Strategic Thinking*, New York: AMACOM.

Rumelt, R. (1974) *Strategy, Structure and Financial Performance*, Boston: Harvard University Press.

... (1982) "Diversification strategy and profitability," *Strategic Management Journal*, 350–369.

... (1984) "The Evaluation of business strategy," in Glueck, W. (ed.), *Business Policy and Strategic Management*, New York: McGraw-Hill.

Sanderson, S.W. and Uzumeri, M. (1997) *Managing Product Families*, Chicago: Irwin.

Schilling, M.C. and Hill, C.W.L. (1988) "Managing the new product development process," *AOM Executive*: 67–81.

Scott, B.R. (1971) *Stages of Corporate Development*, Boston: Harvard Business School.

Senge, P.M. (1990) *The Fifth Discipline*, New York: Doubleday.

Sharpe, W.F. (1970) *Portfolio Theory and Capital Markets*, New York: McGraw-Hill.

Simon, H.A. (1960) *Administrative Behavior*, New York: Macmillan.

Smith, D.K. and Alexander, R.C. (1988) *Fumbling the Future: How Xerox Invented, Then Ignored the First Personal Computer*, New York: William Morrow.

Souder, W. (1988) "Manager relations between R&D and marketing in new product development projects," *Journal of Product and Innovation Management* 5: 6–19.

Staw, B.M. (1976) *Intrinsic and Extrinsic Motivation*, New Jersey: General Learning Press.

Steiner, G. and Miner, J.B. (1977) *Management Policy and Strategy*, New York: Macmillan.

Steiner G. (ed.) (1965) *The Creative Organization*, Chicago: University of Chicago Press.

Sternberg, R.J. (ed.) (1999) *Handbook of Creativity*, New York: Cambridge.

Stopford, J.M. and Wells, L.T. (1972) *Managing the Multinational Enterprise*, New York: Basic Books.

Sull, D.N. (1999) "Dynamics of standing still," *Business History Review* 73: 430–464.

Teece, D.J. (1986) "Profiting from technological innovation: implications for integration, collaboration, licensing, and public policy," *Research Policy* 15: 285–305.

Thomas, R.J. (1995) *New Product Success Stories*, New York: John Wiley & Sons.

Tushman, M. and Anderson P. (1986) "Technological discontinuities and organizational environments," *Administrative Science Quarterly* 31: 439–465.

... (1990) "Technological Discontinuities and Dominant Designs: a cyclical model of technological change," *Administrative Science Quarterly* 35: 604–633.

... (2nd ed., 2004) *Managing Strategic Innovation and Change*, New York: Oxford University Press.

Tushman, M. and O'Reilly, M. (1997) *Winning through Innovation*, Boston: Harvard Business School Press.

United Nations Conference on Trade and Development (2003) *World Investment Report*, New York: United Nations.

Urban, G.L. and Hauser, J.R. (1987) *Essentials of New Product Management*, New York: Prentice-Hall.

... (1993) *Design and Marketing of New Products*, New York: Prentice-Hall.

Von Hippel, E.A. (1988) *The Sources of Innovation*, New York: Oxford University Press.

Welch, Jack (2001) *Jack: Straight from the Gut*, New York: Warner Books.

Wheelwright, S.C. and Clark, K.B. (1992) *Revolutionizing Product Development*, New York: Free Press.

... (1995) *Leading Product Development*, New York: The Free Press.

Wheelwright, S.C. and Sasser, W.E., Jr. (1989) "The new product development map," *Harvard Business Review*, May–June 1989: 112–125.

Womack, J., Jones, D. and Roos, D. (1991) *The Machine that Changed the World*, New York: Harper Perennial.

Woodman, R.W., Sawyer, J.E. and Griffin, R.W. (1993) "Towards a theory of organizational creativity," *The Academy of Management Review* (April) 18: 293–322.

Yamanouchi, A. (1989) "Breakthrough: the development of the Canon personal copier," *Long Range Planning* 22 (October): 11–21.

Zahra, S. (1996) "Governance, ownership, and corporate entrepreneurship: the moderating impacts of industry technological opportunities," *Academy of Management Journal* 39 (6): 1713–1735.

Japanese Language

Akiyama, S. (1975) *Sozosei* (Creativity), Tokyo: Baifu-kan.

Aoki, S. and Ando H. (eds) (2002) *Module-ka* (Use of modules), Tokyo: Toyo Keizai.

Asaba, S. (2002) *Nihon Kigyo no Kyoso Genri* (Competition in Japan), Tokyo: Toyo Keizai.

Asano, N. and Yamanaka, N. (2000) *Shinseihin Kaihatsu* (New product development), Tokyo: Asakura Shobo.

Dentsu Marketing Research (1985) *Kansei Shohi, Risei Shohi* (Sensibility consumption, reasoning consumption) Tokyo: Nihon Keizai.

Eguchi, Y. (2000) *IT Kakumei de Kawaru Marketing* (IT changes marketing), Tokyo: Chukei Shuppan.

Fujimoto, T. (1997) *Seisan System no Shinkaron* (Evolution of the production system), Tokyo: Yukikaku.

Hakuhodo (1985) *Bunshu no Tanjo* (Birth of segmented consumers), Tokyo: Nihon Keizai.

Horii, H. (2003) "Sekai saikou no kenkyu kaihatsu no mezashite," *Business Research*, March.

Ihara, H. (2001) *Kesu de Manabu Marketing* (Cases in marketing), Tokyo: Minerva.

Ikari, Y. (1999) *Hybrid Car no Jidai* (Age of the hybrid car), Tokyo: Kojinsha.

Ikejima, M. (1999) *Senryaku to Kenkyukaihatsu no Togo Mechanism* (Integration of strategy and R&D), Tokyo: Hakuto Shobo.

Imaoka, K. (1986) *Hit Shohin Hasso no Genba* (Concept Formation of Successful New Products), Tokyo: Kodansha.

Inoue, T. (1998) *Joho Gijutsu to Jigyo System no Shinka* (Evolution of information systems and business systems), Tokyo: Hakuto Shobo.

Ishii, M. (2005) *Sozou no joken* (Conditions for creativity), Tokyo: NTT Publishers.

Kanda, N. (ed.) (2000) *Shohin Kikau 7 Dogu* (Seven tools for new product development), Tokyo: Nikka Giren.

Kawade, T. (1989) *Tire to Gomu* (Tire and rubber), Tokyo: Nihon Keizai.

Kawakita, J. (1967) *Hasshou* (Creativity), Tokyo: Chuokoron.

Kojima, T. (1996) *Shinseihin Kaihatsu Senri* (Management of New Product Development), Tokyo: Nikkan Kogyo.

Kondo, S. (1981) *Gijutsu Matrix ni yoru Shinseihin, Shinjigyo Tansakuho* (New product search by technology matrix), Tokyo: Nihon Noritsu Kyokai.

... (1985) *Shinseihin Shinjigyo Tansakuho* (Development of new products and new businesses), Tokyo: Nihon Noritsu Kyokai.

Kono, T. (1965) *Keiei Keikaku no Riron* (Theory of corporate planning), Tokyo: Diamond-sha.

... (1974) *Keieisenryaku no Kaimei* (Analysis of corporate strategy), Tokyo: Diamond-sha.

... (1987a) *Keieigaku Genron* (Principles of management), Tokyo: Hakuto Shobo.

... (1987b) *Shin Seihin Kaihatsu Senryaku* (New product development), Tokyo: Diamond-sha.

... (1999) *Shin Gendai no Keiei Senryaku* (New corporate strategy), Tokyo: Diamond-sha.

... (2003) *Shin Seihin Kaihatsu no Management* (Management of new product development), Tokyo: Diamond-sha.

Kono, T. and Watanabe, F. (1967) *Juyo Yosoku no Riron to Jissai* (Theory and practice of demand forecasting), Tokyo: Diamond-sha.

Mizuo, J. (ed.) (2002) *Visionary Corporate Brands*, Tokyo: Hakuto Shobo.

Muto, S. and Asano, N. (1986) *Shinseihin Kaihatsu no Tameno Research Nyumon* (Introduction to research for new product development), Tokyo: Yuhihaku.

Nihon Noritsu Kyokai (1985) *Shinseihin Kaihatsu Handbook* (Handbook on new product development), Tokyo: Nihon Noritsu Kyokai.

Nishikawa, T. (1990) *Shin Seihin Kaihatsu Program* (Program for new product development), Tokyo: President-sha.

Nonaka, I. and Kiyosawa, T. (1990) *3M no Chyosen* (Challenge of 3M), Tokyo: Nihon Seizai.

Ogawa, K. (1999) *Marketing Johokaihatsu* (Information innovation in marketing), Tokyo: Yuhikaku.

Ogawa, M. (1985) *Shin Kaiso Shohi no Jidai* (Age of new consumers), Tokyo: Nihon Keizai.

Ogawa, S. (2000) *Innovation no Assei Ronri* (Logic of innovation), Tokyo: Chikura Shobo.

Ohe, K. (1998) *Naze Shinjigyo wa Seikoshinaika* (Why new products fail), Tokyo: Nihon Keizai.

Okamoto, S. (1998) *Conjoint Bunseki* (Conjoint analysis), Tokyo: Nakanishi-ya.

Orihata, M. (2001) *Radical Innovation Senryaku* (Radical innovation strategy), Tokyo: Nihon Keizai.

Rukurama, T. (2002) "Global leaders in R&D: the case of Nitto Denko, *Business Research*, March.

Shibata, T., Kuroba, K. and Kodama, F. (2002) *Seihin Architecture no Shinkaron* (Evolution of product architecture), Tokyo: Hakuto Shobo.

Shimaguchi, M. (1998) *Brand Kochiku* (Brand creation), Tokyo: Yuhikaku.

Shimaguchi, M. et al. (1998) *Seihin Kaihatsu Kakushin* (Innovation in new product development), Tokyo: Yuhikaku.

Sugimura, K. (1986) "Responses from 248 researchers at five companies," *Romukenkyu*, January–March.

Takahashi, T. and Hara, K. (1987) *Shinseihin Kaihatsu Management* (Management of new product development), Tokyo: Kia Giren.

Uchihashi, K. (1978) *Takumi no Jidai* (Age of craft), Tokyo: Sankei Shuppan.

Ueda, T. (1987) "Young Setai no Jushi suru Seihin Zokusei (Analysis of product features for the young generation)," *GakushuiOn Daigaku Keisai Ronshu*, Tokyo: Gakushuin Daigaku.

Urakawa, T. (1997) *Kenkyu Kaihatsu Management* (Management of R&D), Tokyo: Diamond-sha.

Waseda University (2001) *Hit Shohin no Marketing* [Marketing hit products], Tokyo: Dobunsha.

Yamaguchi, T. (1992) *Shingijutsu Keieiron* (New R&D management), Tokyo: Nihon Keizai.

Yamaguchi, N. (2001) in "Hit shohin no marketing (Marketing of hit products)," Waseda University (ed.), Tokyo: Dobunkan.

Yamanouchi, A. (1986) *Kigyo Henkaku no Gijutsu Management* (Management of technology innovation), Tokyo: Nihon Keizai.

... (1992) *Shin Gijutsu Keiei Ron* (New research management), Tokyo: Nihon Keizai.

Yasutake, K. (1997) Data in presentation given at Management Planning Research Group, Japan Productivity, Center.

Yoshihara, H. (1986) *Senryakuteki Kigyo Kakushin* (Strategic innovation), Tokyo: Toyo Keizai.

Index

Note: Page numbers in italics refer to charts/figures/tables

5/17